Mea quidem sententia, nemo poterit esse omni laude cumulatus s[criptor nisi erit omni]genarum literarum scientiam consecutus. Etenim ex literarum cognitione efflorescat & redundet oportet pulcherrima literarum scriptio quae nisi subest res a scriptore percepta & cognita, inanem scriptionem et puerilem habet. Henricus Princeps

Mea quidem sententia, nemo poterit esse omni laude cumulatus scriptor nisi erit omnigenarū literarū scientiam consecutus: Etenim ex literarū cogni=tione efflorescat & redundete oportet pulcherrima literarū scriptio: quae nisi subest res a scriptore percepta & cognita, inanem scriptione & puerile habet

Mea quide sententia nemo poterit esse omni laude cumulatus scriptor, nisi erit omnigenarū literarū scientiā cōsecutus: Eteni ex literarū cognitione efflores=cat et redūdet oportet pulcherrima literarū scriptio: quae nisi subest res a scriptore percepta & cognita, inanem scriptione & puerilem habet. H.P.A.

+a

Mea quide sentetia, nemo poterit esse omni laude cumulatus scriptor, nisi erit omnigena=vū literarum scientiā consecutus: Eteni ex literarū cognitione efflorescat & redūdet oportet pulcherima literarū scriptio: quae nisi subest res a scriptore percepta & cognita, inanem scriptionem et puerilem habet. H.P. Henricus B[ ]

Mea quidem sententia Princeps Henricus vix est mediocri laude dignus scriptor, adeo puerilem scriptionem habet.

THE LOST PRINCE

The Life & Death of

HENRY STUART

THE LOST PRINCE

The Life & Death of

HENRY STUART

Catharine MacLeod

WITH

Timothy Wilks, Malcolm Smuts
and Rab MacGibbon

NATIONAL PORTRAIT GALLERY

LONDON

Published in Great Britain by
National Portrait Gallery Publications,
National Portrait Gallery,
St Martin's Place, London WC2H OHE

Published to accompany the exhibition
The Lost Prince: The Life & Death of Henry Stuart
18 October 2012 to 13 January 2013

This exhibition has been made possible by
the provision of insurance through the
Government Indemnity Scheme. The National
Portrait Gallery, London, would like to thank
HM Government for providing Government
Indemnity and the Department for Culture,
Media and Sport and Arts Council England
for arranging the indemnity.

For a complete catalogue of current publications,
please write to the National Portrait Gallery at
the address above, or visit our website at
www.npg.org.uk/publications

ISBN 978 1 85514 458 3

A catalogue record for this book is
available from the British Library.

10 9 8 7 6 5 4 3 2 1

Printed in China

KEY TO CONTRIBUTORS

A.H.	Arnold Hunt
R.M.	Rab MacGibbon
C.M.	Catharine MacLeod
C.A.M.	Catriona A. Murray
D.A.H.B.T.	David A.H.B. Taylor
T.W.	Timothy Wilks

NOTE TO READERS

Literature sections of the catalogue entries are not
intended to be exhaustive, but to indicate key sources.

MANAGING EDITOR Christopher Tinker
EDITOR Sarah Ruddick
COPY-EDITOR Denny Hemming
PICTURE RESEARCH Lucy Macmillan
PRODUCTION MANAGER Ruth Müller-Wirth
DESIGN Philip Lewis
ORIGINATION DL Imaging Ltd.
PRINTING C & C Offset Printing Co., Ltd.

ENDPAPERS *Prince Henry's Copy-book*,
Prince Henry, 1604–6 (detail of cat. 20)
PAGE 1 *Prince Henry in French Armour*,
Nicholas Hilliard, 1607 (cat. 31)
FRONTISPIECE *Prince Henry with Robert Devereux,
3rd Earl of Essex*, Robert Peake the Elder, c.1605
(detail of cat. 14)

Contents

Director's Foreword

A NATION ROBBED of an intelligent and cultured royal leader and a young life lost are the tragic headlines for Henry Frederick, Prince of Wales, dying in November 1612 at the tender age of eighteen. Setting aside the shorthand, the story of this remarkable young man is important to tell 400 years later. Understanding the causes of the extraordinary mass mourning across the nation can now be balanced with a celebration of his precocious achievements and virtuosity. This exhibition therefore aims to present – in biographical and pictorial form – a portrait of this lost prince.

In a historical guessing game, if Henry had lived, his younger brother Charles would not have taken to the throne on the death of their father, James VI of Scotland and I of England, in 1625. And while Charles I was arguably the greatest collector and supporter of the arts ever to sit on the English throne, his achievements in this field were built on foundations laid by his elder brother, from whom he inherited his interest, a significant part of his collections and many of his advisors. Whether Henry – like Charles – would have led the country into civil war is the big, unanswerable question. But for the ten years from the accession of the Stuarts to the English throne in 1603 until his death, Henry was the focus of extraordinary developments in the visual arts, architecture, music and literature, which led to Britain's establishment as a cultural player on the world stage.

An exhibition that would celebrate the life and achievements of Henry Stuart was first proposed by art historian Simon Watney, and I am grateful to him, to Sir Roy Strong, who charted Henry's life in his important book of 1986, and also to Timothy Wilks, who has acted as an external advisor. However, I give special thanks to Catharine MacLeod, Curator of Seventeenth-Century Portraits, who has curated the exhibition and led the project to fruition. She has been ably supported by a number of colleagues, particularly Rab MacGibbon, Associate Curator; Sarah Tinsley, John Leslie, Rosie Wilson and Ulrike Wachsmann in the Exhibitions Department; and Christopher Tinker and Sarah Ruddick in the Publications Department. Many others have contributed to the realisation of the exhibition and catalogue; they are thanked in the Acknowledgements on page 9.

An exhibition such as this is made possible by generous loans and I am very grateful to all those lenders, both private and public, who have been so supportive of this enterprise. Her Majesty The Queen, the British Library and the British Museum, in particular, have been exceptionally generous; without their support the exhibition would not have been possible.

The exhibition and the associated conference have been generously supported by The Weiss Gallery. I am very grateful to Mark Weiss, and for support from individual donors and, in particular, James Stunt. Such patronage of exhibitions is very welcome and greatly helps the Gallery's public programme. I would also like to thank the Paul Mellon Centre for Studies in British Art, which provided a grant towards the publication of the catalogue.

Sandy Nairne
DIRECTOR
NATIONAL PORTRAIT GALLERY,
LONDON

Curator's Preface

WHEN SIMON WATNEY first proposed an exhibition on Henry, Prince of Wales, I thought that the idea was so good I wondered why such a thing had not been done before. The combination of biography, history and art history, and the richness of the artefacts associated with the Prince, seemed to make it perfect for the National Portrait Gallery. When Simon generously handed over the exhibition to me and I began to undertake further research, I realised that Prince Henry's life and the cultural, historical and political activity around him touched on many more aspects of early seventeenth-century British history than I had initially supposed, and indeed than could be explored in an exhibition. I have therefore had to be selective in terms of the aspects of his life I have chosen to examine – a selectivity in fact largely shaped by the survival of artefacts connected with Henry – and I have had to rely hugely on the expertise of others.

My biggest debts are to two scholars who entered this field long before I did, and without whose research and writing on the subject of Prince Henry I simply would not have been able to write this book. The first is Sir Roy Strong, whose immensely rich and stimulating book, *Henry, Prince of Wales and England's Lost Renaissance*, published in 1986, was the first to consider Prince Henry outside of a largely literary context, emphasising particularly his patronage and collecting. It has been my constant companion while I have worked on the book and exhibition, and I have stolen the title of his Epilogue for the last section of the exhibition. The second scholar to whom I am indebted is Timothy Wilks, whose extraordinary DPhil dissertation *The Court Culture of Prince Henry and his Circle 1603–1613* was submitted the year after Sir Roy's book was published. Tim's knowledge of Henry, the

social and political networks within which he lived, his collecting and patronage is, I believe, unsurpassed. His kind agreement to be a consultant for this book and the exhibition, as well as to write a biographical introduction and an introduction to the section on collecting and patronage, made it all possible. He has been unstintingly generous with his knowledge and patient with my ignorance. While any errors and omissions remaining are of course mine, my Henry is truly an edifice built on his.

I owe considerable debts to others. Malcolm Smuts is a senior figure in the field of early seventeenth-century British cultural history and he has produced a thoughtful, nuanced and wide-ranging essay that places Henry in the wider European context, greatly to the benefit of this book. Along with Tim Wilks, he read and made detailed comments on my essay, greatly to its (and my) benefit. I must also record my enormous gratitude to Rab MacGibbon, Associate Curator at the National Portrait Gallery, who has given me extensive assistance with research, written catalogue entries and, for part of the time I have been working on this project, undertaken almost all of my usual day-to-day curatorial tasks at the Gallery. He has been unfailingly good-humoured, thoughtful and intelligent in his approach and it has been a privilege to have such support. In addition I am most grateful to those who generously gave of their time and expertise to write additional catalogue entries: Arnold Hunt, Catriona A. Murray and David A.H.B. Taylor. Many others provided invaluable help; they are listed in the Acknowledgements on page 9. I hope that they, and others who read this book or see the exhibition, feel that the lost Prince has, at least to some extent, been rediscovered on the 400th anniversary of his death.

Catharine MacLeod
CURATOR OF SEVENTEENTH-CENTURY
PORTRAITS

Acknowledgements

A wide-ranging exhibition and catalogue such as this one are the result of a huge amount of work done by a large number of people. My main scholarly debts are indicated in the Curator's Preface, but I would also like to record here my thanks to all those who, in other ways, made the whole project possible.

An exhibition, of course, would not happen at all without the generosity of the owners of the exhibits. We are delighted to be able to thank all those individuals and institutions who allowed us to borrow from them, most of whom are named in the catalogue, but some of whom prefer to remain anonymous. Large groups of material have come from Her Majesty The Queen, the British Library and the British Museum, for which we are particularly grateful, but all the items in the exhibition make an essential contribution, without which the whole would be diminished.

In frequently working well outside my own areas of academic expertise I have been given academic, practical and other kinds of help by many, including: Silke Ackermann, Philip Attwood, Enrico Barbero, Daniela Biancolini, Mark Blackett-Ord, Sir John Boardman, the Duke of Buccleuch, Lorne Campbell, Bridget Clifford, Barrie Cook, Lord Dalmeny, Robin Darwall-Smith, Susan Foister, Amanda Gubbins, Tom Harper, Kate Heard, Karen Hearn, Steffen Heiberg, James Hervey-Bathurst, Gordon Higgott, Robert Hill, James Holloway, Sandra Howat, Nicola Kalinsky, Alastair Laing, Stephen Lloyd, Andrew MacKenzie, Philippa Marks, Jonathan Marsden, Joseph Marshall, Prof. David McKitterick, Simon Metcalf, Tessa Murdoch, Robin and Katie Neilson, Mark Nicholls, Charles Noble, Barbara O'Connor, Sheila O'Connor, Richard Pailthorpe, Sophie Plender, Harvey Proctor, Jim Reeds, Owen Rees, Thom Richardson, The Hon. Lady Roberts, the Earl and Countess of Rosebery, the Duke of Rutland, Janice Sacher, Desmond Shawe-Taylor, Viscount Sidmouth, Chris Stevens, Lesley Thomas, Dora Thornton, Rhodri Traherne, Tony Trowles, Michael Ullyot, Naomi van Loo, Alejandro Vergara, Jeremy Warren, Lucy Whitaker and Bridget Wright. I am particularly grateful to Arnold Hunt, Curator of Historical Manuscripts at the British Library, who not only wrote a catalogue entry but also drew my attention to a number of Henry-related manuscripts of which I was not previously aware.

At the National Portrait Gallery, many have been involved in making the book and exhibition happen. Sandy Nairne, Director, Jacob Simon, formerly Chief Curator, and Sarah Tinsley, Director of Exhibitions and Collections saw the potential of the exhibition and trusted me to curate it; I am most grateful to them. In the exhibitions department, Rosie Wilson, John Leslie and Ulrike Wachsmann have been wonderfully efficient, thorough and supportive in organising the exhibition. It has been beautifully designed by Ian Gardner and Aaron Jones and expertly installed by Karl Lydon and his team of art handlers. Andrea Easey has skilfully edited the exhibition text and also commissioned the interactive elements. Expert conservation of some of the exhibits has been undertaken by Helen White and Polly Saltmarsh. In the Publications Department, Christopher Tinker has deployed his considerable organisational skills and Sarah Ruddick has worked tirelessly with great skill and calm efficiency to make the book happen; Ruth Müller-Wirth has brought her invariably high standards to the management of the production, and Lucy Macmillan and Kate Tolley have ably undertaken the picture research.

Denny Hemming has skilfully copy-edited the text, and the book has been elegantly designed by Philip Lewis at LewisHallam. Pim Baxter and her team in the Communications and Development department, particularly Nick Budden, Neil Evans and Denise Vogelsang, have arranged excellent press and marketing. Liz Smith and her team, especially Catherine Mailhac, Justine McLisky and Helen Whiteoak, have organised an imaginative programme of educational events around the exhibition. I would also like to thank Rob Carr-Archer, Amanda Cropper, Stacey Bowles, Livia Puggini, Richard Hallas and Jude Simmons.

In addition I owe particular, personal thanks to a number of people. Tarnya Cooper, first as Curator of Sixteenth-Century Portraits and more recently as Chief Curator of the National Portrait Gallery, has been especially supportive of this exhibition and catalogue and of me while I worked on it. Diana Dethloff of UCL has generously undertaken the majority of work on our joint research project on Sir Peter Lely so that I could concentrate on Henry. My family – Frank, Alexander and Isobel Salmon and my mother, Marilyn MacLeod – have had a great deal to put up with in having to live with both me and Henry over the past couple of years; they have been unfailingly supportive and I cannot thank them enough. Finally, Kevin Sharpe, one of the most eminent of seventeenth-century historians, wrote a very helpful reference for our application to the Paul Mellon Centre for a grant towards the catalogue; tragically and shockingly he died several weeks later, leaving the whole field diminished. His enthusiasm, irreverence, immense intelligence and knowledge will be hugely missed and I would like to dedicate the exhibition to his memory.

Catharine MacLeod

Prince Henry on Horseback, Robert Peake the Elder, *c.*1606–8? (detail of cat. 28)

G · PRINCEPS ·
RVM · ÆTATIS ·
· 1 5 9 6 ·

Introduction

TIMOTHY WILKS

THE FIRST FACT that one learns about Prince Henry concerns not his life but his death – that it 'came so suddaine and so unexpected'.[1] Henry, the elder son and heir of James VI of Scotland and I of England (1566–1625), died on 6 November 1612, some three months before his nineteenth birthday, and twelve years and four months short of the date when he would have inherited both crowns. Though we may go on to learn much more about Henry,[2] our awareness that his life was cut short will always impinge on our thoughts about him. The sceptically minded will ask what Henry could possibly have achieved in so little time, while those inclined to speculation will wonder what he might have done had he lived longer.

To pursue such questions, however tempting, is to be drawn away from an ultimately more enlightening approach to Henry, which is to seek to understand him as his contemporaries did: as a figure of hope. Henry's father possessed an unconventional set of kingly attributes that were well suited to peacemaking and encouraging harmony between his kingdoms but not to absorbing the energies of an honour-obsessed elite.[3] James was generally glad of the distraction provided by his son, allowing Henry to attract attention and gain a following, anxious only that the Prince would not succumb to the excitable rhetoric to which he would be exposed. When, therefore, with the death of Elizabeth I, the Stuart court moved from Scotland to England in the summer of 1603, it was not the new king but his heir who seemed to many best able to convert national anxiety into expectation.

Anne of Denmark (1574–1619), consort of James, gave birth to her first child, Henry Frederick, at Stirling Castle on 19 February 1594. The infant Henry thereupon became not only heir to the throne of Scotland but also second in line to the throne of England (disregarding the Act of Succession of 1534), being Queen Elizabeth's first cousin thrice removed. His baptism, which also took place at Stirling, residence of the Earl of Mar, was an occasion of great ceremony and celebration, befitting his doubly important status.[4] The construction of his image began immediately, and much of his subsequent life would take the form of a fashioning process from which, it was anticipated, he would emerge as a mirror of princely virtue.

Henry was placed in the care of the Earl of Mar and the Dowager Countess, whom James trusted to provide the child with a secure environment and to bring him up in the reformed faith of the Church of Scotland.[5] The young Prince remained in Mar's care until 1603, when Henry and his mother left Scotland to join James and the Stuart court in England. Thereafter Henry was given his own household and once more lived apart from the other members of the royal family; first, at Oatlands Palace, built by Henry VIII at Walton-on-Thames, then, at Henry VIII's dated but still splendid Nonsuch Palace in Surrey (fig. 1), where the atmosphere of a 'courtly college, or a collegiate court' was created.[6] Appointments to the Prince's early, tight-knit household were made with care – it would be no different when Henry expanded his household after his creation as Prince of Wales in 1610. Francis Bacon, philosopher, statesman and scientist, who schemed unsuccessfully to enter Henry's circle, ruefully observed, 'the masters and tutors of his youth also (which rarely happens) continued in great favour with him'.[7]

It was one of James's greatest desires that relations between the Scots, English and Welsh should be harmonious; indeed, this was essential if his dream of a unified Britain were to become political reality.[8] Although friction between the nations would persist throughout James's reign, relative tranquillity was achieved first within Henry's household and, then, at his larger court. Setting an example, Henry's English governor (later, chamberlain) Sir Thomas Chaloner, and his Scottish cofferer Sir David Foulis, had each married sisters of Henry's English receiver-general, Sir William Fleetwood, to create an Anglo-Scottish marriage alliance at the heart of the household. Henry's influential Scottish tutor and later secretary, Adam Newton, moreover, married a daughter of the late Lord Keeper of England, Sir Thomas Puckering, while Sir Thomas Mildmay, who had married another

FIG. I

Nonsuch Palace, unidentified artist,
*c.*1620

of Puckering's daughters, was confirmed in the 1610 household list as a Gentleman of the Prince's Privy Chamber. Marriage alliances such as these, further strengthened by business and landholding partnerships, did much to bind together Henry's closest followers.

As important as the inclusion of both Scots and English – not that the Welsh, proudly styling themselves 'Cambro-Britaines', were ignored – was the placing of several former followers of the late Robert Devereux, 2nd Earl of Essex.[9] In the new Jacobean spirit of reconciliation those once sympathetic to Essex, even if they had been implicated in his failed coup of 1601, were allowed to seek the Prince's patronage alongside clients of Devereux's political adversaries, the Cecils, and also those of the Howards. Among the rehabilitated Essexians who became attached to Henry were the two surviving Danvers brothers, two younger Heydons, the historian John Hayward and (through the Earl of Rutland) the tutor Robert Dallington. Furthermore, in a conspicuous

display of even-handedness, the young Robert Devereux, 3rd Earl of Essex, was selected to be one of Henry's early companions, paired with John Harington of Exton (later 2nd Baron Harington of Exton), whose family were old political allies of the Cecils.

Henry's routine, from about the age of nine up to his sixteenth birthday, was divided between study (two hours every day) and exercise.[10] He did well enough at his books – a Renaissance prince was not expected to be a great scholar – and he excelled in all physical pursuits. The earliest English portraits of Henry present a pale, slight lad, yet one full of vitality (fig. 2), and his confidence and athleticism is confirmed by numerous contemporary reports, some those of foreign visitors whom Henry was ever eager to impress. For example, in 1605 the soldier and art patron Don Giovanni de' Medici, on a short trip to England, visited Nonsuch where he watched the eleven-year-old Henry dance – this would probably have involved practising the leaps and spins required in the galliard – and

FIG. 2
Prince Henry, Robert Peake
the Elder, 1604

afterwards ride, putting his horse through its drills using spurs. Later, Don Giovanni wrote to his half-brother Ferdinand I, Grand Duke of Tuscany, that Henry had performed everything 'con incredibile disposizione' ('with incredible talent').[11] The following year, the Marchese Vincenzo Giustiniani, one of Rome's collector-princes, met Henry – still 'piccolo, bianco, biondo, disposto' ('small, white, blond, talented') – accompanied by Essex, and discovered that when not in the saddle Henry studied, and that he was learning Spanish.[12] In 1607 Henry demonstrated his riding skills to the Prince de Joinville and dined privately with him.[13] Henry would continue to receive and entertain foreign princes and ambassadors, but as he approached his sixteenth birthday it became necessary for him to emerge into the public gaze and perform as the prince who had been so widely praised, in print and private letter, throughout the previous decade.

On 4 June 1610 Henry was created Prince of Wales by his father at Westminster Palace before both Houses of Parliament, an event preceded and followed by an array of court festivities, their setting the world of Arthurian myth. The preceding Christmas, in the packed Presence Chamber of Whitehall Palace, a ceremonial challenge, issued on behalf of Meliadus, the Arthurian Lord of the Isles, initiated the events to the accompaniment of hammering drums and blaring trumpets. Then, on Twelfth Night, *Prince Henry's Barriers* took place: a masque written in honour of the Prince by Ben Jonson was performed, followed by a mock battle ('barriers' was the term given to a courtly form of martial combat undertaken with pikes and swords).[14] With much skill and exertion, Henry and a handful of companions took on wave after wave of assailants in a contest that lasted all night.[15] Militant Protestants, who dreamt that Henry would one day lead them against the forces of

Catholic imperialism, were heartened by the spectacle, even though the formal combat of the Barriers had little in common with Early Modern warfare. Merlin, moreover, speaking words during the masque that might have been uttered by James himself, had reminded Henry, 'These were bold stories of our ARTHURS age ... it is not since as then'.[16]

This was only the first of a series of performances and ceremonies that would announce Henry as Prince of Wales. The creation itself was celebrated both by public spectacles and by court entertainments. From Richmond Palace Henry was rowed by barge to his investiture at Westminster Abbey, greeted mid-way by the City companies with a river pageant that had Ancient Britain as its theme.[17] This was a simple affair compared to the Queen's masque, *Tethys Festival*, performed later that evening.[18] Written by Samuel Daniel and innovatively designed by Inigo Jones, it contained more martial references but, again, these were countered by words of caution: the sword presented by a Triton to Henry as 'Meliades' was 'not to be unsheathed but on just ground'; nor was Henry to quest for honour abroad but to rule well the empire that he had. The final day of the celebrations saw contests in the tilt yard and a 'sea-fight' on the River Thames, followed by a great firework display, which was watched by half a million spectators.[19]

Henry desired another masque for the next New Year celebrations, and Jonson and Jones delighted with *Oberon, the Faery Prince*, a masque that was more advanced, visually and musically, than any previously performed in Britain. Again, the setting was the world of Arthurian myth, for which Jones juxtaposed classical and imaginatively non-classical design elements to produce a faux Romano-British setting.[20] Unlike the masque performed at the Barriers, this work made no references to past warrior kings, save Arthur; nor was Henry (who played the part of Oberon) given a sword to brandish, as he had been in *Tethys Festival*. King Arthur, meanwhile, was rendered entirely peaceful by the necessity of having him represented by King James, who sat in his chair throughout. In *Oberon*, the urgency of Henry's previous

performances seems to have eased, with style itself assuming greater importance.

As Prince of Wales, Henry began attending meetings of the Privy Council but was not yet ready to influence affairs of state. What else, then, was a Prince of Wales to do? Henry had no intention of creating a political 'opposition court' to that of his father, of the kind created by a later Prince of Wales, George II's heir Frederick Lewis, whose interest in his predecessor – our Henry – may have been misplaced.[21] Though there were very obvious differences in the characters of the two courts – indecorum and intemperateness often prevailing at James's, order and sobriety insisted upon at Henry's – the Prince's court probably gave militants and Puritans rather less, not more, reason to become frustrated with the early Stuart monarchy.

It was observed that Henry retained his independence of thought and action by never allowing any individual to become too close to him, unlike his father who made Robert Carr his favourite while Henry lived.[22] Though Henry may not have been susceptible to favourites, it seems that he was more influenced by Sir Thomas Chaloner than by any of his other uniformly impressive advisers. Chaloner had travelled much and soldiered a little, but had otherwise filled his life by energetically investigating ship design, navigation, colonisation, geographical discovery, mineral extraction, manufacturing processes, and the arts.[23] It was no coincidence that Henry enthusiastically threw himself into all these fields of inquiry, and in doing so became a patron of practitioners in the arts and sciences in general, and of the Virginia Company and the Northwest Passage Company in particular – the latter's first expedition, sailing to Henry's detailed instructions, was probing Hudson Bay at the time of his death.

Henry also began to build ambitiously. Though his worried auditor suggested to him that 'Building much better fitteth old Men, whom Age and infirmity confineth to their Houses', Henry pressed on with alterations at St James's (his Westminster residence) and a complete

remodelling of the grounds between Richmond Palace and
the Thames, intending also to alter much of the fabric
of the palace.[24] For such works he had at his disposal
an excess of talent: French engineer and garden designer
Salomon de Caus, Italian architect Costantino de' Servi,
and the English architect and designer Inigo Jones.[25]
Henry envisaged Richmond Palace as a magnificent,
contemporary setting in which to be announced; one
could stroll in formal water gardens between flanking
grotto houses; attend performances in the central piazza;
and admire the art collection within.[26] There was less scope
to develop St James's Palace, but Henry did create a picture
gallery and library, and a 'riding house', which fulfilled more
successfully the requirements for an academy, attempted
earlier at Nonsuch.[27] Henry was also becoming interested
in public works, and according to his comptroller, Sir John
Holles, he had given priority to the building of the first
bridge across the Thames at Westminster.[28]

Those who encouraged Henry to build were also keen
that he should collect art. Like Henry's building projects,
it was a risk-free operation and would serve to absorb
more of his ample revenues from the Duchy of Cornwall.
Diversionary considerations aside, several of Henry's
most influential advisers, including Chaloner, Holles,
Sir Henry Fanshawe and Sir Edward Cecil, had visited
the magnificent courts of Europe, and understood their
importance in projecting both the virtue and the vigour
of a state. That Henry should now begin to vie with
Continental princes in collecting art would have seemed
to these courtiers more conventional than the relative
disregard for art collecting shown by James VI and I and
his predecessor, Elizabeth I, whose courts reflected their
own idiosyncratic regal styles. The collecting passion,
crucially, seems to have been latent within Henry, and the
person who seems to have fired it was Thomas Howard,
14th Earl of Arundel, a persuasive advocate of art, already

HENRY PRINCE of WALES ELDEST SON [...] KING of GREAT BRITAIN. 86

INTRODUCTION

FIG. 4
Henry, Prince of Wales,
Robert Peake the Elder, *c.*1612

engaged in forming what would become one of the greatest of all art collections (fig. 3).[29] It was Arundel who was called to 'set forth the praise' of paintings for Henry's benefit; a momentous occasion in the history of English art collecting, as it convinced Henry to proceed with a gallery at St James's Palace, soon filled with works from Italy and Holland.[30] By the summer of 1612, Cecil was able to confide to a Florentine ambassador that the finest works of art had the power to 'enchain the soul' of the Prince.[31]

'I have pleasure in over-reaching difficult matters', wrote Henry to John Harington (then touring Italy); something that his friend already knew but which for us is deeply revealing.[32] Henry may only have been informing Harington of a small triumph in reading and copying out an old manuscript of some antiquarian interest, but it serves to indicate his growing belief in his general irresistibility, which led him to seek one challenge after another. Henry's refusal to accept his limits might even have been a contributory factor in the worsening of his final illness.

Then, the unthinkable occurred: Henry died. Holles, finding words for the despondency of many, wrote, 'My hopes and fortunes lie in the grave with him', while a numbed Adam Newton reflected, 'what Weaknes and Uncertainty is in the lykliest of humain things'.[33]

It may seem a heartless discourtesy to a once vivacious youth who inspired the love and loyalty of those who personally knew him, but the idea of 'Prince Henry' has since been used to encompass various resurgent and emergent tendencies in English society at the beginning of the seventeenth century: Puritanism, patriotism, expansionism, classicism and the new science.[34] Each of these tendencies generated hope, much of which was borne like a mantle by the willing Henry. All too easily, the personality briefly at the centre of this post-Elizabethan euphoria has disappeared from view.

NOTES

1 Adam Newton to Sir Thomas Puckering, February 1613, BL Harl. MSS 7004, fol. 68.

2 See Strong 1986; Wilks 2007.

3 See James 1986, pp.308–415; ibid., pp.416–66; Kane 2010.

4 See *A true Reportarie of the most triumphant and royal acomplishment of the Baptisme of the most excellent, right high, and mightie Prince, Frederik Henry* (Robert Waldegrave, Edinburgh, 1594 and Peter Short, London, 1594); Bowers 2005, pp.3–22.

5 See Seton 1915–16, pp.366–79.

6 Birch 1760, pp.32, 35, 97; see also Cleland 1607, ch. VIII.

7 [Francis Bacon], 'Henricum Principem Walliae Elogium', in Spedding 1858, VI, p.328.

8 See Galloway 1986.

9 See Hammer 1999; Mallin 1990, pp.145–79; Council 1980, pp.259–75.

10 Birch 1760, p.76.

11 Letter, 23 June 1605, Archivio di Stato di Firenze, MDP 5157, fol. 377.

12 Banti 1944, p.118.

13 La Boderie to Piusieux, 21 June 1607, *Ambassades de Monsieur de la Boderie,* 1750, II, p.288.

14 'Prince Henries Barriers' in Herford and Simpson 1941, VII; see also Peacock 1987, pp.172–94.

15 Nichols 1828, II, p.270.

16 See Badenhausen 1995, pp.20–37.

17 Nichols 1828, II, pp.315–23.

18 'Tethys Festivall', in Grosart 1885, III.

19 Nichols 1828, II, pp.359–61.

20 'Oberon, The Faery Prince', in Herford and Simpson 1941, VII.

21 See Gerrard 1994, pp.137, 157, 212–15.

22 Bacon, 'Elogium', in Spedding 1858; see also Linda Levy Peck, 'Monopolizing Favour', in Elliott and Brockliss 1999, pp.54–70.

23 For Chaloner, see Thrush and Ferris 2010, 6 vols; John Westby-Gibson and Rev. Kenneth L. Campbell, 'Chaloner, Sir Thomas', ODNB 2004.

24 See Wilks 2001, pp.49–65.

25 See Pagnini 2006; Morgan 2007, ch. 4, 'The Prince's Engineer'; Anderson 2007; Worsley 2007.

26 Eiche 1998, pp.10–14.

27 Worsley 2001, pp.29–47.

28 Sir John Holles to Lord Gray, HMC Portland, IX, pp.8–11.

29 On Henry and Arundel, see Hervey 1921, pp.60–8.

30 T. Wilks, '"Paying special attention to the adorning of a most beautiful gallery": the Picture Gallery at St James's Palace, 1609–49', *Court Historian*, X, no. 2 (December 2005), pp.149–72.

31 K. Watson and C. Avery, 'Medici and Stuart: a Grand Ducal Gift of "Giovanni Bologna" Bronzes for Henry, Prince of Wales (1612)', *Burlington Magazine*, vol. 105 (1973), pp.493–507.

32 Walker 1835, p.xxxvii.

33 HMC Portland, IX, p.33; BL Harl. MSS 7004, fol. 68.

34 Williamson 1978.

E. of Southampton | E. of Bathe | E. of Huntington | E. of Sussex | E. of Cumberland | E. of Rothes | E. of Murray | E. of Glencarne | E. of Eglington | E. of Cassillis | E.

DIEV ET MON DROIT

E. of Northampton | E. of Devonshire | E. of Suffolke | E. of Nottingham | E. of Lincolne | E. of Buchane | E. of Caithnes | E. of Sutherland | E. of Menteith | E. of Wentoun | E.

BLESSED ARE THE PEACE MAKERS

Lord Gray of G. | Lord Peters. 46 | Lord Harington 47 | Lord Danuers. 48 | Lord Gerarde 49 | Lord Spenser. 50 | Lord Saye. 51

Prince Henry and his World

MALCOLM SMUTS

DURING HIS BRIEF LIFE Prince Henry became a potent symbol of hope for Britain's future, a hope coloured by nostalgia for the glories of the country's martial past. As he grew into an athletic teenager, fond of weapons and tournaments, Henry inspired comparisons with Elizabethan heroes, such as Sir Philip Sidney and Robert Devereux, 2nd Earl of Essex, and warrior kings, such as Henry V. Contemporaries anticipated that the reign of Henry IX would bring a renewed war against Spain and perhaps recreate England's lost medieval empire on the continent. During the years following Henry's death, particularly after 1618, as James I refused to enter the Thirty Years War (1618–48) and negotiated instead to marry Prince Charles to the Spanish Infanta, these hopes were transformed into a politically charged sense of lost promise. Henry's martial image and robust Protestantism contrasted with the perceived weakness of his father. The dismal performance of British arms after Charles I declared war on Spain in 1625 reinforced a belief that Henry's death had deprived the kingdom of the vigorous royal leadership needed to revive its ancient greatness.

This seventeenth-century view was perpetuated by Henry's first scholarly biographer, Thomas Birch, in 1760 and then revived in the late twentieth century, above all in Roy Strong's classic 1986 study, *Henry, Prince of Wales and England's Lost Renaissance*. This described an 'inevitable' conflict between 'the bloated, pedantic and middle-aged' James I, with his commitment to 'appeasement [of Spain] at any price' and 'the young Prince, a man-at-arms who shone at tilt and tourney, who courted popularity', and aspired to turn his court into 'a model of virtue'.[1] Strong then added another dimension to the story by stressing Henry's enlightened patronage of the arts. If the Prince had lived, he surely would have led Britain into the mainstream of European visual culture, much as Charles I later attempted to do. But whereas under Charles Britain's artistic Renaissance became associated with William Laud's unpopular High Church ceremonialism and Catholic

alliances, Henry's patronage would have appealed more broadly to the nation and left a deeper imprint.

Although we should not entirely discount elements of truth in this interpretation, for several reasons we should treat it cautiously. It derives in large part from the Early Modern habit of exaggerating the virtues of young princes, which can never be taken at face value. Nor should we accept uncritically contemporary criticisms of James I, even when these coincide with the biases of modern historians. People who contrasted Henry's heroic posture with his father's alleged timidity usually had ulterior motives for doing so. Although we do find occasional hints of tension between James and Henry, Strong's picture of an adolescent Prince who had developed not only oppositionist policies but also the beginnings of an oppositionist court is intrinsically implausible.[2] For James and his ministers had selected Henry's entourage and retained the power to purge it, had they wished to do so. Even in the last years of his life Henry remained an apprentice in the arts of kingcraft, learning the intricacies of European power politics under the watchful eyes of his father and his father's servants. Like many adolescents he seems occasionally to have disapproved of his elders' actions but this does not mean that father and son were fundamentally at odds with each other.

Finally, we need to be wary of oversimplifying the political outlook of James and his court, while conflating the political situation during Henry's lifetime with the much more fraught atmosphere after 1618, when a new religious war in Germany and the issue of the 'Spanish Match' polarised attitudes. Henry approached maturity during a more fluid phase of European politics, following the truce between Spain and the Netherlands in 1609, and the assassination of Henri IV of France in May 1610, when animosities between Protestants and Catholics were complicated by tactical alliances that cut across the religious divide, as well as internal disputes within both Protestant and Catholic societies. It remains true that on some levels debates over James's non-intervention in the Thirty Years War reflected long-standing disagreements over Britain's role in Europe that stretch back through Henry's lifetime into the Elizabethan period. But we should be cautious of portraying those disagreements as a simple choice between unambiguous and unchanging ideological positions, without paying attention to the constantly evolving European situation or the diplomatic, strategic and financial constraints on royal policies. Similarly we need to resist telescoping the story of the British court's artistic 'renaissance' by assuming that Henry had already precociously foreseen the direction that patronage and collecting would take in the 1620s and 1630s.

Instead of speculating about a lost reign, we need to situate the Prince more firmly within his own context by addressing several related questions. How did Henry's evolving image relate to the dynastic aspirations of his father, and the hopes that court panegyrists and others projected upon him as heir to the throne? How did the Scottish political environment of his childhood, and the British and European contexts of his youth, shape that image? How was he trained for his future role as king, and how did his education influence his political outlook? What can we discover about his attitudes towards European affairs as he approached maturity and began to participate more fully in policy deliberations?

The Scoto-Britannic Prince

Henry became a symbol of the future glories of Stuart kingship from the moment of his birth. The aspirations that quickly developed around him reflected both the Scottish politics of the early 1590s and his father's efforts to win Protestant support for his claim to the English succession. Not many years before, James had infuriated Elizabeth I and her Privy Council by appearing to favour the Scottish partisans of his mother, Mary Stuart, and by intriguing with Elizabeth's continental enemies. But in the late 1580s he reversed course, embracing an English alliance while assuming the role of a godly prince who supported the Presbyterian Kirk, sheltered English Puritans fleeing persecution by Elizabeth's bishops, and aided embattled Calvinists in France and the Netherlands. His marriage in 1589 to Anne of Denmark reinforced this stance, since Anne's father, Frederick II of Denmark, was a Lutheran prince sympathetic to Western European Calvinists. During his trip to Denmark to collect his bride, James discussed ways of reducing the doctrinal differences separating Calvinists from Lutherans,[3] while urging the Danish Crown to join the Protestant princes of Germany, Scotland, England and the Netherlands in a grand alliance against Catholic Spain. The Danes, who faced a royal minority since Frederick had recently died, rejected his arguments but James had demonstrated his commitment to the Protestant cause.[4] The lavish welcome and public fast of thanksgiving commemorating Anne's arrival in Scotland reinforced the message.[5]

Other Scots gave an apocalyptic dimension to their King's godly gestures by predicting that in the seventeenth century a British monarch would lead the forces of the Church against the kingdom of Antichrist in the great final struggle that scripture had prophesied.[6] Although James did not endorse these prophecies, he allowed them to be printed and proclaimed from the pulpit. The celebrations surrounding Henry's baptism, in August 1594, placed the Prince within this nexus of religious and dynastic expectations. The baptismal sermon by the Bishop of Aberdeen emphasised 'the genealogies, alliances, league and unities' tying the Stuarts to medieval kings of England and other European rulers. But the most remarkable statement was a Latin poem by the rector of the University of St Andrews, Andrew Melville, entitled *Principis Scoti-Britannorum Natalia* (On the birth of the Scoto-Britannic Prince). Henry, Melville asserted, was destined by his ancestry not only to unite Britain under one sceptre, but also to lead a great coalition of Protestant princes against Spain and Rome:

FIG. 5
*Basilikon Doron, c.*1598
(detail of cat. 11)

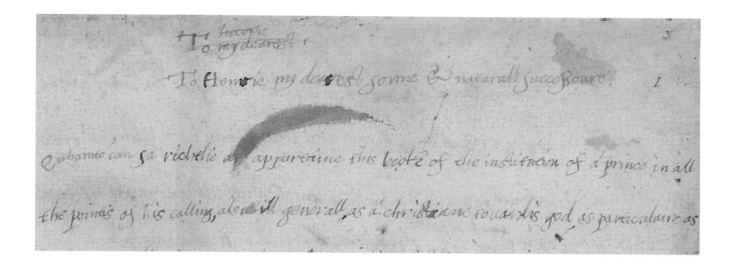

Until with Iberian pride everywhere subdued,
Glorious by triumph over slippery Greyon,
You press under your foot the triple crown of
the papacy.[7]

Published both in the Netherlands and in Edinburgh
by James's official printer, the Puritan exile Robert
Waldegrave, and surreptitiously distributed in England,
the poem elicited a stiff English protest for assuming
Henry's right to inherit Elizabeth's crown before she
had decided the question.[8] The Prince's reputation as a
Protestant warrior did not originate as a protest against
James's policies; it goes back to the very start of his life
in Scotland and originally reflected the King's own
dynastic propaganda.

James had no wish to lead a crusade against Spain
and the Pope at this time; indeed, no one expected an
impoverished Scottish monarch to do any such thing.
James knew, therefore, that he could afford to make grand,
rhetorical gestures that required no immediate action.
Apocalyptic hopes lay with the future, once the Stuarts
had acquired the English Crown. In fact, James's actual
policies were always more equivocal than his language

suggested, and less than three years after Henry's birth, in
December 1596, he broke with the militant wing of the Kirk
after suppressing a Presbyterian tumult in Edinburgh.[9]

Not long afterwards James wrote *Basilikon Doron* as
a book of instruction for Henry on the nature of kingship
and the proper methods for governing Scotland (fig. 5
and cat. 11). Originally published in a private edition of
only seven copies, this treatise was reissued and widely
distributed after James's English accession in 1603. From
its opening sonnet onwards, *Basilikon Doron* emphasised
the fundamentally religious character of kingship.[10] But
it shifted the emphasis away from international religious
wars, which it barely mentioned, to internal reforms
promoted by strong royal authority. It exhorted Henry
to seek solidarity with his fellow princes and to refuse aid
for their rebels, advice that implicitly contradicted James's
earlier rhetorical support for the Dutch and Huguenots.[11]
It criticised the Scottish reformation for promoting itself
through 'popular tumult and rebellion' and producing a
crop of 'rash-heady preachers that think it their honour to
contend with kings and perturb whole kingdoms'.[12] These
comments not only reflected James's efforts to punish
inflammatory sermons but also echoed the criticisms

FIG. 6
Ben Jonson, Abraham van
Blyenberch, *c.*1617

that English conformists, such as Richard Bancroft, had directed against the Scottish Kirk.

Before he ever set foot in England, Henry had therefore become associated with divergent images of Stuart kingship that reflected shifts and ambiguities in his father's political position. In some ways these latent tensions widened after 1603, as English panegyrists welcomed their new royal family. Several hailed James as a monarch whose arrival had saved England from civil war. When James terminated the Nine Years War in Ireland (1594–1603) and the Anglo-Spanish war (1585–1604), they celebrated him as *Rex Pacificus*, the king who healed divisions and prevented bloodshed.[13] Stuart dynastic imagery was adjusted accordingly into a celebration of James's fertile marriage and the royal children it had produced, who would guarantee future peace by securing the succession. Henry's public appearances reinforced this message. He accompanied his mother, and his sister Elizabeth, in a triumphal progress

south from Scotland in June 1603, being lavishly entertained by local dignitaries and civic corporations along the route. He also joined the procession for the King's formal entry into London in March 1604, when the Stuart royal family was praised for bringing peace. But no sooner had Henry arrived in England than the Catholic Ben Jonson (fig. 6) was hailing him as a future conqueror:

> When slow time hath made you fit for war,
> Look over the strict ocean, and think where
> You may but lead us forth, that grew up here
> Against a day, when our officious swords
> Shall speak our actions better than our words.[14]

Jonson would have been the last poet to celebrate Protestant militarism. Why, then, did he choose to proclaim Henry's future European conquests?

Essentially because contemporaries believed that the ability to lead his subjects in war was the prerequisite of a good king, and the heir to the throne therefore had to show promise as a future warrior. Even James acknowledged this, advising Henry on his military education in *Basilikon Doron*.[15] As the Prince matured physically and began to display a natural aptitude for chivalric sports, celebrations of his prowess multiplied. Resplendent tournaments were standard fare at courts throughout Europe and it would have been virtually unthinkable for a vigorous young prince not to engage in them. Henry's household spent the very substantial sum of £2,986 on his debut as a participant in martial sports (or 'barriers') at court in 1610, while London citizens were prevailed upon to lend 'diverse pearls, silks and other necessaries' to grace the occasion.[16] We need not attach any great ideological weight to such events, even if they inevitably reminded spectators of Elizabethan tournaments: they were what people expected.

On the other hand, the speeches Jonson wrote for the Arthurian pageant that accompanied Henry's barriers undeniably seek to balance celebrations of martial exploits with advice that Henry 'restrain' his valour and concentrate on developing his own kingdom by promoting arts and industry.[17] Many scholars have seen this as evidence of the poet's effort to mediate between Henry's bellicosity and James's pacifism. But Jonson may instead have been echoing a more diffuse tension within the court and within the King himself. James's actual policies were always more complex and devious than his image as *Rex Pacificus* suggested. After the end of England's war with Spain, the number of English volunteers fighting in Dutch armies actually increased over and above Elizabethan levels, with James's tacit approval. Although British Catholics were also technically permitted to serve Spain, the Crown discouraged them from doing so, except for Irish fighters who seemed more dangerous at home than in Spanish-controlled Flanders.[18] And the Irish regiment in Spain's Army of Flanders created endless suspicion, bordering on paranoia, among Jacobean diplomats and politicians. No one knew for certain if the peace with Spain would endure, or what challenges the future might bring. James realised that kings sometimes had to fight wars, although as he had written in *Basilikon Doron*, and as Jonson repeated in the speeches for *Prince Henry's Barriers,* it was foolhardy to enter a conflict without sufficient cause or the money to sustain an army.[19] As a future king Henry needed to 'restore British chivalry' in case war became necessary, while simultaneously acquiring the prudence to know when not to fight. We need not interpret this nuanced message as evidence of overt conflict.

A Princely Upbringing

But the devil lay in the details: how should the British Crown respond to the specific conditions of early seventeenth-century European politics? The Jacobean court and Privy Council included figures of widely differing views, ranging from crypto-Catholics sympathetic to Spain, such as the 1st Earl of Northampton, to committed supporters of international Protestant alliances. From an early age Henry was subjected to attempts at persuasion by various interested parties. Queen Anne, who secretly converted to Catholicism around 1600, reportedly lobbied

him to favour pro-Spanish and pro-Catholic policies.[20] James's leading minister, Robert Cecil, 1st Earl of Salisbury, assiduously cultivated him.[21] The Prince's chaplains also weighed in. 'The eyes, the hearts, the hopes of all the Protestant world be fixed upon your Highness,' one of them proclaimed, 'all expecting your gracious faithfulness and readiness in the extirpation of that man of sin. March valiantly on.'[22] Authors dedicated books to Henry, often promoting a political agenda, while foreign states tried to woo him through gifts and other methods. The French seem to have been particularly assiduous. One of their ambassadors suggested bribing members of his entourage with pensions to encourage his Francophile tendencies, while Henri IV dispatched his best riding master, Pierre Antoine Bourdon, seigneur de St Antoine, to teach the Prince horsemanship.[23] Cosimo II, Grand Duke of Tuscany, reportedly distributed bribes in England in 1612 to encourage support for a marriage between his daughter and Henry[24] and also sent the Prince a fine collection of small bronze statues (cats 52 and 53).[25] Maurice of Nassau (cat. 70) gave Henry presents and offered to dispatch a book on fortifications that a Dutch engineer wanted to dedicate to the Prince.[26] The Huguenot Duc de Rohan sent Henry horses, while Marshal Schomberg wrote to him about the need for the French, Dutch and British to join in 'a grand design' to attack Spain in Flanders and the West Indies.[27]

To understand Henry's response to these attempts to mould his outlook, we need to know something about the people who oversaw his upbringing and education. It is significant that James appointed a leading aristocratic supporter of the Scottish Kirk, John Erskine, 2nd Earl of Mar, as Henry's first governor and confirmed Lord Mar's appointment when Queen Anne tried to dislodge him in 1597. The Prince's tutor, Adam Newton, also had a Presbyterian background, in addition to being an accomplished Latinist. Despite its criticism of impertinent Puritans, *Basilikon Doron* prescribed a programme of princely education infused with religious and moral principles. James exhorted his heir to turn his court into

FIG. 7
Les raisons des forces mouvantes
by Salomon de Caus (title page),
unidentified artist, 1615

'a pattern of godliness' and punish moral lapses among his servants. He admonished Henry to remain chaste before marriage and monogamous thereafter, as well as temperate, upright and pious, and to exercise his body with sports like tennis and riding, since a king must be a horseman. He must study scripture, law, history and the military arts, although with an eye to acquiring useful knowledge rather than scholarly proficiency, which is unnecessary in a prince.[28] When Henry later fined servants for swearing, encouraged diligent preachers, patronised the writings of scholars such as the historian John Hayward, and

demonstrated a passion for both tennis and horsemanship, he was following his father's advice to the letter.

Even after moving to England the Prince's household always contained a substantial contingent of Scots, as originally appointed under Mar, who must have fostered an atmosphere of Calvinist piety and moral probity. The new English servants added after 1603 would not have altered this orientation. Sir Thomas Chaloner, who replaced Mar as Henry's governor, was a veteran of several Elizabethan military campaigns and a staunch Protestant. The Prince's clergy were mainly committed Calvinists.[29] They were decidedly more prone to employ 'prophetic' and 'apocalyptic' language in their sermons than the King's preachers, whom James had mostly inherited from the previous reign. A relatively late addition to Henry's entourage, his household Treasurer Sir Charles Cornwallis (cat. 17), would have further encouraged anti-Spanish biases. Although Cornwallis came from a recusant family and served James as ambassador to Madrid between 1605 and 1609, he provided a deeply sardonic commentary on religious observance at the Spanish court in a letter to the Prince. Cornwallis thought Spain more vulnerable than many people supposed, with overstretched resources, unreliable soldiers, an administration riddled with corruption, weak coastal defences and an American empire open to attack by any adversary with a strong navy.[30]

Since James had vetted all these appointments, we can only assume that he approved of his son's solidly Protestant environment, which seems to have inoculated Henry against Catholic influences, while predisposing him to admire Calvinist heroes like Maurice of Nassau. The entourage must have shaped his outlook in more specific ways, although his own personality also played a role. Even before leaving Scotland, Henry began to receive a conventional Early Modern education, under Newton's guidance, in Latin grammar, rhetoric and composition, supplemented by lessons in French and Italian.[31] It was considerably less rigorous than the training his father and other sixteenth-century royals, such as Edward VI and Elizabeth I, had received. Even so, Henry proved a mediocre pupil. He mastered Latin slowly and although he must have read the Bible, nothing indicates that he ever took a deep interest in theology. He preferred physical exercises like riding and shooting.[32] In this respect he genuinely differed from his father, whose love of learning and passion for theological argument were famous.

But this does not mean Henry lacked intellectual interests entirely. He simply preferred subjects that seemed relevant to the life of action and practical leadership that he imagined for himself, subjects he could master through direct observation rather than learning. His education in such pursuits took place under the supervision of Chaloner, who had been instructed by James to turn the Prince's household into a 'court college'. For Henry was to be educated alongside young aristocrats of his own age as a future leadership cohort. The plan reflected James's attempts to unify his kingdoms by creating a cohesive community of landed families within the court's orbit. Henry's young entourage included both Scots and English, drawn from families like the Devereux, Howards and Cecils, who had quarrelled violently in the recent past but were now encouraged to ally with each other. The Prince would have every opportunity to form close bonds with this group and together they would develop a common outlook through their communal studies.

Henry's generation was the first to grow up in a period of peace with Spain, and the winding down of religious warfare on the continent made it easier for British Protestants to tour freely throughout Europe, including Flanders and Italy. Chaloner had travelled unusually widely for an Elizabethan Protestant, even visiting Rome, and was thus ideally placed to encourage members of the court college to take full advantage of this opportunity. The Prince told a French ambassador that he dreamed of going to Paris incognito, to see Henri IV and his court, although he knew his father would never permit such an adventure.[33] Instead Henry had to experience foreign lands vicariously, through the letters sent to him by his entourage as they went on the grand tour. Even this

indirect exposure piqued his curiosity and stimulated his desire to emulate the court cultures of Europe. Strong and others have emphasised Henry's collection of paintings, and his interest in architecture and court spectacles. But the Prince may have been even more attracted to mechanical devices and natural philosophy. The three most highly paid 'artists' in his household – the Italian Costantino de' Servi, the French garden designer Salomon de Caus and the Dutch 'engineer' Abraham van Nyevelt – specialised in such pursuits.[34] De Caus tells us that he instructed Henry in the arts of perspective and he must also have explained the principles of hydraulic engineering, in which he was an expert (see cat. 21). Some of the 'devices' he designed for Prince Henry are illustrated in his book, *Les raisons des forces mouvantes* (fig. 7). Chaloner's strong interest in chemistry, alchemy and experimentation may also have influenced Henry, who was praised for his 'quick and delightful apprehension of the fundamental causes of all secrets, both natural and artificial that have been brought to your view'.[35]

Although these pursuits may have possessed an aesthetic dimension they were essentially extensions of the practical and chivalric education James had prescribed for his son. Inevitably Henry was especially fascinated by military theory and tactics. He assiduously practised manoeuvres with the pike and developed a close relationship with the naval architect Phineas Pett (cat. 61), who built him a ship and showed him around the royal navy.[36] Henry reportedly became furious upon learning that James had decided to appoint Charles rather than himself as nominal Lord Admiral of England when the aged Earl of Nottingham retired from the post in 1612. Although essentially honorific, Henry coveted the position so ardently that the French ambassador thought his disappointment might 'foment a jealousy between the two brothers that can only harm the State'.[37] Henry became the patron of a company interested in searching for a northwest passage to China, and associated with London merchants and aristocratic supporters of maritime expeditions.[38]

Henry and Royal Foreign Policy

The Prince's upbringing and developing interests led him to favour a strong Protestant court and an interest in military and nautical pursuits. By 1610 many with a similar orientation had begun to look back nostalgically on the previous reign, and to regard Henry as a leader who might restore the old Elizabethan spirit. But to take this imagery at face value is to exaggerate and distort the differences between Elizabethan and Jacobean policies. Elizabeth I had never wanted to engage Spain in all-out war and, when forced to do so, she often infuriated her generals by underfunding their campaigns and attempting to limit their strategic options. As Sir Walter Ralegh alleged in a revealing pamphlet that he wrote for Henry, she 'did all by halves', squandering her opportunity to reduce Philip II to a 'king of figs and oranges' by preventing her commanders in the field from overwhelming his maritime defences and seizing his American empire.[39] The supposed 'Elizabethan war policy' was not that of the Queen but that of an aggressive group, often bitter rivals, whom she generally kept on a short leash. Their strategic plans may have appealed to a segment of the political nation but no major statesman would have wished to provoke a new war with Spain just to put them to the test.

The practical problem facing James I and his Privy Council was how to counter potential Spanish threats to Britain and its allies at an affordable cost. Relations with Spain remained relatively chilly after the peace treaty, warming up only after about 1613. The King's ambassadors in Madrid – Cornwallis, Francis Cottington and George Digby – all reported serious tensions, which they blamed on Spanish ill will.[40] James told a Venetian ambassador in 1606 that 'it is a very remarkable fact that every plot against myself and my kingdom has had its roots in Spain or in [Spanish] Flanders'.[41] Although there were also tensions in James's relations with France, he generally cooperated with Henri IV and the Dutch to curb Habsburg ambitions. In 1610 the three powers joined to support the Protestant claimants in a dispute over the strategically located German principalities of Cleves and Jülich.[42]

The involvement of the Catholic French blurred the religious nature of this policy without changing the fact that it promoted Protestant interests. Ever since Henri IV's conversion to Rome in 1593, the anti-Spanish cause had ceased to be unambiguously Protestant, becoming instead a fight by both Protestants and some Catholics against Spanish and papal 'tyranny'. The religious character of British policy became even more ambiguous in the seventeenth century, as James extended diplomatic support to Catholic opponents of papal interference and Jesuit influence in France, once telling Henri IV's ambassador de Rosny (the future Duc de Sully) that 'he hated the Jesuits ... considering them as his personal enemies'.[43]

Rather than abandoning the fight against Spanish and papal power, the King had chosen to pursue it by different methods, which ranged from theological argument to tactical alliances with both Catholic and Protestant states and politicians, in various localised conflicts. James's obsession with the Jesuit order and extreme papalists evoked memories of sixteenth-century political conspiracies and assassination plots, against Elizabeth and other European rulers and statesmen, in which the order had been involved. Like many Protestants, James suspected that the Jesuits had never fully abandoned these methods. He also knew that Jesuits were often at the forefront of efforts to roll back concessions to Protestants in France and the Holy Roman Empire.[44] This made it easy to see them and their secular political allies as the real enemy.

James knew that, when fighting extreme Catholics and Spain, it was always better to have moderate Catholic allies, especially the King of France. France's formidable power provided a shield behind which weaker Protestant states might shelter. But the murder of Henri IV in late April 1610, as he prepared for a new war against the Habsburgs, threatened to overturn this strategy. Long-term prospects looked ominous. At the very least, a prolonged minority promised to neutralise French power for nearly a decade. At worst, Henri's death might allow a resurgence of the militant pro-Spanish Catholicism he had defeated

FIG. 8
Letters Patent of James 1, creating his son Henry Prince of Wales and Earl of Chester, attributed to Isaac Oliver and two other unidentified hands, 1610 (detail of cat. 27)

in the civil war of the 1590s. The dismissal of the Huguenot minister Sully and reports of growing Jesuit influence at the French Regency court magnified these fears[45] – even before the double marriage alliance with the Spanish Habsburgs, which was soon to be negotiated by the Regency government.

As these alarming events transpired, it became clear that James's accumulating debts threatened to hamstring Britain's military capacity. As a solution, Lord Salisbury proposed to Parliament the Great Contract, by which the Crown's rights of wardship and other vexatious feudal privileges would be surrendered in exchange for a permanent parliamentary tax. As historian Pauline Croft has shown, Salisbury also arranged for Henry's creation as Prince of Wales to take place during the opening of the 1610 session (fig. 8), in the hope of creating an atmosphere of good will in which his reform might succeed.[46] But although the magnificent ceremonies, featuring a procession of barges on the Thames, court jousts and fireworks, increased Henry's own popularity, the Great Contract failed.

Henry now entered a new phase in his life, during which he was encouraged to take a more active interest in affairs of state, at a challenging moment for a British statesman. Although the kingdom faced no immediate threat, the European situation looked volatile, while financial problems weakened the British Crown. Quarrels among

Britain's Protestant allies added to these difficulties. Following the 1609 truce with Spain, conflicts over theology and politics erupted within the Netherlands. In a letter to Henry, the diplomat Edward Conway warned that these dissensions threatened to destroy the unity of a state that had never managed to develop 'a formed and grounded government'. Although he hoped that the Stadtholder, Maurice of Nassau, might hold the Republic together, he warned that 'if Count Maurice cannot effect the work our state must foresee the evil and their interest in it and his majesty must interpose his authority in time'.[47] At Conway's urging and perhaps that of others, Henry tried to strengthen Maurice by nominating him to the Order of the Garter[48] but this provoked yet more controversy in the Netherlands, implying too close an allegiance to the British sovereign.

A second intra-Protestant dispute erupted in 1612 when Henry's uncle, Christian IV of Denmark, went to war with the King of Sweden. Christian demanded that James honour their alliance and the Crown cobbled together a force of 4,000 conscripts who duly went off to fight Lutheran Swedes.[49] Conway found this war especially alarming because of the opportunities it afforded the King of Poland, 'in religion a Jesuit, in league and combination with the Pope and Spain and so not only a dangerous and fearful neighbour but likely to be presently a declared enemy to the reformed churches and neighbour states, which concerns the King of Great Britain'. Since the Swedish king was young and inexperienced, the German princes distracted by problems within the Empire and the Dutch hobbled by internal divisions, Conway thought Britain needed to broker a peace. In a letter to Newton, now the Prince's secretary, he urged Henry to lobby his father to do so.[50]

Henry was learning from a staunchly Protestant diplomat that European politics could not be reduced to a simple pattern of religious animosities; as a future king he would need not only to fight Catholics but also to cajole and pressure wayward allies. Indeed, some Catholics would help combat Spanish and Jesuit policies. In France this apparently included the Duke of Guise, who in June 1610 sent an emissary to London to assure James that, despite his own Catholicism, he recognised that 'the state' of France required toleration for Protestants, as granted under the Edict of Nantes.[51] James responded warmly and helped broker an alliance between Guise, the Prince de Condé and Huguenot nobles, in opposition to the Regency government that had negotiated the alliance with Spain.[52] Henry evidently kept informed about the progress of this French coalition, since two years later he provided the British ambassador in Paris, Thomas Edmondes, with an assessment. He thought that 'if the princes of the blood and those of the religion do stick the one with the other firmly ... they may have a very great stroke in the greatest and most important business of State', but that attempting to remove royal ministers would provoke efforts 'to clip their wings'. He therefore advised Edmondes to approach the princes and Huguenot leaders, not as an ambassador but 'as a private man that wisheth their welfare', and urge them to proceed with caution.[53] The Prince was learning to play the role of a royal politician who knew how to cover his tracks while meddling in the politics of another kingdom.

Henry's views on France were also shaped by conversations with the Huguenot Duke of Bouillon, during an embassy to the English court in the late spring of 1612. Bouillon had been sent to reassure James that the Bourbon-Habsburg marriage treaty did not threaten British interests. But he also wanted to consult the King about the affairs of the Huguenots and German Protestants, with whom he had close ties, and strategies for containing 'the House of Austria'.[54] Before leaving for London he asked Edmondes secretly to arrange for him 'some private conferences' with Henry to discuss 'what means were fit to be used to meet with any indirect proceedings' in Paris and 'prevent great future inconveniences to our State [i.e. Britain]'.[55] We have no direct information about what transpired during these interviews, or even whether they took place. But we do know that in England Bouillon promoted a marriage between Henry and the nine-year-old Princess Christine of France, as well

as a second match between Princess Elizabeth and the German Elector Palatine, Frederick V, who had grown up in Bouillon's household in Sedan.

While it is clear that Henry supported the Palatine match, his attitude towards his own marriage is murkier. In a eulogistic memoir written after his death, Cornwallis claimed that the Prince had resolutely declined to marry a Catholic.[56] Some historians have accepted this statement, treating it as evidence that Henry rejected his father's alleged strategy of seeking marriage alliances with both Catholic and Protestant Europe, so that he might play the role of peacemaker between them. Contemporary evidence, however, indicates that this was never James's intention and that Henry's attitude was more flexible than Cornwallis made out. The British court received several overtures regarding marriages for James's children, including a suggestion that Elizabeth marry the recently widowed Philip III of Spain and Henry his younger daughter. Few seasoned diplomats thought the Spanish were serious, however. More earnest offers arrived from two other Catholic states, Tuscany and Savoy. None of these matches would have significantly strengthened James's ties with the Habsburgs, or his ability to broker a European peace involving them. But in different ways the French and Savoyard marriages might have gained him other political advantages.

Bouillon argued that a French marriage for Henry would significantly strengthen the domestic opponents of the Hispanophile faction in Paris, perhaps allowing them to stop the French-Spanish marriages, which had not yet taken place.[57] In Bouillon's mind the Palatine marriage for Elizabeth and a French match for Henry were complementary elements in a single strategy, of strengthening French and German opponents of Jesuit and pro-Habsburg policies by allying them to the British Crown. But, as would transpire, he had almost certainly misread French politics, over-estimating both the Hispanophile tendencies of the French Secretary of State and the principled motives of figures like Condé,[58] but given these miscalculations his strategy made sense.

In addition to a very large dowry that would have helped clear James's debts, the Savoy marriage offered different opportunities and risks. Although a Catholic with dynastic ties to the Habsburgs, the Duke of Savoy had recently become openly antagonistic towards Spain. Ralegh summed up the case against the Savoy match in a memorandum directed to Henry, arguing that whatever the Duke pretended, his Catholic religion and family ties to the Spanish monarchy would always turn him into a Habsburg client in the long run. Not all Protestant diplomats shared this view, however; the prospect of drawing Savoy into a coalition against Spain seemed alluring and Sir Henry Wotton was dispatched to North Italy to promote the project.

When asked by his father whether he favoured the French or Savoyard match, Henry replied, 'if your majesty look to the greatness of the dowry then it is likely you will make choice of Savoy'. But if he was concerned with 'which of these two will give the greatest contentment to the general body of Protestants abroad, then I am of opinion that you will sooner incline to France'.[59] In another letter, however, he stated that the main reason to pursue the French match 'was the hope, which the Duke of Bouillon gave your majesty, of breaking their other match with Spain'.[60] Henry therefore opposed making concessions to the French over matters like his future bride's freedom to practise the mass outside 'her most private and secret chamber'.[61] In the end, he agreed to accept James's decision, writing that 'your majesty may think that my part to play, which is to be in love with any of them, is not yet at hand'.[62] Although one might read these comments as veiled expressions of reticence about either match, they also suggest Henry's pragmatism and flexibility.[63] By October 1612 the balance seems to have tilted towards the Savoy match, which would almost certainly have been celebrated alongside Elizabeth's marriage to the Elector Palatine early in 1613, had Henry lived.

We can never know for certain how the Prince's survival would have altered the course of history, although a few things do seem clear. Negotiations for Prince Charles's Spanish marriage would have seemed far less significant, if they had gone forward at all, removing one contentious issue that marred the last years of James I's reign. Henry also seems far less likely to have supported the so-called Arminian clergy, such as William Laud, who caused so much trouble between Charles I and his Parliaments. But the fiscal problems that deterred James from entering the Thirty Years War and later crippled Charles's military endeavours would have remained. We can only speculate whether Henry IX would have done a better job than his younger brother at persuading Parliament to remedy those deficiencies, or devising a viable strategy for fighting Spain with a limited budget. Henry's close ties to nobles like Essex might have helped, but how much difference this would ultimately have made is an unanswerable question.

What we can say is that by dying when he did, Henry escaped having to confront the realities of seventeenth-century politics. He passed into the realm of memory and myth – where ideological choices became radically simplified, and intractable political and financial problems disappeared – a symbol of thwarted ambitions and lost hopes. His impressive funeral, and the outpouring of sermons and eulogies that followed, solidified his image as the Stuart prince who would have fulfilled the dreams of the Elizabethan war party, perhaps even leading a British army against Rome, as Melville had predicted in 1594. This picture of an unfulfilled reign appeals to the romantic belief that heroic leaders can solve major political problems, merely through devotion to principle and force of personality. Early Modern cults of royal virtue and glory encouraged this attitude, while modern fascination with the stories of great men who 'make' history by building, or saving, nation states has perpetuated it.

In an age of personal monarchy the temperament and outlook of a king mattered: Henry's survival would have made a difference, even if we cannot know how, or how much. Even in death, through his legend and his ghost, sighted in St James's Palace as early as 1615,[64] he influenced contemporary attitudes. But we need to distinguish between the legend and the actual Prince, who died in November 1612, aged eighteen.

NOTES

1 Strong 1986, p.15.
2 Ibid., pp.52, 71–85, esp. 84.
3 SP52/45, fol. 33, Robert Bowes to Lord Burghley, 24 April 1590: 'The King of Scots hath had long disputation in Latin with Hemingius of Denmark, tarrying with him one night and found him conformable in all the articles of religion, saving only in predestination, wherein the King hath hope that he shall be reformed'.
4 SP52/45, fol. 290, Bowes to Burghley, 9 May 1590.
5 BL Add. MSS 33531, fol. 235; Egerton MSS 2598, fols 16, 63 and 90.
6 Napier 1593.
7 [Alan Melville],'Principis Scoti-Britannorum Natalia' (1594), McGinnis and Williamson 1995, pp.278, 280.
8 SP52/54, fol. 34.
9 Goodare 2010, pp.21–48.
10 I have used the edition in McIlwain 1918, comparing it to the 1599 Scottish original; quotation at p.3.
11 Ibid.
12 pp.6, 23.
13 Malcolm Smuts, 'The Making of *Rex Pacificus*: James VI and the Problem of Peace in an Age of Religious War' in Fischlin and Fortier 2002, pp.371–87.
14 Herford and Simpson 1941, p.137.
15 McIlwain 1918, pp.29, 40.
16 TNA SO3/4, warrant of February 1609; SP14/5/63.
17 Orgel 1969, pp.142–58, quotation at p.157.
18 David Trim, 'Calvinist Internationalism and the shaping of Jacobean Foreign Policy' in Wilks 2007, pp.239–58. This is a subject in need of further detailed investigation.
19 Cf. McIlwain 1918, p.29 and Orgel 1969, p.155.
20 Birch 1760, p.44.
21 BL Harl. MSS 7002 *et passim*.

22 Price 1610, sig. A1v.
23 TNA, PRO31/3/41, fol. 217.
24 Birch 1760, p.224.
25 Birch 1848, p.212.
26 BL Harl. MSS 7008, fol. 112.
27 BL Harl. MSS 7008, fol. 209.
28 *Basilikon Doron*, pp.33, 34–8, 39–40, 48.
29 McCullough 1998, pp.183–94.
30 'Discourse on Spain' in BL Add. MSS 36444, fols 18–47; Birch 1749, pp.284–5.
31 Ayshna Pollnitz, 'Humanism and the Education of Henry, Prince of Wales' in Wilks 2007, pp.22–64.
32 Birch 1760, p.27.
33 TNA PRO31/3/41, Verteau dispatch of 14 November 1609.
34 For de' Servi and de Caus see Strong 1986, pp.86–110. Van Nyevelt is a more mysterious figure ignored by Strong who appears in a household list reproduced in Birch 1760, p.363, with a pension of £200 a year, equivalent to de' Servi's, double that of de Caus and four times that of Henry's Surveyor, Inigo Jones.
35 Pearsall Smith 1907, I, p.497.
36 Timothy Wilks, 'The Pike Charged: Henry as Militant Prince' in Wilks 2007, pp.180–211; Strong 1986, pp.57–60.
37 TNA PRO31/3/44, fol. 202v.
38 Ibid., fols 201v–202.
39 BL Cotton MSS Vitellius CXVIa, fol. 338.
40 BL Add. MSS 36444, fol. 47, Stowe MSS 169, fol. 110; Library of Congress microfilm LC041. camb202/2/35 (Trumbull MSS, old numeration, v. 21), Cottington to Trumbull, 19 August 1610; BL Stowe MSS 173, fol. 222v.
41 *CSP Venetian 1603–7*, XI, p.378.
42 A succinct modern account is Wilson 2009, pp.229–38.
43 Bouwsma 1968.

44 Cf. Wilson 2009, pp.28–31.
45 Trumbull Correspondence, old numeration, v. 4, fol. 98.
46 'The parliamentary installation of Henry, Prince of Wales', *Historical Research* 65 (1992), pp.177–93.
47 BL Harl. MSS 7002, fol. 73v.
48 Ibid., fol. 105.
49 TNA PRO31/3/44, fol. 207, 236, 244 bis.
50 BL Harl. MSS 7002, fol. 184.
51 BL Stowe MSS 171, fol. 206.
52 Ibid., fols 258, 268v–9.
53 Birch 1749, p.362.
54 BL Stowe MSS 172, fol. 284v.
55 Ibid., fol. 184.
56 Cornwallis 1641, p.2.
57 Birch 1749, p.352, Edmondes to James I, 20 June 1612, reporting a conversation with Bouillon.
58 The best modern account of this confusing period is Dubost 2009, pp.295–495.
59 Birch 1760, p.235.
60 Ibid., p.219.
61 Ibid., p.234.
62 Ibid., p.235.
63 TNA PRO31/3/45: 'Et quant à lui il ne fait pas beaucoup de démonstrations de s'en émouvoir et semble s'en remettre au jugement de son père.'
64 Online catalogue summary of Biblioteca Real MSS II/228, doc. 218, accessed June 2011.

Portraits of a 'most hopeful Prince'

CATHARINE MACLEOD

He was tall and of an high stature, his body strong and well proportioned, his shoulders were broad, his eyes quicke and pleasant, his forehead broad, his nose bigg, his chinne broad and clouen, his haire inclining to bleeke, whereas before it had been of a whitish colour, the colour of his face some what swarte and scorched with the sunne, his whole face and visage comely and beautifull, looking for the most part with a sweete, smyling, and amiable countenance, and withall full of grauity, and Princely majesty, resembling much in shape of his body, and diuers actions the King of Dennemark his Vncle.[1]

This verbal portrait of Henry, Prince of Wales, written by a contemporary, provides a close literary counterpart to perhaps the most well-known visual portrayal of the young Prince: Isaac Oliver's miniature (opposite, see also cat. 32). It shows the Prince not in rich clothing or official robes but in an elaborate, gilded suit of armour, apparently standing in a tent with a military encampment behind. His 'Princely majesty' is expressed not only through his physiognomy but also through his presentation as a knight, about to perform glorious deeds on the battlefield. The consistency with which Prince Henry was portrayed, both visually and verbally, is remarkable. Paintings and biographies reinforce one another, the former showing him as a warrior prince, the latter stressing his interest in all things military, including designs for fortifications, martial sports and contemporary conflicts.[2] Both support the image that has been preserved for posterity: in appearance, like his mother Anne of Denmark and his Danish uncle Christian IV; in character, brave, noble, athletic, intelligent, serious, majestic and wise. The biographies of the Prince, however, are all posthumous, and while they reflect a degree of first-hand knowledge, they were written with hindsight, in a context of loss and nostalgia, and were published later still, at a time when the image of the Prince was intended to serve new political purposes (see cat. 81). The majority of the surviving portraits are, on the other hand, contemporary. By exploring the most significant of these works, this essay considers the nature of Prince Henry's visual image during his lifetime, the existing iconographical conventions that his portrait painters drew upon and the new kinds of iconography that they developed for it. In so doing, it questions traditional assumptions as to who was generating this royal image, and what purpose it was intended to serve.

While a complex web of influences – including the relationships between and agendas of sitter, artist and patron – contributes to the shaping of every portrait of every individual, there were additional, particular factors at work in Prince Henry's portraiture. As the heir to the thrones of England and Scotland, the only person regarded as being of greater importance than Henry was his father, King James. Yet as king-in-waiting there was little scope for Henry to express publicly his real wishes and desires, to make manifest in his actions or visual imagery the priorities he intended for his reign, or even to reveal a great deal about his personality, unless these inclinations coincided with the agendas of his father and his advisors. Under the watchful care of tutors and attendants, and ultimately of the King, Henry's image – in the abstract and as shown in individual portraits – was created to convey political and social objectives that were specific to certain circumstances (often obscure today) and to express more general hope for a new age. Portraiture provided a medium, along with masques, tournaments and other elaborate festivals, by means of which the Prince could be presented as a symbol of an idealised future. In a sense, what the Prince actually was, as a child and teenager, only mattered in so far as it foretold what he would become – or what it was hoped he would become – when he was King. The concern of those around him was with 'you most hopefull Prince, not as you are/But as you may be', as Samuel Daniel put it in his dedication to the Prince in *The Tragedie of Philotas*.[3] The extent to which the Prince himself was involved in the development of this prophetic, propagandistic imagery might be easier to gauge today if he had

FIG. 10
The Whitehall Mural Cartoon:
detail showing Henry VIII,
Hans Holbein the Younger, *c.*1536

lived to become king and, in the context of hugely increased autonomy, had revealed his own priorities in the development of his image. As it is, his early death has made it impossible now to untangle fully the young Prince's own image-making agenda from that of his advisors and of other courtiers who may have commissioned his portraits.

A sense of the importance of Henry's image as conveyed through portraiture emerges early in his life. While there are few portraits dating from his childhood in Scotland,[4] surviving works and payments in royal records indicate that there was a steady production of pictures from his arrival in England in 1603. From the beginning there are indications that the models provided by extant royal portraiture were regarded as inadequate. Excluding his father, James, whose inheritance of the English throne was not a certainty during his childhood, Henry was the first male heir to the throne since Edward VI, so any precedents in English portraiture of heirs apparent were sixty years old. The solution to the problem of portraying the king-in-waiting in the mid-sixteenth century had been to create an iconography that mirrored that of the king, his father. But Prince Henry had grown up in very different circumstances from Edward. The intervening decades of relative peace and stability under Elizabeth I were followed by a wave of optimism, after the arrival in England in 1603 of a ready-made royal family – the Stuarts. This optimism, combined with a relative lack of anxiety over the succession, compared with Tudor times, seemed to demand a new, more ambitious kind of painted image for the young Prince.

This new kind of portraiture was to be neither a reflection of that of Henry's predecessor as Prince of Wales, nor of that of his father. Whereas the majority of Edward VI's portraits, such as the portrait in the Royal Collection of Edward when Prince of Wales, were based on the full-length image of Henry VIII by Hans Holbein the Younger (figs 10 and 11),[5] Henry's portraits were in the main completely different from those of his father, James I. By contrast with Henry VIII, whom Holbein had famously painted with legs wide apart, face turned fully to the front,

challenging the viewer to meet his intimidating stare, James I was depicted in his first English royal portraits in a much less confrontational and more elegant pose, turned at an angle to the viewer. Positioned beside a draped table or an upholstered chair, he has an air of superiority and distance, appears richly dressed and is placed in a sumptuous setting, but there is little to distinguish him from his own courtiers in their portraits. The artist who created these images of James, convincingly identified as John de Critz (d.1642), was following the well-established fashions of continental European court portraiture, created by Anthonis Mor and Titian for the

FIG. II
Edward VI when Prince of Wales,
attributed to William Scrots, *c.*1546

inspired him with new vigour and stimulated an unexpec-tedly innovative group of paintings.[8] The opportunity to paint Henry arose very shortly after the Prince's arrival in England, with a commission that presumably came from John, 1st Baron Harington of Exton, guardian of Henry's sister, Princess Elizabeth.[9] Peake painted Henry with his close companion, Harington's son, also called John, in 1603, in an extraordinary and unprecedented composition (fig. 12). Nothing in Peake's earlier portraiture suggests that he was about to produce a painting of this kind; it must have appeared startling in the extreme to his contemporaries. The outdoor setting was in itself a novelty, and the grouping of the ancillary figures around the Prince – horse, groom, dog, deer and kneeling attendant, not ranged formally and statically but as part of an implied narrative – has no precedent in large-scale royal portraiture in England. Moreover, the Prince is shown in the act of sheathing his sword, caught in action rather than stasis, another remarkable innovation. This striking work (of which Peake and his workshop produced a later variant, replacing Harington with another of Henry's companions, Robert Devereux, 3rd Earl of Essex; see cat. 14) was the first in a series of three painted by the artist in which, in response to the challenge of portraying the young Prince, he appears to be trying to out-do himself in inventiveness.

The subject of the painting is a significant, and specific-ally English, moment in the royal hunting ritual. The portrait may derive from an earlier woodcut, or from a lost, more direct and closely related print source (see cat. 14 and fig. 16). No doubt it was intended in part to be a graceful compliment to James, who was well known to be extremely fond of hunting. It has also been pointed out that the wide-legged pose of the Prince echoes the full-length portraits of Henry VIII and Edward VI, but with his right arm raised, holding his sword, Prince Henry's stance and the sense of being caught in action appear to derive more directly from the traditions of narrative or religious paintings than from British portraiture.[10] In the former category, images of the Archangel Michael are perhaps closest in type; traditionally depicted as a winged

Habsburg rulers of the sixteenth century.[6] But although Prince Henry was painted once, as far as is now known, in this format (see cat. 45), the series of strikingly original compositions that followed suggests that this conventional type of image was regarded as an inadequate means of expressing the promise that Henry embodied.

The artist most closely associated with Prince Henry throughout his life in England was Robert Peake the Elder (*c.*1551–1619), who, like John de Critz, was already a well-established painter when James succeeded to the English throne, but does not seem to have worked as a portraitist for the previous monarch.[7] Indeed, Peake must have been in his fifties in the early years of the seventeenth century, and the major part of his career was already behind him. But the arrival of the young heir apparent seems to have

knight in armour, St Michael is usually shown standing, legs apart, drawing or raising his sword to defeat the Devil, often in the form of a dragon at his feet. While this might seem an unlikely visual reference in a court associated strongly with Protestantism, St Michael was, along with St George, an exemplar of virtuous, militant Christianity. In spite of its hunting rather than military theme, this painting, when viewed in this context and particularly when considered in relation to Peake's subsequent portraits, can be seen as introducing a new dynamic, chivalric type of imagery of the Prince.[11]

The second remarkable portrait of Prince Henry by Peake is a work now in the collection of the Palazzo Reale in Turin (see cat. 60). It shows the Prince once again standing in a wooded landscape setting, with a bridge and part of a building in the background. He wears green, as in the double portrait, which is not only a hunting colour but also the colour of hope.[12] This time he is apparently in the act of unsheathing his sword, in a pose that again echoes depictions of the Archangel Michael. He stands with one foot on a shield of the type used in tournaments and entertainments at the Jacobean court, elaborately shaped, with scrolled edges. The knights taking part in such

tournaments generally had symbolic images and mottoes, or *imprese*, on their shields. At the centre of Prince Henry's shield are the three white feathers and the motto 'Ich Dien' ('I serve'), usually associated today with Princes of Wales but, strictly speaking, the badge of the heir apparent. Both are known to have been used in connection with Henry prior to his official creation as Prince of Wales, which took place in 1610.[13]

It seems likely that this portrait, in spite of the fact that it appears to have been painted somewhat earlier (probably between about 1605 and 1608; see cat. 60), came into the collection of the Dukes of Savoy as part of the marriage negotiations on behalf of Prince Henry and the Infanta Maria, daughter of Charles Emmanuel I of Savoy, which began early in 1611. There is a direct source for the composition in Hendrick Goltzius's print of Titus Manlius Torquatus from his series Roman Heroes (see fig. 24, p.142), published in 1586.[14] Goltzius (1558–1617) was an admired and influential artist of the period; Henry acquired at least one painting by him for his own collection.[15] Thus the use of this pose would have suggested, to those knowledgeable in the field, parallels and associations between the young Prince and a Roman military hero. While the Prince is obviously small and young by comparison with the implausibly muscular Roman, for those inclined to pin their hopes of military triumph on the Prince the comparison would have promised great things to come. But by contrast with Goltzius's complex, receding landscape, Peake's woodland looks like a series of stage flats, set at intervals behind Henry.[16] Peake's painting can thus be interpreted as alluding to the promise of a heroic, military future, as symbolised by the young Prince, and yet also as echoing the artificial, often literally theatrical context within which his militarism was, for the present, confined.

The third of Peake's adventurous compositions, painted probably *c*.1608, is the most dramatic and most mysterious of all (see cat. 28). A full-size, full-length portrait of the Prince on horseback, its basic equestrian composition would have been familiar in some circles from prints and royal seals, and from a well-established tradition of

FIG. 13
Knight, Death and the Devil,
Albrecht Dürer, 1513

equestrian paintings of continental, especially Italian and French, rulers.[17] But again, it was entirely novel in large-scale British portraits of royalty. Henry is depicted fully armed, accompanied by a figure who appears to be a personification of Time amalgamated with Opportunity, whom he pulls along by means of the favour on his arm, which is tied to Time's forelock.[18] Peake seems to have used Albrecht Dürer's print of 1513, *Knight, Death and the Devil* (fig. 13), as a source for his composition and, as with the Turin portrait, the knowledgeable viewer might well have understood the parallel being drawn between Dürer's virtuous knight, riding bravely onward, undeterred by the figures of Death and the Devil alongside him, and the young Prince. As Gail Weigl has pointed out, the painting echoes lines written by Ben Jonson years before and addressed to Henry: 'O shoot up fast in spirit, as in yeares; .../And when slow Time hath made you fit for warre/ Looke ouer the strict Ocean, and thinke where/you may but lead us forth ... .'[19] But the sense of Henry's fitness for and progress towards war is undermined by the fact – which would have been immediately recognisable to his contemporaries – that his elaborate armour was made for display in the tilt yard, not for the feats of battle, and he rides alongside a brick wall, not before a battlefield. Henry's urgent progress, accompanied by a representation of a mythological character rather than a real squire, is towards a mock battle, not a real one.

These three remarkable works by Peake share a number of elements in common: in each, Peake is striving to do something compositionally new in English royal portraiture; in each, Henry is depicted as a prince of action, caught in movement rather than stasis; in each he is shown with armour, weapons, or both. In different ways, each portrait seems simultaneously to promote Henry as the embodiment of military hope for the future, and yet to draw attention to his youth, and to the artificial, symbolic, theatrical context within which his military promise was contained. Peake's uncompromisingly Elizabethan style of painting, with its emphasis on elaborate, decorative surfaces rather than convincing spatial recession, has

the effect of emphasising the artificiality of these scenes. His portraits are, in a sense, the descendants of sixteenth-century cabinet miniatures of Elizabethan heroes such as the Earls of Leicester and Essex and Sir Philip Sidney, shown in their tournament armour, and they suggest links between Henry and these figures of the past (fig. 14).[20] These Elizabethan soldiers can be regarded as exemplars of the transference of tilt yard prowess to the real field of battle, and for those who hoped that Henry would augment this tradition, his portraits would have symbolised – in effect acted as emblems of – the great feats that he would perform as an adult. But they suggested this from the safe distance of a present in which Henry was quite clearly a boy performing within the constraints of the hunt, the tilt yard and the theatre.

There has been a tendency in the literature on Prince Henry to assume that he himself must have both devised the elaborate compositions in which he is depicted, and, at least in the case of the latter two, commissioned the paintings.[21] It has been extrapolated from this and from Henry's known interest in martial endeavour that his intention was to present himself as the champion of militant Protestantism, ready to join in battle on the continent in opposition to the policies of his relatively pacific father. However, there is no written evidence about the commissions for any of the three portraits, and whatever Henry's own intentions may have been, it is, as noted earlier, now impossible to isolate them from the complex network of influences being brought to bear on him. But it is worth considering the probable contexts for the production of these portraits, as they have an important bearing on the development of the Prince's image, and who is likely to have been behind this image-making, both literally – in terms of the pictures – and metaphorically – in terms of the propaganda being put out about the Prince.

The double portrait with Harington (see fig. 12 and the later version with Essex, see cat. 14) is most likely to have been commissioned by the family of the Prince's companion; there is no evidence that the Harington portrait was ever in the Royal Collection (and the Essex portrait joined that collection much later). King James I, whose own portraiture was conservative in nature (see cats 3 and 5), does not seem a likely source for this innovative composition, but as this portrait of Henry was produced so early in James's reign in England, and was so large and important, it seems possible that the King gave it his royal approval. Certainly those in charge of Henry, men appointed and trusted by the King, must have approved the scheme and given access to the Prince. James was known to be aware of the power of portraits and he had demonstrated concern about the misuse of images of his own family.[22] Likewise, the Turin portrait must have had official approval if it had been sent directly to the Duke of Savoy from the English court in connection with the Prince's marriage negotiations, or even, as has been recently suggested, if it was passed by Sir Henry Wotton from his own collection in Venice to the Duke of Savoy during the negotiation process (see cat. 60). The third portrait, the equestrian image of Henry, is first recorded in the collection of Henry Howard, Earl of Northampton, after the Prince's death.[23] It is most likely that it was commissioned by a courtier, perhaps Northampton himself, wishing to compliment the young Prince, and its iconography was probably approved by Henry himself and by implication,

given the Prince's age and lack of autonomy, by the King or his representatives.[24]

The desire to see Henry as the originator of this type of composition derives partly from a traditional narrative about the Prince, in which he is seen as at odds with his father and somehow beyond the latter's control.[25] But as all the contemporary biographies record, however different his personality and inclinations may have been, Henry had a strong sense of obedience to his father.[26] And it must be asked how likely it really is that the young Prince, probably no more than about fourteen years old in the Turin portrait, would have or could have devised an iconographic scheme for a painting with the intention of communicating a military and political policy in opposition to that of the King. Moreover, as far as the equestrian portrait is concerned, while Henry was undoubtedly genuinely responsive to art, it seems unlikely that he had the knowledge and confidence in artistic matters to come up with a whole new direction for large-scale royal portraiture. What seems more plausible is that those who commissioned the portraits, perhaps together with Peake, found the print sources and suggested them as models for the compositions. Henry was surrounded by advisors and tutors, who, we must remember, were chosen for him by his father, many of them highly knowledgeable about both classical literature and contemporary art (see, for example, cats 15 and 18). It may be that one or more of these men were involved with this process. Henry no doubt had a role in acquiescing, or not, to the plans put forward, and the intention of the patron was undoubtedly to honour the Prince by having him depicted in a manner that accorded with his conception of himself and the propagandistic agendas of his court. The patron, however, was the man or woman with the money, and his or her exchange with the artist was of critical importance; moreover, among his courtiers, obedience and deference to the King was paramount. Prince Henry may not even have sat for each of these portraits; although he does appear slightly older in each successive painting, the basic similarity in the angle and structure of the heads makes it possible that

Peake simply adjusted and aged the face using a face pattern that he kept in his studio.

Henry may have played a more active role, however, in the series of portrait miniatures by Isaac Oliver (*c*.1565–1617). Oliver was an official limner (miniature painter) to Henry's mother, Queen Anne, from 1605, but was described in Henry's funeral accounts as the Prince's 'Painter'. The survival of a relatively large number of repetitions by Oliver of one miniature type of the Prince suggests that he was creating a standard portrait with the approval of Henry and his advisors. It is also significant that Henry's brother, Charles, is recorded later as owning two miniatures of Henry of this type.[27] Oliver's portraits show Henry as a young man rather than a boy, clearly at a slightly later date than the three Peake paintings considered above, and almost certainly after his creation as Prince of Wales at the age of sixteen, when the Prince gained a more extensive household and more autonomy with regard to his finances. As a younger boy Henry had been painted by Nicholas Hilliard (1547–1619), the favoured miniaturist of Elizabeth I (see cat. 5), but the choice of Oliver at this stage was significant; it linked Henry's patronage to that of his mother, rather than his father, who continued to be painted by Hilliard until the artist's death. It suggests, as does much of Henry's collecting, a concern to be connected with the most

up-to-date, fashionable and even novel developments in art. Oliver was a generation younger than Hilliard and his softer, more fully modelled style had strong links to the work of avant-garde continental painters of the period.[28]

Oliver's most famous miniature of the Prince, alluded to at the start of this essay (see p.32 and cat. 32), is the most magnificent survivor of this group. They are relatively straightforward portraits, in which the Prince, dressed in elaborate tournament armour, looks out at the viewer, his face turned slightly to one side, against the background of a red velvet curtain. Only in the larger, rectangular example (cat. 32) is there any significant variation, in the form of the distant military encampment. The format of the rectangular miniature, cutting off the Prince at chest level, combined with Oliver's soft and rounded, yet precise style, echoes the approach of certain Dutch artists of the period, perhaps particularly Michiel van Mierevelt (1566–1641), the Delft painter whom Henry tried to bring to England (see cat. 50). It would seem that after Peake's experimental but distinctly English portraits, there was a move, at least in the case of this miniature, to link Henry's iconography to the visual culture of continental Europe. In this context, Henry's visual image reflected a wider agenda that sought to present him as a prince on the European stage through his acquisition of princely collections of paintings, sculpture, antiquities and books (see pp.118–9).

Oliver also produced a more adventurous composition for the Prince, in which he is presented as a Roman hero, in profile, against a shell-shaped niche (see cat. 44). This portrait seems to be one in a series by Oliver of sitters depicted in a similar setting and style; its iconography is exclusively classical and it may have been inspired by the Prince's acquisition of an important collection of antique coins, medals and cameos.[29] The Prince is implicitly compared with great Roman military leaders, or emperors; at the same time the echoes in the miniature of antique works of art may be seen as alluding to his classical knowledge and precocious collecting of antique objects.[30] At least three versions of this miniature survive, but it was clearly not as widespread in terms of ownership as the more conventional miniature type. The profile portrait came into much wider circulation, however, as the head of a full-length figure of the Prince. Oliver used the head as the basis for a drawing that showed the Prince standing, dressed in contemporary armour, practising a military exercise with a pike. Oliver's original drawing is now lost, but it is known through an engraving after the work by William Hole (see cat. 26), which was first published as the frontispiece to Michael Drayton's *Poly-olbion*, dedicated to the Prince, in 1612. The striking qualities of the composition, as well as its appropriateness in the context of the Prince's martial image, ensured that it continued to be produced in a number of variant prints for some years after Henry's death.[31]

Like Peake, Oliver draws on and makes reference to both classical sources and the chivalric traditions of performance, portraiture and literature. This eclecticism was entirely characteristic of the age, and a notable feature of the elaborate entertainments in which the Prince took part.[32] It has been argued that Ben Jonson and Inigo Jones used classical references in their masques to promote humanist educational and civic values as a counterbalance to Henry's militaristic leanings, creating a new kind of chivalry.[33] While this may well be the case, and there undoubtedly were moments in the last couple of years of Henry's life when James also seemed to think that his

son's military interests needed checking,[34] Oliver's easy transfer of his classical profile head of Henry on to a body dressed in tilting armour suggests neither conflict between the implications of Roman heroism and chivalric heroism, nor anxiety over the depiction of Henry in military guise.

Oliver seems to have had, in the later years of Henry's life, a virtual monopoly over his portraiture in miniature.[35] Numerous other oils were painted, many coming from Peake's studio, others by both known and unknown artists (see fig. 4 and cat. 7). By far the majority of these show the Prince either in armour or in the robes of a Knight of the Order of the Garter, the most significant chivalric order of the period. The latter works, while not showing the Prince actually armed, do of course allude to his role as a knight, ready to take arms on behalf of noble and virtuous causes, like the Order's patron saint, St George.

Prince Henry's portraits, then, both small and large-scale, show remarkable consistency in depicting him as a military champion, using a wide and innovative range of iconographic material, drawn from chivalric traditions, classical literature and imagery, and contemporary visual sources. It is, however, implausible to see this visual image-making as primarily generated by the Prince, or indeed created in order to promote a policy of militant Protestantism in opposition to that of the King's avowed pacifism, particularly in the case of those portraits painted, like the three by Peake discussed here, when Henry was very young. Henry's image as a militant prince must have been a collective, collaborative creation, undertaken with the full knowledge of his advisors – men put in place by the King – and with the acquiescence of the King himself, whose concern with Henry's education and self-presentation is amply testified to in his letters and his book on kingship, *Basilikon Doron* (see cats 11 and 12). Undoubtedly there were those who wanted to encourage Henry to pursue a more aggressive foreign policy than that of his father, and Henry's martial image, as generated by the literature, diplomatic correspondence and visual arts of the period, ideally suited their purposes. It also reflected the Prince's real concerns; his enthusiasm for martial exercises and his wider interest in military matters was much commented on,[36] as was his devotion to Protestantism, and the consistency with which this is reported by a wide range of commentators is evidence that this was not just image-building or wishful thinking. It seems likely that he actively colluded in a campaign to present himself as a potential militant Protestant hero.

But ultimately, just as Henry's martial visual image must be associated with a broad spectrum of patrons, advisors and artists, in addition to the Prince and the King himself, so, with its numerous references, it is susceptible of numerous interpretations. It can be seen as an extension of Elizabethan traditions, as Malcolm Smuts has indicated (p.26);[37] as a promise of militant action in the future; or as a means of emphasising the Prince's cultural links with continental Europe and classical antiquity. Such malleability in the interpretation of Henry's portraits had distinct advantages for James. As Kevin Sharpe recently put it, 'By acting as the focus and symbol for one policy, while

James himself more represented another, Henry enabled the Stuart Family, indeed the king himself, to represent both peace and war, a pacific diplomacy with the prospect of militant action; as one elegist put it, "halfe love, halfe warre"',[38] or, as he wrote elsewhere, Henry's image enabled 'the Stuart dynasty simultaneously to stand for quite contrary values, to represent the aims and ambitions of different factions, and to embody the differing hopes of subjects'.[39] James benefited from this approach not solely in relation to his own subjects; foreign ambassadors tended to report on divisions between the Prince and King, advising that whereas the King might not support their cause, the Prince would do so if he were old enough, or might do in years to come.[40] Yet while so many of Henry's portraits seem to promise military endeavour, this action is located in an unspecified, fictive, symbolic setting. The Prince is a knight in an arena built from the stories of Arthurian chivalry and myths of Roman heroes, and there is no certainty that he will ever move beyond it.

NOTES

1 W.H., *The True Picture and Relation of Prince Henry* [...] Leiden, 1634. W.H. may have been a Groom of the Prince's Bedchamber by the name of William Haydon; see Strong 1986, p.227.

2 Two other biographies of the Prince were published in 1641, one by Sir Charles Cornwallis, *A Discourse of the most illustrious prince, Henry, late Prince of Wales*, published by John Benson, London, from a manuscript of 1626; and a second, also purporting to be by Cornwallis, but not by him, entitled *The Life and Death of our Late most Incomparable and Heroique Prince, Henry, Prince of Wales* [...], from a manuscript of 1613, published by Nathanael Butter. See pp.20–1 of the latter in particular for the Prince's martial interests, and cat. 81. Francis Bacon also wrote a brief description of Prince Henry entitled 'The Praise of Henry, Prince of Wales'; see Joseph Devey (ed.), *The Moral and Historical Works of Lord Bacon* [...], London, 1866, pp.493–5.

3 Samuel Daniel, dedication to *The Tragedie of Philotas*, published in *Certaine small poems lately printed with the Tragedie of Philotas*, London, 1605.

4 Roy Strong records only one portrait of Henry from before the accession of James VI of Scotland to the English throne. See Strong 1969, p.162, and here, cat. 7.

5 See Millar 1963, vol. 1, p.66, no. 49 and vol. 11, pl. 33.

6 For de Critz, see cat. 3.

7 A painting depicting Elizabeth I in procession at Sherborne Castle has been attributed to Peake, but it has little in common with the securely attributed works and seems unlikely to be by him. Peake was attached to the Office of Revels under Elizabeth. See Hearn, 'Peake, Robert', ODNB 2004.

8 It seems likely that Peake's inventiveness was at least in part motivated by the hope of attracting further patronage at the new court. His success

can be measured by the fact that he was appointed to the important job of Serjeant-Painter, jointly with John de Critz, in 1607. Although Peake and his studio produced the majority of the oil portraits of Henry that survive, and he is listed among those who received allowances of mourning cloth for the Prince's funeral (Wilks 1987, p.281), it is not clear that he actually held a post in Henry's household.

9 This is now in the Metropolitan Museum, New York. The portrait of Princess Elizabeth by Peake belonging to the National Maritime Museum, London (cat. 8) appears to have been painted as a companion piece. See Hearn 1995, pp.185–6.

10 See Williamson 1978, pp.28–9.

11 The meaning and nature of chivalry in the Middle Ages and subsequently has been much debated. For the purposes of this essay, I am using the term to denote the concept of the virtuous, noble knight, ready to enter battle on behalf of God,

associated with the literature of King Arthur and related British mythology.

12 For example, Job:14: 'A tree hath hope, if it be cut, it waxeth green againe'.

13 I am grateful to Bridget Wright of the Royal Library for pointing out that these are correctly known as the heir apparent's feathers. There are a number of examples of the feathers and motto being used in relation to Henry before his creation as Prince of Wales. For example, they are used on the frontispiece of John Norden's *A Description of the Honor of Windesor ...*, of 1607 (Royal Library, Windsor); also the embroidered velvet cover of the illuminated manuscript presented to Prince Henry in Oxford in 1605 (see cat. 59).

14 See Strong 1986, p.114; also Bertana 1983, pp.423–6.

15 See Strong 1986, p.201, fig. 91.

16 This was pointed out by Ellen Chirelstein (see Chirelstein 1990, p.51).

17 See Gail Capitol Weigl, '"And when slow Time hath mad you fit for warre": The Equestrian Portrait of Prince Henry', in Wilks 2007, pp.146–72.

18 See Strong 1986, p.115.

19 See Weigl, op. cit., p.157 and Ben Jonson 'The Entertainment at Althorp' in Herford and Simpson 1941, p.131.

20 Roy Strong, in Strong 1986, p.223, writes of Henry in an 'ideological line of descent' from these three figures, noting that 'All three acted as a focus of attempts to introduce the fruits of Renaissance civilization while maintaining an extreme Protestant and anti-Spanish stance.' But as he also notes, the Prince was equally linked with opponents of these men and members of rival factions, such as Sir Walter Ralegh and Robert Cecil, 1st Earl of Salisbury, the latter also a great collector.

21 For example, John Peacock, 'The Politics of Portraiture', in Lake and Sharpe 1994, pp.213–14 and p.215; Strong 1984, p.114; and Williamson 1978, p.69, 'In honor of his own elevation to the Principality of Wales, Henry commissioned a magnificent equestrian portrait of himself.'

22 See Campbell 1985, p.xxxiii.

23 See Timothy Wilks, '*Henry Prince of Wales, on Horseback:* A note on patronage and provenance', in Wilks 2007, p.173.

24 Wilks discusses the possibility that Northampton could have commissioned the portrait, art. cit., pp.173–9. It appears that the painting was in Northampton's 'Lower House' by 1614, one of two houses he had in Greenwich (correspondence with Timothy Wilks).

25 Differences between the two were played up in some of the diplomatic correspondence of the day, such as the *Relazione* of 1607 by Nicolo Molin, CSP Venetian, 1603–7, pp.513–14, cited in Strong 1986, pp.14–15 and p.230, note 27. This and other accounts of James I's criticism of his son have led commentators to exaggerate the extent to which Henry wilfully defied his father. Strong is surely going much too far in stating 'To the King, terrible though it may seem, the premature death of the Prince was to come almost as a relief', Strong 1986, p.15.

26 Sir Charles Cornwallis, Henry's Treasurer and biographer, refers to 'maligners of true vertue', hinting at rumours of disagreements or disrespect, and he contradicts this strongly, asserting the Prince's true loyalty and obedience to his father, in thought and action (Cornwallis 1641, pp.3–4). Strong also notes, in Strong 1986, p.83: 'Obedience to the King was a central facet of the Prince's make-up.'

27 These two miniatures are cat 32; and Reynolds 1999, no. 55. Both are recorded in Charles I's collection in the catalogue written by Abraham van der Doort; see Reynolds, op.cit., pp.91–3.

28 See Reynolds 1988, pp.21–23.

29 See p.133.

30 See p.118.

31 Timothy Wilks, 'The Pike Charged: Henry as Militant Prince', in Wilks 2007, pp.188–211.

32 As John Peacock has commented on the masques and tournaments of the period, 'The synthesis of neo-medieval chivalric [military] exercises and the forms of classical antiquity had become a characteristic feature of Renaissance court culture. In the classicising intellectual milieux of [Ben] Jonson and [Inigo] Jones the connexion was intrinsically established.' Peacock 1995, p.280. Strong also refers to the eclecticism of Henry's portraiture, in which he is shown as 'Spenserian knight and Roman imperator rolled into one', see Strong 1986, p.117.

33 Council 1980, pp.259–75, especially p.269: 'Jonson's efforts to accommodate Prince Henry's apparent desire to identify himself with a revival of chivalric grandeur conflicted so significantly with Jonson's own assessment of the model offered by chivalry that throughout the *Barriers* he criticizes and redefines its terms.' Council is building on Williamson's analysis of 'the rival myth' to that of Henry as conqueror, which he sees as particularly promoted by Jonson: Williamson 1978, ch. 4, pp.75–107.

34 For example, in *c.*1609/10, after Henry received a tract entitled *Arguments for War*, James had Robert Cotton write a response, later published as *Wars with foreign Princes dangerous to our Commonwealth* [...] (1657) and in another edition as *An Answer to such Motives, as were offered by certain Military men to Prince Henry, inciting him to affect Arms more than Peace* (1675).

35 Henry's official 'limner' or miniaturist, however, was the mysterious Mark Belford or Bilford (see Wilks 1987, pp.101–2).

36 For example, the French ambassador La Boderie recorded in 1606 that Henry 'studies two hours a day, and employs the rest of his time in tossing the pike, or leaping, or shooting with the bow, or throwing the bar, or vaulting, or some other exercise of that kind; and he is never idle'. Quoted in Birch 1760, p.76.

37 Frances Yates, in an important study, first argued that the promotion of Henry as a chivalric hero was part of a revival of an Elizabethan interest in chivalry that centred on a group of militant courtiers, who wanted to push James I into war on the continent. Even if we now accept that James's policy, at least in the first part of his reign, was not the 'appeasement' that Yates claimed it to be, she was right to associate the chivalric image with Elizabethan traditions. See Yates 1975, especially ch. 1, 'The Elizabethan Revival in the Jacobean Age', pp.17–37.

38 Thomas Heywood, *A Funerall Elegie* [...], 1613, quoted in Sharpe 2010, p.110.

39 Sharpe 2010, p.108.

40 See, for example, the correspondence of Sir Henry Wotton, Paulo Sarpi and the Doge of Venice, referred to in Strong 1986, pp.75–6.

A New Royal Family

On 24 March 1603 Elizabeth, Queen of England and Ireland, died at the age of sixty-nine. There had been much discussion during her lifetime as to who would be successor to the childless Queen; in the event the throne passed swiftly and with little controversy to James VI of Scotland, whose grandfather, James V, had been Elizabeth's first cousin. James VI had inherited the Scottish throne on the abdication of his mother, Mary, Queen of Scots, at the age of just thirteen months. His reign in Scotland had been relatively successful in a difficult political context, and his arrival in England was eagerly awaited, not least because, for the first time in living memory, the new monarch had a family, which comprised an heir, a 'spare' and a marriageable daughter.

James had married Anne, or Anna as she was known in Scotland, the second daughter of Frederick II of Denmark, in 1589. The early years of their marriage seem to have been relatively happy, although Anne was to become involved in various unfortunate political intrigues and also suffered several miscarriages. On 19 February 1594, in Stirling Castle, she gave birth to a son, Henry Frederick, amid much rejoicing. Henry, Duke of Rothesay, as he was then known, was baptised on 29 August that year in a new Chapel Royal, built specially for the occasion. The baptism ceremony, attended by the Earl of Sussex as proxy for Queen Elizabeth, was of unprecedented splendour; banquets, tilts and masques were held in the Prince's honour and poetry celebrated the hope for the future that he represented.

Shortly after his birth Henry was removed from his mother's care and he remained at Stirling in the charge of John Erskine, 2nd Earl of Mar, and his mother, the Dowager Countess. The principle of fostering royal children was well established in Scotland and elsewhere, and it seemed the most sensible and safest course of action to James, who had grown up without seeing his own mother after the age of ten months. This separation brought enormous distress to Anne, however, and marked the beginning of a deterioration

Prince Henry, Marcus Gheeraerts
the Younger, *c*.1603 (detail of cat. 7)

in her relations with James. Four more children were born to the couple in Scotland: Elizabeth (1596–1662), Margaret (1598–1600), Charles (1600–49) and Robert (born and died 1602). Two more daughters, Mary (1605–07) and Sophia (born and died 1606), were born after James's accession to the English throne; like Margaret and Robert, they also died young.

A month after James's accession to the English throne, he made a long and slow journey south to London, greeted at each stage by jubilant crowds. Anne followed in the summer with her two eldest children, having successfully wrested Henry from the control of the Earl of Mar under dramatic circumstances. Once in England, the children were again separated from their parents and each other. Henry had his own household, which was based mainly at the palace of Nonsuch during his early years in England; after his creation as Prince of Wales in 1610, he divided his time mainly between St James's and Richmond Palaces. Princess Elizabeth was sent to live briefly with Frances, Lady Cobham, and then in the household of John, 1st Baron Harington of Exton and his wife Anne. Charles, who, owing to ill health, had followed the family to London a year later, lived in the household of Sir Robert and Lady Carey. Although Henry did see his parents periodically, particularly his mother, much of his communication with them was by letter. Henry's surviving correspondence with his parents is formal, dutiful and correct, written in English, Latin or French; it also reveals that he found himself from time to time caught up in disputes between them. James's letters to Henry by contrast appear spontaneous, swinging between parental severity, advice and affection.

James had clear views about the responsibilities and privileges of kingship, and also had well-established credentials as an author. He combined these two interests in a practical manual on how to rule, entitled (in Greek) *Basilikon Doron* (Royal Gift), which he addressed to Henry.

In its first Edinburgh edition of 1599, only seven copies were printed. James's arrival in London prompted great curiosity about the new king, however, and once a publisher by the name of John Norton had obtained a copy, new editions flooded the market. It is estimated that between 13,000 and 16,000 copies of *Basilikon Doron* were printed in the space of about two and a half weeks.

Interest in the new royal family expressed itself in other ways, including the desire for portraits. Courtiers, eager to show their loyalty, commissioned images of the new monarch, his wife and children, and the royal family had portraits painted to send to political allies at home and abroad. Robert Peake the Elder became the favoured painter for depictions of the children; John de Critz produced the earliest English portraits of the King and Queen. Miniature portraits were also required; the artist Nicholas Oliver supplied the earliest of these but, although Hilliard continued to produce portraits of James until the artist's death, Isaac Oliver soon became the favoured artist for miniatures of the Queen and her three children.

Not all subjects greeted the arrival of the Stuart family with unalloyed joy, however. James's approach to religious difference was relatively tolerant for the time, and his Queen had converted to Roman Catholicism, which she was allowed to practise privately. But a small group plotted for the establishment of Catholic rule in Britain, and thus the Gunpowder Plot was born. The plan was to blow up the House of Lords, containing the King, Prince Henry and all the ruling elite, at the opening of Parliament in the autumn of 1605. Meanwhile Princess Elizabeth would be kidnapped, to be placed on the throne as a Catholic puppet queen. The plot was uncovered, the plotters killed or captured and executed, and the famous celebration of 5 November established. The episode served to increase James's popularity – for a time. C.M.

I

Prince Henry Frederick (1594–1612)

UNIDENTIFIED ARTIST, 1596

Oil on canvas, 686 × 521mm
Inscribed top left: *FHREDERICVS + HENRI/CVS + D + G + PRINCEPS +/SCOTORVM + ÆTATIS +/SVAE + 2 +1596+*
Private Collection

The birth of a son to James VI of Scotland and his Queen, Anne of Denmark, on 19 February 1594 was an event of great importance to both the Scottish and the English royal dynasties. Not only was he the heir to the throne of Scotland, but by this stage his father, James VI, was also considered the most likely successor to Elizabeth I, ruler of England, Wales and Ireland. Thus the young Prince was seen as the probable heir to the whole of Britain. He was named Henry Frederick (not Frederick Henry as the inscription on this painting puzzlingly implies). Henry was the obvious name; it was not only that of his paternal grandfather, Henry Stuart, Lord Darnley, but it also alluded flatteringly to Queen Elizabeth's father, Henry VIII, and also to her grandfather, Henry VII, from whom the baby Prince was directly descended (see cat. 2), and in addition to his godfather, Henri IV of France. Frederick was the name of his maternal grandfather, Frederick II of Denmark.

It was a mark of the Prince's significance – and of his father's inclination to spend lavishly on magnificent events – that Henry's baptism at Stirling Castle was one of the most spectacular occasions to take place in Scotland. The whole celebration, including the rebuilding of the Chapel Royal, cost £100,000 Scots, which was raised through a special tax. The banquet included, among other spectacles, the arrival of courses in a gilded model ship on an artificial sea, complete with Neptune standing on the deck (William Fowler, *A True reportarie*, Edinburgh 1594, cited by Howard 1995, pp.30–4). Henry was to remain at Stirling in the care of the Earl of Mar after the departure of his father and mother, much to the dismay of the latter (see cat. 4).

This is the only known portrait of Prince Henry to have been painted in Scotland before his father James VI acceded to the English throne as James I. The artist has not been identified, although the lack of sophistication in the portrayal of the child, and the flattened, decorative nature of the composition, suggest a painter who specialised in heraldry or decorative painting (Thomson 1975, p.35). The Prince is shown in elaborate clothing, heavily encrusted with jewels, signifying his wealth and status. His depiction seated on a chair may be intended to allude to the expectation of his future coronations. The object in his left hand is unclear, but in his right hand he holds cherries (also scattered on the table), symbols of innocence and virtue that were often included in portraits of children in the sixteenth and seventeenth centuries. C.M.

PROVENANCE
Early provenance unknown; probably the Bingham Mildmay sale, Christie's, 24 June 1893 (lot 52, as 'Frederick, Prince of Wales'); purchased by the 5th Earl of Rosebery through Agnew's; by descent.

LITERATURE
Strong, *Tudor and Jacobean Portraits*, 1969, I, p.162, II, pl.315; Thomson 1975, no. 26, p.35.

2

The most Happy Unions Contracted betwixt the Princes of the Blood Royall
of theis towe Famous Kingdomes of England & Scotland

RENOLD ELSTRACK (1570–after 1625),
probably after JOHN SPEED (1552–1629), 1603

Engraving on paper, 372 × 270mm
The British Museum, London (1856·6·14·149)

When James VI of Scotland inherited the throne of England from Elizabeth I, there was a need to explain to the wider public just how the Scottish Stuart royal family connected with the Tudor royal family. This was particularly important since James's Catholic mother, Mary, Queen of Scots, had been executed by Elizabeth I for treason; although James – who had been brought up a Protestant, apart from his mother – was not particularly tainted by association, there was a need to rehabilitate the Stuart monarchy and to stress its links with England, as well as to elucidate James's position in the succession. James was, strictly speaking, Elizabeth's first cousin twice removed. His grandfather, James V, and Elizabeth had been first cousins. In fact James was descended directly from Henry VII on both his father's and his mother's side. This family tree also shows an earlier connection between the thrones of England and Scotland when Joan Beaufort, a granddaughter of John of Gaunt, married James I of Scotland in 1424.

John Speed was a renowned cartographer and author of the period, well known for his skill in genealogy. He designed the family tree, which was then engraved by the prolific and skilled engraver Renold Elstrack (see also cat. 10). It was probably Elstrack who provided the portraits of the various individuals. Some of the images of the earlier figures are undoubtedly fictional, but the heads of James VI and Anne of Denmark (top) were probably based on portraits painted in Scotland, such as the portraits by Adrian Vanson in the Scottish National Portrait Gallery. Speed operated for a brief period as a publisher as well, and he published both this print and the large image of James and Henry in Parliament (see cat. 10). The demand for family trees of the Tudor and Stuart families in 1603 is testified to by the fact that two similar prints were published at the same time, engraved by Benjamin Wright (*fl.*1596–d.1613) and William Kip (*fl. c.*1585–d.1618) (see Griffiths 1998, pp.45–6). C.M.

PROVENANCE
Purchased by the British Museum
from Messrs Graves, 1856.

LITERATURE
Griffiths 1998, no. 4, pp.45–6.

THE MOST HAPPY VNIONS CONTRACTED BETWIXT THE PRINCES OF THE BLOOD ROYALL OF THEIS TOWE FAMOVS KINGDOMES OF England & Scotland, contynewed from the Normans conquest to our most gracious Soueraigne Iames the .1 King of England. Scotland. France. & Ireland. Defender of y fayth.

49

CAT. 3

CAT. 4

3

James VI of Scotland and I of England (1566–1625)

JOHN DE CRITZ THE ELDER (d.1642), *c.*1606

Oil on canvas, 2030 × 1160mm

Dulwich Picture Gallery, London (DPG 548)

James, only son of Mary, Queen of Scots, ascended to the Scottish throne as James VI at the age of thirteen months, on his mother's abdication. His accession to the English throne as James I came in 1603, on the death of Queen Elizabeth, who had been the first cousin of his grandfather, James V. In the centuries since his lifetime he has been the subject of criticism as a man and a king, much of which now seems unfair. He was undoubtedly extravagant, creating serious financial problems, and he had ambiguous and unpopular relationships with a series of problematic young men. On the other hand, he was one of the most intellectual and scholarly of all British monarchs, and he showed toleration towards different religious standpoints and a commitment to European peace, both of which were read as signs of weakness in the past but might be judged today as more laudable qualities.

James is usually regarded as not having been interested in art, in part because he is recorded as having been reluctant to sit for his portrait by a contemporary, Sir Anthony Weldon, who wrote 'This Kings Character is much easier to take then [sic] his Picture, for he could never be brought to sit for the taking of that' (Weldon 1650, p.177). However, Weldon was a hostile witness and, while the surviving portraits suggest that James did not sit very often, there is some evidence that he was not as uninterested in paintings, or other forms of artistic production, as has been assumed (see Campbell 1985, pp.xxxiii–xxxiv and Chaney 2003, pp.50–1).

John de Critz was one of a number of painters of Flemish and Dutch origin active at the English royal court during the reigns of James I and Charles I. Born in Antwerp, he was brought to England as a boy, and was apprenticed to the artist and poet Lucas de Heere (1534–84). By the late 1590s de Critz had established himself as an independent artist. He held the important court position of Serjeant-Painter to James I from 1605 until the king's death in 1625, and then to Charles I, for two periods jointly with other artists, Leonard Fryer (d.1605) and Robert Peake the Elder (*c.*1551–1619) until de Critz's own death in 1642 (see Edmond, 'Critz, John de, the Elder', ODNB 2004 and also Town 2012). In this role de Critz had many and varied responsibilities, including decorative painting of all kinds, and he was in charge of a large and sophisticated workshop. His portraits of James I and Anne reflected the conventions of continental court portraiture, depicting the King and Queen standing at a slight angle to the viewer, leaning on a richly draped table or upholstered chair.

In the first half of his reign in England, James was painted primarily by de Critz and his studio (see Strong, *Tudor and Jacobean Portraits*, 1969, vol. I, p.179). The portraits of James by de Critz fall into two basic variants: standing, leaning on a table, wearing a fur cloak (represented notably by the present portrait) and standing by a chair, wearing a jewelled cloak (see Hearn 1995, pp.184–5). Many versions exist, in different sizes, all of which use the same facial type, which would have derived from a pattern kept by de Critz in his studio.

James is presented in this portrait as a European ruler, in a pose developed and then used repeatedly for court portraits in the previous century, notably by Anthonis Mor and Titian for members of the Habsburg family. Rather than signalling his regal status through symbolism or attributes, the painting alludes to James's wealth and power through his rich surroundings and elaborate attire, including his magnificent hat jewel. Known as 'the Feather', it consisted of a large 'table' diamond and twenty-five smaller diamonds set in gold (see Scarisbrick 1995, p.19). Although new poses – and other artists – were used for James's portraits in the later part of his reign, his portraiture in general is notably different from that of his eldest son in almost never including any military allusions, other than the ubiquitous sword at his side. C.M.

PROVENANCE
Countess of Warwick of Holland House, who married Joseph Addison of Bilton Hall, Warwickshire in 1716; Miss Addison (d.1797); bequeathed to the Hon. John Simpson; by descent to the Rev. Bridgeman-Simpson at Bilton Hall; Bilton sale, Christie's, 28 June 1898 (lot 12); bought by Henry Yates Thompson and given by him to Dulwich Picture Gallery, London, 1898.

LITERATURE
Strong, *Tudor and Jacobean Portraits*, 1969, vol. 1, p.179; Ingamells 2008, p.200.

4

Anne of Denmark (1574–1619)

JOHN DE CRITZ THE ELDER, *c.*1605–10

Oil on canvas, 2210 × 1310mm

National Portrait Gallery, London (NPG 6918)

In 1589, at the age of fifteen, Anne, the second daughter of Frederick II of Denmark, married James VI of Scotland. Tall and blonde, she was chosen by James over a French princess, Catherine of Navarre, reportedly after meditating in front of their portraits in his chamber for three days (see Meikle and Payne, 'Anne of Denmark', ODNB 2004). Perhaps more significantly, she provided James with a generous dowry and a useful Scandinavian alliance. Although she involved herself in various unfortunate political manoeuvres during her early years at the Scottish court, and suffered miscarriages, her life with James appears to have been generally happy at first and its crowning achievement was the birth of Prince Henry in 1594.

Shortly after Henry's birth, however, relations between James and Anne deteriorated when, following Scottish royal tradition, James insisted that the baby be removed from his mother's care and brought up by John Erskine, 2nd Earl of Mar and his mother, the Dowager Countess. The King and Queen continued to produce children, however, including Elizabeth in 1596 (later Elizabeth of Bohemia) and Charles in 1600 (later King Charles I). Four other children died young, and Anne suffered further miscarriages. During her time in Scotland Anne had gradually moved away from her Lutheran faith towards Roman Catholicism; by the time she settled in London she had become a practising Catholic. James was tolerant of her religious beliefs but popular feeling towards Catholicism, particularly at such a high level of society, was such that she was forced to practise in secret.

The issue of Anne's control over Henry came to another crisis point in 1603, when James ascended to the throne of England as James I.

James travelled to London without Anne, and in his absence she went to Stirling Castle and demanded the release of Henry into her care. Initially she was refused, but she persisted. She then suffered a miscarriage; James eventually relented, and Anne subsequently travelled to England with Henry and Elizabeth.

With much greater funds at her disposal in London than had been the case in Scotland, Anne became one of the most important cultural patrons of her day. She was a patron of Ben Jonson and Inigo Jones as well as other writers, influential composers and choreographers, through her commissions for lavish court masques, in which she also performed (see pp.92–3 and cats 34–43). Anne was moreover an accomplished musician, and she became an important early collector of paintings (Wilks 1997).

In 1606 de Critz was paid for portraits of the King, the Queen and 'the prince' (presumably Henry) to be sent to the Archduke of Austria; the present portrait may perhaps be connected with this commission, as it seems likely to have been painted at about this time. Previously unknown and unpublished, this painting emerged recently on the art market, having for generations been mis-identified as a portrait of Elizabeth I. Anne's three sisters all married members of German princely families and there are numerous routes through which the painting could have descended to its most recent owners. Three-quarter length versions of this portrait are known (at Blickling Hall, Norfolk and at the National Maritime Museum, London) and de Critz also produced an earlier portrait of Anne, of which several versions exist, including a full-length example (Loseley Park, Surrey). C.M.

PROVENANCE
Schaumburg-Lippe family at Schloss Bückeburg since at least 1880 (October 1880 inventory, Schloss Bückeburg, no. 1153); Sotheby's sale 8 December 2010 (lot 13), unsold; purchased by the National Portrait Gallery, London.

5

James VI of Scotland and I of England

NICHOLAS HILLIARD (1547–1619), *c.*1609–15

Watercolour and bodycolour on vellum laid on a playing card, 46 × 38mm

The Royal Collection (RCIN 420039)

Miniature portraits played as important a role as large-scale oils in the sixteenth- and early seventeenth-century English courts. While they could not be admired by large groups of people at the same time, their intimacy – and indeed secrecy – in a sense added to their prestige. They were often mounted in elaborate lockets set with precious jewels, and could be presented as valuable gifts to favoured courtiers, or commissioned to show devotion to a political patron, family member or lover.

Nicholas Hilliard was an immensely skilled and famous miniature painter, originally trained as a goldsmith, who had flourished during the reign of Elizabeth I. As her favoured miniaturist, he seems to have had a monopoly of her portraiture in this medium (see Strong 1963, p.7). Hilliard also designed medals and seals for her, and she granted him a £40 annuity (1599). When James VI acceded to the English throne he continued this strand of royal patronage, renewing Hilliard's salary. Hilliard and his assistants produced numerous portraits of the King over the years, all of which are versions

of three basic 'types', as identified by Graham Reynolds. All three types are closely related but the face progressively ages; this miniature is an example of the second type.

Hilliard's style was characteristically graphic and linear, with minimal use of shadow in the modelling (although in many of his miniatures, including the present work, the effect is increased by the fading of the red and pink tones) and great attention paid to the details of the costume and jewellery. His approach is explained in his remarkable work, *A Treatise concerning the arte of limning* (see Thornton and Cain 1981). It gave the miniature itself a jewel-like quality, and Hilliard's skill was such that his reputation spread across Europe in his own lifetime. It was, however, a style that was becoming rather old-fashioned by the early years of the seventeenth century, especially by comparison with that of his pupil Isaac Oliver (see cat. 6), and it is significant that James continued to patronise Hilliard while the more artistically adventurous Anne and her son Prince Henry soon came to favour Oliver (see cats 6 and 32). C.M.

PROVENANCE
Possibly the miniature bought by Charles I and recorded in his catalogue as 'king James of famous memory picture w^{th}out a hatt in a bone lac'd falling band in a Lavender Cloth suite' (Millar 1960, p.113, no. 44, note 3 and p.217); by descent in the Royal Collection.

LITERATURE
Reynolds 1958, pp.14–26; Reynolds 1999, p.70, no. 28.

6

Anne of Denmark

ISAAC OLIVER (*c*.1565–1617), *c*.1612

Watercolour and bodycolour on vellum laid on to card, 51 × 41mm
Signed, upper left: *IO* (in monogram)
National Portrait Gallery, London (NPG 4010)

Queen Anne appears to have been significantly more interested in the visual arts than her husband, and her appointment of Isaac Oliver as her 'limner' or miniature portrait painter on 22 June 1605, at a salary of £40 a year, marked a distinct shift in royal patronage. Elizabeth I had employed Nicholas Hilliard, who, in the last decade of his life, also supplied the standard miniature portraits of James I (see cat. 5). Anne's patronage of Oliver, however, along with painters in oils such as John de Critz (see cat. 3), Marcus Gheeraerts the Younger (1561/2–1636; see cat. 7) and Paul van Somer (1577/8–1621/2), suggested that she favoured artists who had closer connections with continental portrait practice rather than the more distinctively English artists favoured by Elizabeth I.

Isaac Oliver was the son of Huguenot refugees who had come to England in 1568, and trained in Hilliard's workshop. Oliver's stippled, softly modelled manner, particularly in his depictions of faces, departs significantly from the linear, flat, graphic style of his master. The connections between Oliver's work and contemporary developments in continental painting, particularly what is often described as Mannerism, are especially obvious in the miniatures he painted of allegorical, historical or biblical scenes, but

are also apparent in his portraits. His use of pronounced areas of light and shade, and his depictions of sometimes rather elongated and even contorted anatomical features, are seen as reflecting these aspects of continental practice. He had been in Venice in 1596, and his travels, and perhaps more importantly his study of continental prints such as the works of Hendrick Goltzius, clearly had an impact on his style.

Oliver produced numerous miniatures of Anne, often probably intended as gifts for her family, favoured courtiers or foreign monarchs (examples are in the Royal Collection and the Victoria and Albert Museum, London). Dressed in elaborate costume and jewellery, she is often depicted with her hand to her heart, a pose also used in a few miniatures of her by Nicholas Hilliard or members of his studio (see Strong 1983, nos 243, 244). The crowned 'S' jewel she wears probably refers to her mother, Sophia of Mecklenburg; Anne spent lavishly on jewellery and was immensely proud of her Danish family, also owning a jewel that took the form 'C4', for her brother, King Christian IV of Denmark (see Scarisbrick 1986, p.23–4). In this miniature she also appears to be wearing a jewelled locket, which probably contained another miniature, perhaps of the intended recipient of this portrait.
C.M.

PROVENANCE
Parry Walton (dealer, restorer and Keeper of the Pictures in the Royal Collection; d.1702); purchased 1691 by James Sotheby of Ecton for £1 16s. od. (*Sotheby Notebooks*, V&A); seen in the collection of Sotheby's son by George Vertue, *c*.1742 (*Notebooks*, V, p.11); by descent in the Sotheby family; sold at the sale of the Sotheby collection, Sotheby's, 11 October 1955 (lot 72); purchased by the National Portrait Gallery, London, with help from the Art Fund, 1957.

LITERATURE
Strong, *Tudor and Jacobean Portraits*, 1969, I, p.8; Strong 1983, p.153, no. 254.

7

Prince Henry

MARCUS GHEERAERTS THE YOUNGER (1561/2–1636), *c*.1603

Oil on canvas, 1619 × 1168mm

National Portrait Gallery, London (NPG 2562)

This portrait, which was at one time extensively overpainted and believed to depict Prince Charles, is in fact a portrait of Prince Henry, painted at about the time the Stuart royal family came to England in 1603 (reidentified by Roy Strong based on the provenance, style and costume dating; memo in NPG file, 31 March 1976). The painting's provenance suggests strongly that it was commissioned by Sir Henry Lee (1533–1611), who had been a prominent courtier and favourite of Elizabeth I, and who had an important role in developing magnificent chivalric entertainments in her honour (see cat. 29).

Henry is depicted in his robes as a Knight of the Order of the Garter. The highest order of chivalry in Britain, the Order of the Garter dates back to the fourteenth century. It had particular significance in the sixteenth and seventeenth centuries, when Knights of the Order (limited to twenty-five in addition to the monarch) were almost always shown in their portraits wearing at least their garter badge, depicting St George and the dragon on a collar or ribbon, and the garter itself, with the motto *Honi soit qui mal y pense* ('Shame on him who thinks evil of this') written around it. Henry was made a Garter Knight in 1603 and it seems likely that Lee commissioned the portrait not only to commemorate this moment, but also to hang as a companion to at least two portraits of almost identical composition, both also painted by Gheeraerts, that he already owned: one of Robert Devereux, 2nd Earl of Essex (1565–1601), Elizabeth's disgraced and executed favourite (National Portrait Gallery, London; fig. 15), and one of Lee himself (Worshipful Company of Armourers and Brasiers, London). It seems likely that Lee saw Henry as the successor to, and focus of, Elizabethan chivalric values.

Marcus Gheeraerts the Younger was a member of the closely connected network of immigrant painters from the Low Countries working in

England in the late sixteenth and early seventeenth centuries. He was one of the most highly skilled and admired artists of his generation in England, and he seems to have been a particular favourite of Sir Henry Lee, who, in addition to the paintings already mentioned, commissioned an important portrait of Queen Elizabeth I from the artist, known today as 'The Ditchley Portrait' (National Portrait Gallery, London). Although the present portrait is the only one of Prince Henry attributed to Gheeraerts, the artist was paid £79 in 1611 by the Treasurer of James I's Chamber for portraits of King James, Queen Anne, Princess Elizabeth and Prince Charles; in the accounts he is referred to as 'His Ma[jes]ties Paynter' (Edmond 1978–80, p.138). A full-length portrait of Queen Anne is at Woburn Abbey, Bedfordshire; a half-length version (Royal Collection) is dated 1614. Although there are further payments for royal portraits up to 1618, and Gheeraerts was among those listed as attending the Queen's funeral, there are no surviving portraits of the King by him. C.M.

PROVENANCE
Presumably commissioned by Sir Henry Lee; by descent in the Lee and subsequently Dillon families at Ditchley to Harold, 17th Viscount Dillon; bequeathed to the National Portrait Gallery, London, and accepted February 1933.

LITERATURE
Hearn, 'Marcus Gheeraerts the Younger', ODNB 2004.

FIG. 15
Robert Devereux, 2nd Earl of Essex, Marcus Gheeraerts the Younger, *c*.1597

56

Elizabeth Queen of Bohemia daughter of James the First

8

Princess Elizabeth, later Queen of Bohemia (1596–1662)

ROBERT PEAKE THE ELDER (*c*.1551–1619), 1603

Oil on canvas, 1359 × 953mm
Inscribed at bottom: *Elizabeth Queen of Bohemia daughter of James the First*;
inscribed on fan handle: *Æ 7*; inscribed on bridge: *1603*
National Maritime Museum, London

Elizabeth, named after her godmother, Elizabeth I of England, was the eldest and only surviving daughter of James VI of Scotland and I of England, and his wife Anne of Denmark. She was born two years after her brother Henry, later Prince of Wales, and like him was put into the care of another family as an infant. In Elizabeth's case her guardian was Alexander, Lord Livingstone, later Earl of Linlithgow. At the accession of her father to the English throne in 1603 she was brought by her mother to England, where, after a brief period with Lord and Lady Cobham, she was settled in the household of John, 1st Baron Harington of Exton (1539/40–1613) and his wife, Anne. It was from their house, Coombe Abbey, that the Gunpowder plotters intended to abduct her in 1605. The plan was to place her on the throne as a puppet queen, after the destruction of Parliament, and her father and older brother with it. Harington was alerted to the danger, however, and was able to remove Elizabeth to safety in Coventry with just a few hours to spare. During this early period in her life the main evidence of Elizabeth's contact with her brother is a number of formal letters, although their relationship would later become more close and affectionate (see cat. 77).

Robert Peake was, like Nicholas Hilliard (see cat. 5), a native-born English artist who had trained as a goldsmith (see Hearn, 'Peake, Robert', ODNB 2004). He emerged as the favoured portraitist of the royal children shortly after their arrival in London in 1603. By this stage he was a mature and well-established artist, but his work during the Elizabethan period is difficult to pin down with confidence. Two portraits, however, act as touchstones for his style as a painter. One, *Unknown Military Commander* (Yale Center for British Art,

Connecticut), has a contemporary inscription or signature naming the artist and giving the date as 1593. The other, painted towards the end of his career, is catalogued here (see cat. 80). It is clear from technical examination of Peake's portraits, however, that many of the works associated with him were the product of a large studio in which various hands were employed on different parts of each painting (analysis undertaken as part of the Making Art in Tudor Britain project at the National Portrait Gallery). This must have been increasingly the case when he took on the huge workload that was the responsibility of the Serjeant-Painter, a post to which he was appointed jointly with John de Critz in 1607, and which involved decorative painting of all kinds.

This work, showing the Princess at the age of seven, was probably commissioned by Harington and appears to be a companion portrait to one of Prince Henry and Harington's son, John (Metropolitan Museum, New York; see pp.35–6). The two paintings appear to share their provenance, and have similar landscape backgrounds; the depiction of small figures hunting in the background of this portrait forms an additional link with the double portrait, in which the two boys are shown taking part in a ritualistic moment during the hunt. Unlike Prince Henry, however, Princess Elizabeth is presented here, as in all her early portraits, in a traditional, static, full-frontal pose. This reflects her role in the royal family, primarily as a very important asset in the diplomatic and political game of royal marriage negotiations, and it echoes earlier paintings produced in similar contexts, such as Hans Holbein the Younger's 1538 portrait of Christina of Denmark (National Gallery, London). C.M.

PROVENANCE
Probably commissioned by John, 1st Baron Harington of Exton; perhaps by descent to Anne Montagu, wife of Dudley, 4th Baron North, whose son Francis North acquired Wroxton Abbey in 1680; presumably by descent at Wroxton Abbey to William, 11th Baron North; bought by Agnew's, October 1914; bought by Henry P. Davidson, 14 October 1916; by descent; sold at Christie's, 17 November 1989 (lot 39); bought by The Weiss Gallery; bought by the Trustees of the National Maritime Museum, with help from the Art Fund and the National Heritage Memorial Fund, 1991.

LITERATURE
Hearn 1995, pp.185–6, no. 126.

9

Charles I, when Duke of York and Albany (1600–49)

ROBERT PEAKE THE ELDER, *c.*1610

Oil on canvas, 1270 × 857mm
Inscribed (later), upper right: *Henry, P. of Wales*
Scottish National Portrait Gallery, Edinburgh (PG 2212)

Charles was born at Dunfermline Palace in Fife, the second son of James VI of Scotland and Anne of Denmark. Like his elder siblings, Henry and Elizabeth, the young Prince was raised away from court in the household of a trusted courtier. Charles stayed in Scotland with his guardians, Lord and Lady Fyvie, until July 1604 when he left for England, over a year after the rest of his family as he was not considered to be physically ready to make the journey south. His new guardian, Elizabeth Trevanion, the wife of Sir Robert Carey, supposedly taught him to overcome his speech impediment and his inability to walk properly (he probably suffered from rickets).

Once in England, however, Charles spent more time at court and in the company of his family. Although Charles adored Henry, Henry would sometimes tease him. Mocking the attention Charles paid to his devotional studies, Henry once claimed he would make him Archbishop of Canterbury when he became king. Charles's letters to his 'sweet, sweet brother' underline his adulatory feelings towards Henry – 'I will give anything that I have to you, both my horses, and my books, and my pieces, and my cross-bows ... Good brother love me, and I shall ever love you and serve you' (British Library, Harley MS 6986, 154).

This portrait was painted by Robert Peake the Elder around 1610, when Charles was still second in line to the throne, possibly commissioned in connection with the festivities surrounding Henry's creation as Prince of Wales. The luxurious setting and his expensive clothes, including the stuffed bird of paradise (*Paradisaea minor*) pinned to his hat, indicate the sitter's social importance, although the picture is devoid of any specific visual reference to his royal status. Peake painted Charles's portrait a number of times: in 1613, for instance, he was paid £13 6s 8d for a full-length portrait; in 1616, the year Charles was created Prince of Wales, he was paid £35 for three more pictures of him. In the present picture Charles's pose is similar to that in Peake's portrait of him in his Garter robes, painted around 1611 (private collection), and to the portrait painted to commemorate his visit in 1613 to Cambridge (University of Cambridge, see cat. 80). This rather formulaic standing posture, with the sitter in front of pulled-back curtains and next to a table, is quite unlike the dynamic poses in many of Peake's innovative images of Charles's elder brother.
D.A.H.B.T.

PROVENANCE
Bequeathed to the Scottish National Portrait Gallery (as Prince Henry) by Major J. A. Erskine-Murray, 13th Baron Elibank, 1973.

LITERATURE
Strong, *English Icon*, 1969, p.250, no.230.

10

James I in Parliament

RENOLD ELSTRACK, 1604

Engraving, on a sheet of paper comprising four sections:
main section 427 × 505mm; left section 143 × 526mm;
right section 143 × 538mm; lower section 126 × 510mm

The British Museum, London (1856·6·14·148)

This exceptional print was made in 1604 to mark James I's first Parliament in England, which opened on 19 March that year. It shows the King in the centre with, on his right, the Lord Chancellor, Thomas Egerton, Lord Ellesmere (1540–1617), and, on his left, the Lord Treasurer, Thomas Sackville, Earl of Dorset (c.1536–1608). In front of Dorset sits Prince Henry. On either side are various peers including other officers of state and bishops. The borders of the print illustrate the coats of arms of the peers of England, Scotland and Ireland. The scene depicted in the print was one that, a year and a half after this impression was issued, was to assume even greater significance as it narrowly missed becoming a memorial to a lost building and numerous lost lives, including those of James and Henry.

James's accession to the English throne had not been greeted with joy by everyone. Life for Catholics in England on the whole became some-what easier than it had been under Elizabeth I, as the King reduced the fines payable for non-attendance at services of the established Church and made peace with Spain, the main Catholic power in Europe. But a small group would settle for nothing less than Catholic rule in England, and thus, the Gunpowder Plot was born in 1605. The ringleader was Robert Catesby

(c.1572–1605), a Warwickshire landowner. Catesby assembled a group of like-minded Catholic gentry, including the famous Guy Fawkes (1570–1606), to carry out his plans, which involved blowing up the House of Lords, killing the King, Prince Henry and many peers of the realm, and putting Princess Elizabeth on the throne as a Catholic puppet ruler. As Catesby later explained, 'In that place [Parliament] have they done us all the mischeif, and perchance God hath desined that place for their punishment' (Salisbury MS 113/54, cited in Nichols, 'Catesby, Robert', ODNB 2004). As it transpired, the plot was disclosed via a letter to a Catholic nobleman, Lord Monteagle, warning him not to attend the opening of Parliament in the autumn of 1605. Famously, Guy Fawkes was discovered in the cellars beneath the House of Lords with eighteen hundredweight of gunpowder during the night of 4–5 November 1605; Parliament was to have opened the following day.

In the short term, the effect of the plot was to increase James's popularity, or certainly protestations of support for him, from Catholics both in Britain and abroad. James suggested sending Henry back to Scotland for his own safety, but was dissuaded by his counsellors, who saw the advantages of keeping the popular Prince in England. C.M.

PROVENANCE
Henry Graves (formerly in the collections of Richardson, Scott, Caulfield, Colnaghi, Lloyd; see Griffiths 1998, p.46); purchased by the British Museum, London, 1856.

LITERATURE
Griffiths 1998, p.46, no.5.

II

Basilikon Doron

JAMES VI OF SCOTLAND
(later JAMES I OF ENGLAND), *c.*1598

Ink on paper, ff. ii + 34, in the original purple velvet binding (rebacked)
with decorative plates, corner pieces and clasps of gold, some of
these broken or missing, 333 × 238mm

The British Library, London (MS Royal, 18.b.XV)

Basilikon Doron (the title is Greek for 'royal gift')
is King James's handbook on the art of kingship,
addressed to Prince Henry 'my dearest son, and
natural successor'. Written in 1598, when Henry
was only four years old, it was intended as an
advice-manual in case James should die before his
son reached adulthood. Like James's other works,
it expresses his conviction that, like all kings, he
was divinely appointed as a 'little God' to rule
over other men. But *Basilikon Doron* is not a work
of abstract political theory; it is a highly practical
book, almost a how-to guide, covering every
aspect of a ruler's character and behaviour.
James approves of card games but disapproves of
chess; he encourages Henry to take up fencing,
wrestling, tennis and archery, but prohibits
'all rumling violent exercises, as the football'.
Underlying this advice is James's awareness
that the king is like an actor on the stage, his
words and gestures constantly exposed to
public scrutiny. As he warns Henry: 'the people,
that see you not within, cannot judge you but
according to the outward appearance of your
actions and company, which only is subject
to their sight'.

The autograph manuscript of *Basilikon Doron*
is a highly personal document, written in
vigorous Middle Scots and full of revisions
and corrections; in it, as Jenny Wormald has
commented, we can glimpse James 'searching
for words and ideal expression of arguments,
scribbling, scoring out, scribbling again'. The
first edition, printed in Edinburgh in 1599, is
said to have been limited to seven copies (only
two survive today) for private circulation among
James's most trusted advisers. Very soon, however,
the work started to circulate more widely, and
James may even have encouraged this as he
came to appreciate its propaganda value. The
English courtier Sir John Harington of Kelston
noted in 1602 that 'there passeth among friends
a copy of an advice or admonition to his son the
young Prince, which I had a short view of, but
I found it a thing which affected all the judicious
readers exceedingly' (Markham 1880). Harington
believed that it strengthened James's claim to
the English throne, by showing him to be
'a man of spirit and learning, of able body, of
understanding mind'. When *Basilikon Doron*
was published in London in 1603, it became an
instant bestseller, and is estimated to have sold as
many as 16,000 copies as the English clamoured
to find out more about their new king. A.H.

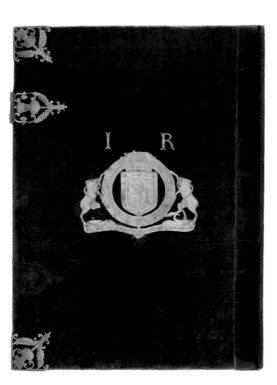

PROVENANCE
By descent in the Royal Collection;
transferred to the British Museum
by George II in 1757.

LITERATURE
Craigie 1944–50; Wormald 1991,
pp.36–54.

LEFT: Back cover
OPPOSITE: First folio (fol. 1r)

To henrie
my dearest

To Henrie my dearest sonne & naturall successoure:

Quhonic can sa richelie & appearaine this booke of the institution of a prince in all

the pointis of his calling, als weill in generall, as a christiane coueatis god, as particulaire as

a king touardis his people: quhonic I saye can it sa weillie apparteine as unto you my

dearest sonne, since I the authoure thairof, as youre father am all sueltis man be cairfull for

youre godlie & vertuouse education as my eldest sonne & the first fruictis of

godlie blessing touardis me in my posteritie, & as king man tymouslie prouyde for youre

training up in all the pointis of a kings office, sen ye are naturall & lauefull successoure

thairin, that being richelie informed heirby of the weche of youre burthen ye maye in

tyme beginne to consider, that being borne to be a king ye are rather borne to onus then

honos, not excelling all youre people sa farre in ranke & honoure, as in daylie caire &

hazardouse pr gainis taking for the lauefull administration of that greate

office that god hes layed upon youre shoulderis; giuing so a iuste simmetrie & propor

tion betuixt the heiche of youre honorable place, & the heauie weche of youre greate charge

& consequentlie entaice of faillie (quhilk god forbidd) of the sadnesse of youre

fall according to the proportion of that heiche: I haue thairfore for the greater ease

to youre memorie, & that ye maye at the firste caste up any pairt that ye haue to doe with,

deuydie this haill booke in thrie pairtis; first youre deutie touardis god as a christiane

the next youre deutie in youre office, the thridde teaches you how to behaue youre

self in indifferent thingis, quhilk of thame selfs are nather richt nor wrong but

according as they are richtlie or wrong usit & ye will self serue according to youre

12

*Letter from King James I
to Prince Henry*

1604

Ink on paper, 290 × 194mm

The British Library, London (Harley MS 6986, fol. 67r)

James I was deeply concerned with his son's education and the extent to which he was following the precepts James had laid out for him in his manual of kingship, *Basilikon Doron* (see cat. 11). Henry was expected to provide evidence of his academic progress, and this letter from the King was written in response to one from the ten-year-old Henry in which he had included a poem in Latin. The King was not, however, impressed by Henry's work. He explains here that, while he is pleased that Henry's handwriting has improved, he suspects that the Prince has not composed the poem himself, but has copied someone else's work. He says that he longs to receive a letter from him 'as well formid by youre mynde, as drawin by youre fingers', and refers the Prince to a passage 'in my booke to ye'.

Although James's letter reprimands the Prince, it is not unaffectionate. By comparison with the formal style employed by Henry (see cat. 13), James's writing style is informal and lively, written in his native Middle Scots, interspersed with phrases in Latin, often sayings, such as, 'fortune favours the brave'. The mixture of affection on James's part, respect on Henry's and tension resulting from the differences between them, which marks this exchange of correspondence, was to characterise their relationship throughout Henry's life. C.M.

PROVENANCE
As cat. 13

LITERATURE
Strong 1986, p.14; Pollnitz 2007, pp.47–8.

13

*Letter from Prince Henry
to Queen Anne*

22 September 1603

Ink on paper, 148 × 203mm

The British Library, London (Harley MS 7007, fol. 20)

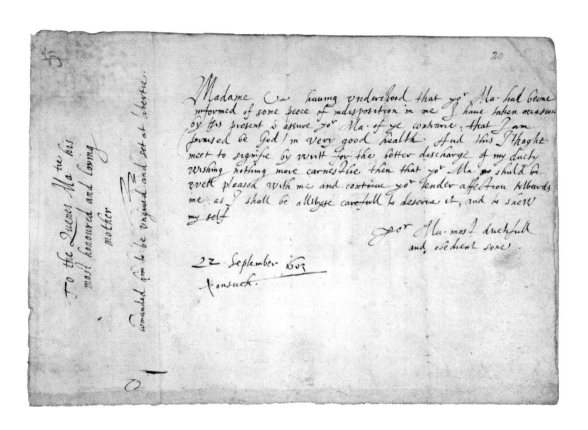

This short and formal letter written by Prince Henry in September 1603, at the age of nine, was to reassure his mother that he was, contrary to what she might have heard, in good health. It was written from Nonsuch Palace, where Henry's household was established at that time. It may be that Adam Newton, the Prince's tutor, saw this as an opportunity for Henry to practise his formal letter-writing style, but its formality also reflects the distance between mother and son, both emotionally and physically. More

than half the letter is taken up with the closing words, in which Henry assures his mother of his obedience and wish to please her. It has been suggested that this letter may have been written in order to dissuade Anne from coming to visit Henry, and as such it also illustrates the struggle for control of, and access to, Henry that dominated Anne's relationship with her son (Wilks 1987, p.289). The fact that it was retained by Adam Newton suggests that it was a first draft, rather than the final letter sent to the Queen.
C.M.

PROVENANCE
Sir Adam Newton, Prince Henry's tutor; by descent to his son Sir Henry Puckering (formerly Newton); acquired, perhaps as a gift, by a Cambridge landlady; purchased by George Paul of Jesus College, Cambridge, 1713; given or sold to Robert Harley, 1st Earl of Oxford and Mortimer; by descent to his daughter-in-law Henrietta, Countess of Oxford, and granddaughter Margaret, Duchess of Portland, by whom sold to the nation, 1753; British Museum, London.

LITERATURE
Wilks 1987, p.289; Pollnitz 2007, pp.22–64.

The Making of the Prince

After Prince Henry's arrival in England in 1603, a household was formed for him, which from 1604 was based mainly at Nonsuch in Surrey, a magnificent Tudor palace that had moved in and out of royal ownership and was at that time leased to John, 1st Baron Lumley. Henry's household included both those who had been with him in Scotland, such as David Murray, a Gentleman of the Bedchamber, with whom he was particularly close, and new appointees, including his governor, Sir Thomas Chaloner. A particularly influential figure in Henry's life at this point was Adam Newton, a Scots classical scholar, who had been his tutor since 1599. The agenda for Henry's education had been set out by his father, King James VI and I, in his *Basilikon Doron* (see cats 11 and 19) but the details of its organisation were the responsibility of Newton. At Nonsuch, Prince Henry and Newton had access to Lumley's enormous library of approximately 3,000 books, an important resource that eventually passed into the Prince's ownership in 1609 (see pp.119 and 136).

Henry's education initially followed a similar course to that of a child at an English grammar school of the day. He learned to read and write in Latin, studying the works of standard classical authors such as Cicero, Terence and Virgil.[1] In addition he learned French, probably Italian, a little Greek, and italic handwriting. After this grounding, Henry's education became more particular to the circumstances of his life and future role. He studied more history and politics, as well as having lessons in mathematics, theology, cosmography, geography and music, among other subjects. The resources of his library were supplemented by gifts and acquisitions of books (see p.119), and also, as he grew older, by treatises and tracts on various political subjects. Henry was also regularly updated on both domestic and foreign issues by Robert Cecil, 1st Earl of Salisbury, the most powerful politician of the day.

Prince Henry with Robert Devereux, 3rd Earl of Essex, Robert Peake the Elder, *c.*1605 (detail of cat. 14)

Henry was required by King James to achieve a certain level of academic competence but he was not to aim to be a 'passmaister' in all the 'liberal arts and sciences', as this might distract him from his role as a monarch.[2] Henry seems to have followed this advice, perhaps too literally, showing little natural inclination for the classical, literary studies of his early education. James's own academic enthusiasm led him to judge Henry's work harshly on more than one occasion. The Venetian ambassador reported an incident in 1607 in which James compared Henry's approach to his studies unfavourably with that of his younger brother, Prince Charles. Henry countered, 'I know what becomes a Prince. It is not necessary for me to be a professor, but a soldier and a man of the world.'[3] As his studies became more obviously a preparation for his future role as a political and military leader, however, Henry became more interested.[4] And his passion for the physical side of his education – James prescribed 'running, leaping, wrestling, fencing, dancing' and especially 'such games on horse-back as may teach you to handle your armes thereon, such as the Tilte' – was never in doubt.[5]

Henry was joined for at least part of his education by a group of boys regarded as the next generation of potential leaders. This arrangement reflected a scheme of Salisbury's father, Lord Burghley, during Elizabeth I's reign to educate noble boys together[6] and it was favoured by King James, who intended to create a 'collegiate court' around Henry, under the direction of Chaloner.[7] Among those educated with Henry were Salisbury's son, William Cecil, Lord Cranborne; Robert Devereux, 3rd Earl of Essex, son of Elizabeth I's disgraced last favourite; and Sir John Harington, son of Princess Elizabeth's governor, John, 1st Baron Harington of Exton. Unlike the Prince, however, these boys were able to complete their education with a period of foreign travel. This deficiency in Henry's experience – foreign travel being deemed too risky for the heir apparent – was made up in part through the reading of travel books and the correspondence of his friends abroad, notably Sir John Harington, who was described as 'the right eye of the prince'.[8] Plans were also made to establish a more formal academy under Henry's patronage, in order to give young Englishmen an education that would rival that of their continental counterparts, but this never came to fruition.[9]

Henry's household expanded when he became Prince of Wales in 1610, though many of his previous attendants remained. New offices reflected the Prince's increased autonomy and maturity: Newton became his Secretary, for example, Murray his Groom of the Stole, and Chaloner his Chamberlain. Henry now had new establishments, primarily at St James's Palace and Richmond Palace, and additional officials were required, including Sir Charles Cornwallis, as Treasurer of the Household. Others, without official positions, were also formative influences on the young Prince: men such as Edward Cecil, later Viscount Wimbledon, whose military and cultural experiences abroad fed and helped to shape Henry's interests. Henry represented hope for the future, and those with ambitions for a role in that future jostled for his patronage and attention. C.M.

1 See Pollnitz 2007, pp.32–48.
2 James VI and I, *Basilikon Doron* 1599, p.113.
3 *CSP Venetian, 1603–7*, XI, p.513.
4 Pollnitz 2007, pp.49–54.
5 James VI and I, *Basilikon Doron* 1599, pp.143–4.
6 Wilks 1987, pp.56–7.
7 Birch 1760, p.97.
8 *CSP Venetian, 1603–7*, XI, pp.215–16.
9 Wilks 1987, pp.57–60.

14

Prince Henry with Robert Devereux,
3rd Earl of Essex (1591–1646)

ROBERT PEAKE THE ELDER, *c.*1605

Oil on canvas, 1905 × 1651mm
The Royal Collection (RCIN 404440)

Robert Devereux, son of the disgraced and executed 2nd Earl of Essex, favourite of Elizabeth I, was one of Prince Henry's chosen companions (see Wilks 1987, pp.54–60). It is likely that he, or someone connected with him, commissioned this painting. When James VI of Scotland acceded to the English throne, Essex was living in the care of the mathematician and classical scholar Henry Savile (1549–1622). His father was dead and his mother had since married Richard Burke, 4th Earl of Clanricarde and later 1st Earl of St Albans (1572–1635). James sought out associates of the 2nd Earl, who had supported his succession, and honoured them. The young Robert was sword-bearer at James's entry into London and at his coronation, and his titles and property were restored to him; Henry Savile was knighted in 1604 (Morrill, 'Devereux, Robert, third Earl of Essex', ODNB, 2004).

This portrait is a repetition, with some differences, of a slightly earlier painting by Robert Peake showing Prince Henry with, as his companion, Sir John Harington, later 2nd Baron Harington of Exton (dated 1603; Metropolitan Museum, New York; see fig. 12). The outdoor setting of both pictures was extremely unusual and the dynamic pose of the Prince entirely new in large-scale royal portraiture in England at this time. Peake, or the patron of the painting, clearly felt that royal portraiture had in a sense to be reinvented for the young Prince; this was the first of three novel compositions undertaken by the artist in portraits of Prince Henry (see pp.35–7 and cats 28 and 60). The scene depicted is a ritual moment in a royal hunt in which the prince cuts a slit in the throat of the already dead deer. Henry is sheathing his sword, having already made his cut. The ritual is described in *The Noble Art of Venerie, or Hunting* ..., a book of the period comprising a translation of two French treatises with a few additions, now generally attributed to George Gascoigne (1534/5?–1577). The section

in which this ritual is described is entitled 'An Aduertisement by the Translatour, of the English manner, in breaking vp of the Deare'. It is illustrated with a woodcut showing Queen Elizabeth in the first (1575) edition and James I in the second (1611) edition. James was known to be exceptionally fond of hunting, and so the composition of the painting – which may derive from the woodcut or from a lost, related print – was probably intended as a compliment to him.

In addition to his appointment as Serjeant-Painter (see cat. 8), Robert Peake may have held a position in the household of Prince Henry, but there is no surviving record of this, except the description of him as the Prince's 'paynter' in the funeral accounts (Wilks 1987, p.281). The majority of surviving portraits of the Prince are by him or members of his studio, as are most portraits of Princess Elizabeth and Prince Charles from this early period in their lives. C.M.

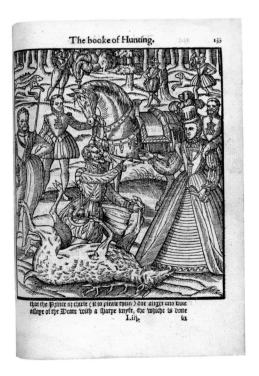

PROVENANCE
Possibly acquired by Frederick, Prince of Wales (1707–1751); in the collection of George III by *c.*1785; by descent in the Royal Collection.

LITERATURE
Gardner 1945, pp.113–17; Held 1958, p.145; Millar 1963, I, p.79, no. 100; Strong 1986, p.114; Wilks 1987, pp.88–9; Evans 1998, p.25, no. 1.

FIG. 16
Illustration from p.133 of *The Noble arte of Venerie, or Hunting* ...,
George Gascoigne, 1575

15

David Murray of Gorthy (1567–1629)

UNIDENTIFIED ARTIST, 1603

Oil on canvas, 541 × 438mm
Inscribed upper left: *1603/Æ^te 36/Sr David Murray*
Scottish National Portrait Gallery, Edinburgh (PG 3538)

In 1599, David Murray was appointed by James VI to Prince Henry's household at Stirling Castle, becoming one of his Gentlemen of the Bedchamber. The King had written the first version of his instructive manual *Basilikon Doron* for Henry the year before, and Murray's appointment was part of the King's ongoing programme of educating and influencing his five-year-old heir. Murray moved to England with the Prince in 1603 and remained in his service until Henry's death in 1612. He was knighted in 1605, and when the Prince's household was increased in size in 1610 following his investiture as Prince of Wales, Murray was appointed Groom of the Stole.

It was, however, as Keeper of the Privy Purse and Keeper of the Robes that Murray played a role in Prince Henry's cultural interests. Through these important court positions he was responsible for the Prince's finances, which included making payments to artists and for his wardrobe and regalia. His account books record payments to jewellers and to the painters most closely associated with the Prince's portraiture – Isaac Oliver for miniatures and Robert Peake The Elder for large-scale portraits, including 'pictures made by His Highness' command'.

The young Prince appears to have been significantly attached to Murray, and on his deathbed he 'would many times call upon Sir David Murray, Knight (the only man in whom he had put choice trust) by his name, David! David!

David!' (Nichols 1828, vol. 2, p.482). In Henry's funeral procession, Murray rode in the chariot carrying the Prince's coffin. Afterwards, Prince Charles sought to have Murray installed in his own household, but this was refused by the King, 'alleging he was a puritan, seducing his late master to that schism' (British Library, Add. MS 32464).

Murray was also a noted poet. The year before the Prince's death he published his best-known work, *The Tragicall Death of Sophonisba* (1611), which he dedicated to Henry. Likewise, several literary works were dedicated to Murray, including the motto 'Virtus Romanet Antiqua' in Henry Peacham's 1612 emblem book *Minerva Britanna* (p.36).

This portrait of Murray, wearing a fashionable black, winged doublet, with a lace-edged standing collar, is the only known contemporary depiction of this important courtier. The style of the inscription, giving the sitter's age and date, is close to that of inscriptions on various portraits attributed to Peake, including *Unknown Military Commander* (Yale Center for British Art, Connecticut), but this portrait does not appear to be by the same artist. It may be that both the artist of this painting and Peake were using the same specialist to paint inscriptions on their portraits. Dated 1603, the present work commemorates a momentous year for Murray's royal master. D.A.H.B.T.

PROVENANCE
Possibly at Wemyss Castle; David Laing bequest to the Society of Antiquaries of Scotland in 1878; gifted to the Scottish National Portrait Gallery, 2009.

LITERATURE
Laing 1867, p.35.

1603
Æ 36

Sʳ David Murray.

16

Robert Cecil, 1st Earl of Salisbury (1563–1612)

JOHN DE CRITZ THE ELDER, 1602

Oil on panel, 902 × 734mm
Inscribed: *SERO, SED SERIO*, upper left and *1602*, top right
National Portrait Gallery, London (NPG 107)

Robert Cecil was the most powerful politician and courtier of the first part of James I's reign in England. The son of the greatest of Elizabethan statesmen, William Cecil, Lord Burghley, he eventually held three of the most important political offices simultaneously: Secretary of State, Lord Treasurer and Master of the Wards (Croft, 'Robert Cecil, first Earl of Salisbury', ODNB, 2008). In addition, he undertook almost all foreign diplomacy himself and kept a close eye on the activities of all the royal family, especially Prince Henry. Towards the end of his life, Salisbury paid particular attention to the Prince; the Venetian ambassador wrote in 1611 that Henry was 'almost always with the Earl of Salisbury' (*CSP Venetian, 1610–13*, XII, p.227, 21 October 1611). Salisbury ensured that Henry was supplied with information about foreign affairs and he conducted the important marriage negotiations with foreign courts that were undertaken on behalf of both Princess Elizabeth and Prince Henry.

In addition to his immensely busy life as a bureaucrat and politician, Cecil found the time to commission masques and festivals, and spectacular architecture, notably his great house and garden at Hatfield, as well as to amass a large and important collection of paintings. He was undoubtedly one of those who influenced Prince Henry in his collecting. A letter of March 1610 from Sir David Murray, the Prince's Groom of the Stole, refers to an arrangement whereby Cecil was to bring some of his own pictures to show to the Prince (HMC Salisbury; see also p.119). The link between their collecting activities is also reflected in a letter of January 1611 from Sir Walter Cope to Sir Dudley Carleton in Venice, in which Cope says, 'Yf you meete with any auncient Master peeces of paintinge at a reasonable hand, you cannot send a thinge more gracious, either to the Prince, or to my Lord Treasurer' (Auerbach and Adams 1971, p.79).

Cecil was probably the source of an important Italian picture in Henry's collection, *Prometheus* by Palma Giovane (1554–1628) (Shearman 1983, p.123, and Wilks 1997, pp.35–6).

Cecil was a patron of John de Critz before James came to the English throne, and it may be that it was through him that the artist was brought to the attention of the new King of England, and came to produce his standard portrait (see cat. 3). The earliest portrait of Cecil, presumed to be by de Critz, is dated 1599, but there is also a payment to de Critz in 1607 for five portraits, including one of Cecil himself to be sent to Sir Henry Wotton, English ambassador to Venice (Hatfield, Cecil papers, Box U/81; cited in Bracken 2002, p.134, note 16). All Cecil's portraits by de Critz have the same facial type as the present portrait; it may be, as other authors have suggested, that he was sensitive about his appearance (he was of short stature and had a hunch back) but it is also very likely that he was simply too busy to spend hours sitting for a variety of different portraits. C.M.

PROVENANCE
Given by David Laing to the National Portrait Gallery, London, 1860.

LITERATURE
Hearn 1995, no. 119, pp.174–5; Bracken 2002, pp.121–37.

FIG. 17
Prometheus Chained to the Caucasus, Palma Giovane, *c*.1570–1608

SERO, SED SERIO

1602

17

Sir Charles Cornwallis (c.1555–1629)

ROBERT PEAKE THE ELDER and STUDIO, c.1610

Oil on canvas, 1130 × 832mm
Inscribed (in a later seventeenth-century hand): *S^r: Cha: Cornwallis Kn:/(Embass^r:
into Spain and/Treas^r: to Pr: Henry whose/Daughter maried S^r: W^m: Fytche Kn^t: of Garnets/Essex*
National Portrait Gallery, London (NPG 4867)

Sir Charles Cornwallis was a courtier and diplomat who was appointed Treasurer of the Household to Prince Henry on his creation as Prince of Wales in 1610. He was one of a number of men appointed by the King to official positions in Henry's household, who had considerable influence on the young Prince and were in turn highly impressed by him (Wilks 1987, pp.31–2). Cornwallis was a relation by marriage of Robert Cecil, 1st Earl of Salisbury (see cat. 16), and it was no doubt in part owing to this connection that he found great favour under James I. He had been knighted by James in 1603, shortly after the King's arrival in England, and subsequently was sent as an ambassador to Spain. After four purportedly difficult years protecting British (and specifically Protestant) interests and supplying intelligence to Salisbury, he returned home, and was appointed to the Prince's household. In 1626, fourteen years after Henry's death, he wrote a biography of the Prince, *A discourse of the most illustrious prince, Henry late Prince of Wales. Written Anno 1626. by Sir Charles Cornwallis, Knight, sometimes Treasurer of His Highnesse house*, which was published in 1641 by John Benson (this should not be confused with the other biography of Henry published in 1641, also said to be by Cornwallis; see cat. 81). Cornwallis explicitly states on page 4 that his account is based only on first-hand knowledge of Henry: 'my purpose and desire is to deliver nothing but verities knowne to myself, not things received by tradition from others'. This is not to say, however, that it does not follow the conventions of writing about princes, and it does not in any real sense contradict the other biographies.

This portrait of Cornwallis, which shows him holding his white rod of office as Treasurer, has not previously been attributed to Robert Peake, but there is much physical evidence to suggest that it came out of his workshop. The costume is very finely painted, using techniques – such as those creating the effect of metallic fabric – that are characteristic of other portraits generally accepted as being by Peake (information obtained by microscopic and other analysis as part of the Making Art in Tudor Britain project at the National Portrait Gallery). The head, however, is weak in execution as well as being damaged; clearly it was painted by a distinct hand, presumably using a studio pattern. Two other portraits of Cornwallis exist, which use the same facial type but vary the pose (photographs in the Heinz Archive and Library, National Portrait Gallery, London); these were also presumably painted by Peake or members of his studio. C.M.

PROVENANCE
Probably Sir Charles Cornwallis; probably by descent to his daughter, Dorothy, who married Sir William Fytche of Garnets, Essex; probably by descent in the Fytche family; [...]; Dr W. Katz, from whom purchased by the National Portrait Gallery, London, 1972.

Sr Cha: Cornwallis Knt
Embass: into Spain and
Treas: to Pr: Henry whose
Daughter maried Sr Wm
Hytche Knt of Garnets
Essex

77

18

Edward Cecil, Viscount Wimbledon (1572–1638)

MICHIEL JANSZ. VAN MIEREVELT (1566–1641), 1610

Oil on panel, 622 × 508mm
Inscribed upper left: *Colonel Cissil/Viscount Wimbleton/Ætatis suae 37/An° 1610*
Private Collection

A professional soldier and an ardent Protestant, Edward Cecil was much admired by Henry and became a leading member of the circle that developed around the young Prince. He was the nephew of the most powerful politician of the day, Robert Cecil, 1st Earl of Salisbury (see cat. 16), and distinguished himself as a commander of English forces fighting in the Dutch War of Independence (1568–1648) alongside Prince Maurice of Nassau (see cat. 70). In 1610 he led the British contingent sent to defend German claims to the duchies of Jülich and Cleves in a succession dispute with the Holy Roman Emperor, Rudolf II.

The conflict between northern Protestant states and Catholic Habsburg forces was followed with great interest by Prince Henry. Cecil sent him a series of letters from the siege of Jülich over the summer of 1610. His dispatches include detailed descriptions of siege warfare suitable for the instruction of a future military leader. Cecil also declared his wish 'to be able in your happiest days to become a pore instrument

in some remarkable and princely undertakings of your owne' (Dalton 1885, p.204).

In addition, Cecil cultivated the Prince's humanist interests; he sent sycamore trees from the Netherlands for Henry's park at Richmond and encouraged his enthusiasm for the visual arts. He was closely involved in the arrangements for fifteen bronze statuettes to be sent to the Prince from Florence as part of the marriage suit of the Medicis (see cats 52 and 53). Cecil admired Italian culture and supported the Medici match, having stayed in Florence in the 1590s.

This portrait seems to be the first to have been commissioned from the Dutch artist Michiel van Mierevelt by an English patron. It was painted in Delft at the time of the Jülich campaign and shows Cecil in field armour, wearing a sash of command. Cecil was involved in attempts to persuade Mierevelt to work for the Prince. The court's enthusiasm for the artist was no doubt influenced by this portrait, which was later owned by Charles I. R.M.

PROVENANCE
Collection of Charles I, branded with his cipher 'CR' (*Carolus Rex*); sold to Sir David Murray on 23 October 1651; recovered at the Restoration; lost from the Royal Collection at an unknown date; [...]; collection of Colonel George Anson MC at Catton Hall, Walton upon Trent and thence by descent; on loan to the National Portrait Gallery, London (L164), 1977–90.

LITERATURE
Wilks 1987, p.18; Strong 1986, pp.46–7; Hearn 1995, pp.203–4; Jansen 2011, p.77.

19

Basilikon Doron in Basilica Emblemata totum versum

HENRY PEACHAM (1578–*c*.1644), *c*.1610

Ink and watercolour on paper, bound in leather, 42 folios (including
3 unfoliated paper flyleaves at the beginning and 4 at the end), 300 × 200mm
(open at book 2, folio 30r, emblem XXXV)

The British Library, London (BL Royal 12.A.LXVI)

Henry Peacham was a writer and illustrator on the fringes of the court who, like many in his position, saw Prince Henry as a means to further his career. This book, which he presented to the Prince in about 1610, was made to this end. Using James I's text of *Basilikon Doron* (see cat. 11), Peacham turned the King's words of advice into a series of 'emblems'. These consisted of a quotation from the 1603 edition of *Basilikon Doron*, a symbolic image representing the advice given in the quotation, a Latin quatrain interpreting the image, and a motto, sometimes in Greek. Books of emblems of this type were very popular in the sixteenth and seventeenth centuries, particularly in continental Europe. It was intended that in unpicking the meaning of the emblem the reader would ponder deeply its significance and use it as a means of self-improvement. Peacham's book was never published but he made three variant manuscript copies: the first in 1603–4, dedicated to Prince Henry (Bodleian Library, Oxford), and the second a year or so later, dedicated to James I (British Library, London). This is the third version; it has the greatest number of emblems and they are fully coloured, unlike those in the other versions.

The emblem reproduced here illustrates a passage in *Basilikon Doron* in which James refers specifically to Henry's education. He advises that Henry should be 'reasonably versed' in the liberal arts and sciences, 'but not preassing to bee a passmaister in any of them', as this will distract him from his other responsibilities. He cites the case of Archimedes, who, according to Plutarch's account, was so absorbed in working on a mathematical problem when his city was captured that he refused to come and meet the victorious Roman general, and was consequently killed.

Peacham also dedicated his emblem book *Minerva Britanna* (1612) to Prince Henry; the Prince's death was a blow to his hopes. He wrote a poem, 'A Period of Mourning' (1613), lamenting his loss, and subsequently, while travelling on the continent, wrote another poem, 'Prince Henrie Revived' (1615), on the birth of Prince Frederick Henry, son of Princess Elizabeth and Frederick V, Elector Palatine. He is best known, however, for his treatise on drawing, *Graphice* (1612; first published in 1606 as *The Art of Drawing* and published in expanded form as *The Gentleman's Exercise* in 1634) and for *The Compleat Gentleman* of 1622. C.M.

PROVENANCE
Presented by the author to Henry, Prince of Wales; by descent in the Royal Collection; presented to the British Museum by George II in 1757 as part of the Old Royal Library.

LITERATURE
Warner and Gilson 1921, II, p.9; Young with Verstraete 1998, pp.xviii–xix, pp.127–205 (especially p.181), pp.233–4; Horden, 'Peacham, Henry', ODNB 2004.

Emblem . XXX V .

Inopportuna studia.

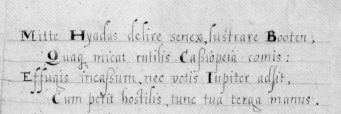

Mitte Hyadas delire senex, lustrare Booten,
 Quaq̃ micat rutilis Caßiöpeiä comis :
Effugis incassum, nec votis Iupiter adsit,
 Cum petit hostilis tunc tua terga manus .

As for the studie of other liberall artes and sciences, I would
have you reasonably versed in them, but not preaßing to bee
a paßemaister in any of them : for that cannot but distract
you from the pointes of your calling, as I shewed you before
and when by the enemie winning the Towne, ye shalbee —
interrupted in your demonstration, as ARCHIMEDES was
your people (I thinke) will looke very bluntly vpon it. ⁓

20

Prince Henry's Copy-book

PRINCE HENRY, 1604–6,
bound probably in 1610

Ink on paper, bound in white vellum
tooled with gold; 16 written leaves,
spine height 200mm
(open at folios 5v and 6r)

Trinity College, Cambridge
(Wren TC MS R.7.23, vol. I)

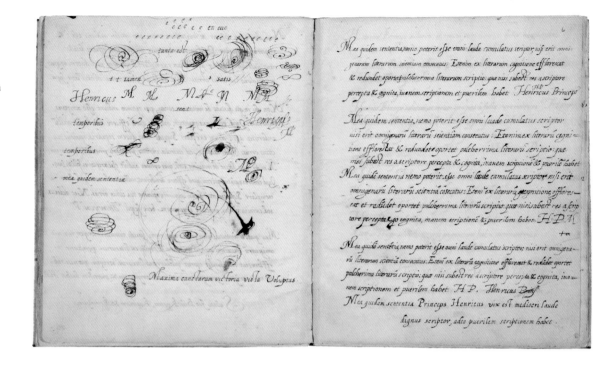

This is a copy-book in which Prince Henry
practised his handwriting, under the supervision
of Peter Bales (*c*.1547–1610?), his writing master
from 1604 to 1606. On the left-hand page Henry
has been practising flourishes, letters, Latin
phrases and his own signature. On the right-hand
page he has copied out, repeatedly, a passage of
Latin adapted from Cicero about the importance
of having knowledge of 'all important letters
and learning' in order to be a good scribe. The
last two lines on the page appear to have been
composed by Bales for his (and perhaps Henry's)
amusement; they can be translated as, 'indeed,
in my opinion, Prince Henry has such a childish
hand that he is hardly worthy of even mediocre
praise as a writer' (Pollnitz 2007, p.47).

Henry's education seems to have been
conventional for the time, at least at first; he
learned Latin and French and italic handwriting.
He composed Latin letters, read Latin texts
and made translations. As Aysha Pollnitz points
out, the only difference between Henry's letter-
writing in Latin and that of his contemporaries at
grammar schools was 'that Henry's letters were

addressed and sometimes sent to continental
heads of state, establishing his presence on the
European political landscape' (Pollnitz 2007,
p.43). As time went on Henry's education
broadened, and he learned mathematics and
perspective, music, history and some Italian
and Greek, among other subjects, although it is
difficult to know to what extent he was actually
taught by all those who were referred to as his
'tutors' (see Pollnitz 2007, pp.28–9).

This book was kept, along with other
exercise books and papers of the Prince's, by
Adam Newton (d.1630), a scholar of Scots origin
who was Henry's tutor from 1599. When Henry
was created Prince of Wales in 1610, Newton was
made his Secretary. He was a very important
influence on Henry, not just through his formal
educational role, organising a programme of study
for the Prince and undertaking much of the
teaching, but also as one of those, like Sir David
Murray, who was personally close to Henry and
could control access to others. Newton also
seems to have been knowledgeable about and
interested in art (see Wilks 1997, pp.43–4). C.M.

PROVENANCE
Sir Adam Newton; by descent to
his son, Sir Henry Puckering,
formerly Newton (*c*.1618–1701);
given by Puckering to Trinity
College, Cambridge, 1691.

LITERATURE
Pollnitz 2007, pp.22–64.

*La perspective avec la raison
des ombres et miroirs*

SALOMON DE CAUS (1576–1626)

printed by John Norton, London, 1612

Printed book; 170 pages, spine height 422mm
(open at folio 6, 'Perspective Lesson',
engraved by Cornelis Boel (b. *c.*1576))

The British Library, London (747.d.26.)

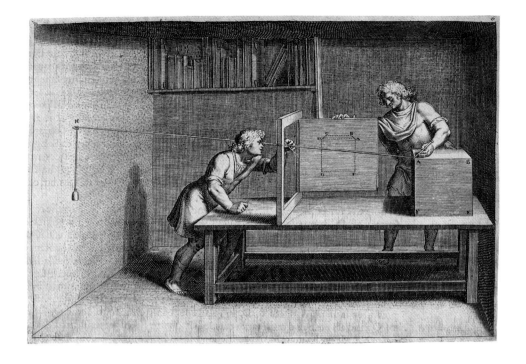

Salomon de Caus was born in Dieppe to a Huguenot family. His dedication to Prince Henry in *La perspective* indicates that he first came into contact with the Prince whilst employed in Brussels by the Archdukes Albert and Isabella when, either in person or by correspondence, he began teaching the Prince perspective. By the end of 1610 de Caus had joined Henry's household at Richmond. He was employed alongside the Surveyor of the Prince's Works, Inigo Jones, and the Italian designer Costantino de' Servi, in the ambitious project to transform the palace and its grounds into a showpiece to rival the courts of Henry's continental contemporaries (see Appendix, pp.180–3).

La perspective was based on the lessons de Caus gave to the Prince and was the first book on perspective to be published in England. It is a testament to the quality of Henry's education, both for its theoretical complexity and as evidence of the Prince's fluency in French. It was produced in one edition with three issues: firstly by the King's printer, Robert Baker, in 1611, secondly by John Norton in 1612, and thirdly by Anne van Hulsen of Frankfurt for the

international market (Marr in Wilks 2007, p.229). The illustration shows classicised figures of a prince and tutor engaged in a lesson; it is based on Albrecht Dürer's woodcut *Draughtsman drawing a lute* from his treatise *Underweysung der Messung* (Instruction in Measurement), 1525.

Through richly illustrated exercises, de Caus demonstrates the rendering in perspective of progressively more complex forms, from simple shapes to explanations of *trompe l'oeil* and anamorphosis. The later chapters deal with the perspectival rendering of shadows and the reflections of objects in a mirror. Along with the English translation, published by Robert Peake the Elder, of Serlio's *First Book of Architecture*, also published in 1611 and dedicated to the Prince, de Caus's treatise responded to a need amongst English patrons and practitioners for a better understanding of Vitruvian architectural theory and Euclidian geometry. These publications not only expressed the cultural ambitions of Henry's court but were also viewed as practical guides, whose application, be it architectural, artistic, military or technological, would enhance England's honour and prosperity. R.M.

PROVENANCE
Horace Walpole collection; [...] purchased by the British Library, London, 1845.

LITERATURE
Strong 1986, pp.109–10; Morgan 2007, pp.53–8, 143–8; Marr 2007, pp.212–38.

HENRICUS PRINCEPS FECIT
letter square

THOMAS HARRIOT (*c*.1560–1621), *c*.1605–10

Ink on paper, 310 × 200mm (f. 27)

The British Library, London
(Additional MS 6782 vol. 1[a])

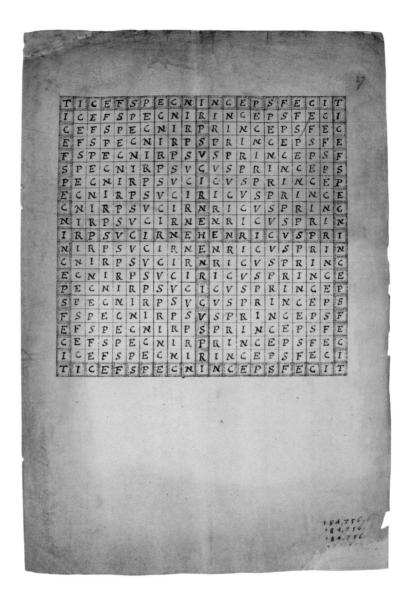

This letter square is a mathematical exercise based on the Latin words *Henricus Princeps Fecit* ('Prince Henry made this'), devised by the mathematician Thomas Harriot. As explained by Dr Jim Reeds, 'It illustrates a combinational calculation, namely, the number of paths spelling out the phrases in question, starting from the middle cell of the diagram and ending at any corner, always moving vertically or horizontally through neighbouring cells. The number of such spellings ending in any particular corner cell is always a binomial coefficient ... since there are four corner cells, the final answers are four times the appropriate binomial coefficient' (Reeds 1999). The calculation of the number of pathways is written out bottom right: 184,756 added together four times. The answer (739,024) has been cut off. Harriot was imitating a similar square based on the words *Silo Princeps Fecit*, cut into the foundation stone of the church of St John the Apostle and Evangelist in Pravia, Spain, commemorating Silo, King of Asturias from AD773 to 784; Harriot also made a copy of the Silo square. Reeds noted that the paper used for this square was of higher quality than Harriot usually used, and speculated that it might have been made for presentation to the Prince.

Thomas Harriot was one of the most important mathematicians of his day; like that of many of his contemporaries, his work extended into other areas of 'natural philosophy' including astronomy and navigation. Harriot was part of the expedition to Virginia in 1585 and he settled briefly on Roanoke Island, where he studied the language and customs of the local Algonquian Indians, as well as the flora and fauna (Roche, 'Harriot, Thomas', ODNB 2004). It is not known how, or even if, he knew Prince Henry, although he was in close contact with others in Henry's circle, including George Chapman and John, 2nd Baron Harington of Exton, so it is conceivable that he knew, or even taught, the Prince at some point. C.M.

PROVENANCE
Thomas Harriot; bequeathed to Henry Percy, 9th Earl of Northumberland (1564–1632); by descent at Petworth House to George O'Brien Wyndham, 3rd Earl of Egremont (1751–1837); deposited by Lord Egremont with the majority of Harriot's papers in the British Museum, London, 1810.

LITERATURE
Shirley 1983, pp.419–20; Reeds 1999.

23

Homer Prince of Poets: Translated according to the Greeke in Twelve bookes of his Iliads

GEORGE CHAPMAN (1559/60 – 1634), printed by Humphrey Lownes for Samuel Macham, 1609

Printed book, 154 pages, spine height 240mm (open at title page: engraving by William Hole (*fl.*1607–d.1624))

The British Library, London (c.39.g.24)

George Chapman was a playwright, poet and classical scholar, a contemporary of Shakespeare and an important literary figure in Elizabethan and Jacobean England. In about 1604 he obtained the relatively minor position of Sewer-in-Ordinary, an attendant at table (and food taster) to Prince Henry, and from this time the Prince was the focus of a number of his literary works. Chapman worked on his translation of Homer throughout much of his career. He published a translation of the first seven books of the *Iliad* in 1598, with a dedication to the 2nd Earl of Essex. Essex was executed for treason in 1601 and when Chapman published the full translation of all twelve books in 1609, it was dedicated to Prince Henry. In his poem, 'Corollarium ad Principem', printed at the end of another book published in the same year (*Euthymiae raptus; or the teares of peace with interlocutions*), Chapman claimed that the Prince had commanded the completion of Homer's works, which he called 'your Homer' and 'my Princes Homer'.

By commissioning a translation of Homer, Prince Henry would have boosted his reputation for scholarship, a reputation that was of some importance to his father and probably also to him. Henry seems to have learned a little Greek (see Pollnitz 2007, p.43), but probably not enough to read Homer in the original. Chapman's translation also made the *Iliad* accessible to a much wider public, and it was a major contribution to contemporary English literature. Chapman himself saw Homer's text as an important part

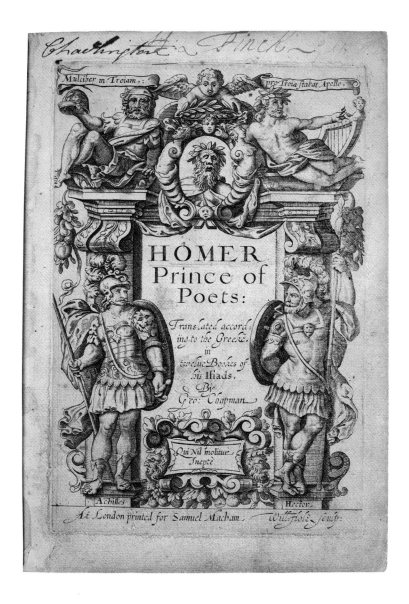

of the Prince's education, providing him with 'princely presidents' (i.e. precedents). Appealing to Henry's martial interests and image as a potential military hero, he compared him with Alexander the Great and asserted that Alexander 'would affirme that *Homers* poesie/Did more advance his Asian victorie,/Then all his Armies' (second page of dedication).

After Henry's death, Chapman wrote *An Epicede or Funeral Song* (1612), and he finally published *The Whole Works of Homer* in 1616. C.M.

PROVENANCE
Formerly in the collections of 'Charrington' and 'Finch' (names inscribed on title page); purchased by the British Library, London, 1838.

LITERATURE
Strong 1986, pp.130, 180; Wilks 1987, pp.74, 251–4; George Chapman, *Chapman's Homer: The Iliad,* 1611 edn, Allardyce Nicoll, Bollingen Series 41, 1998; Bertheau 2007, pp.134–45.

24

Coryats Crudities

THOMAS CORYATE (?1577–1617)

printed by William Stansby for the author, London, 1611

Printed book; engraved illustrations hand-coloured in watercolour, 942 pages and 5 engraved plates, spine height 230mm
original red velvet binding set on new boards
(open at title page: engraving by William Hole)

The British Library, London (G.6750)

Foreign travel was considered an important part of a noble education in the early seventeenth century. It was a means of learning more about political and religious contexts that might have a bearing on domestic politics; of acquiring languages and manners, which might serve important diplomatic purposes; and of increasing knowledge of the art, architecture, scientific wonders and history of other lands, thus making oneself 'more Compleat in all things', as the travel writer Sir Thomas Palmer put it in 1606 (quoted in O'Callaghan 2007, p.85). As heir to the throne, Prince Henry could not travel abroad; it was considered simply too risky. He therefore had to rely on others to convey the requisite knowledge to him. Friends, such as Sir John Harington (see cat. 25), would write to the Prince while on their own travels; Robert Cecil, 1st Earl of Salisbury, ensured that the Prince was kept abreast of political and diplomatic developments. Travel books were another means by which Henry could pursue this aspect of his education.

Coryats Crudities was a remarkable addition to this genre. A humorous and lively account of the European travels of Thomas Coryate, it combines detailed descriptions of art and architecture, local events and history, with tales of Coryate's own adventures. The text is supplemented with illustrations by William Hole, an engraver who was associated with various members of the Prince's circle (see Wilks 2007, p.182). The title page is illustrated with various amusing and dramatic incidents on the journey, and this is followed by a series of mock-panegyric verses written by various friends and acquaintances (many from Henry's court), but the volume actually conveys a great deal of useful information. Firmly Protestant in tone, the French section has an emphasis on the political and religious situation. The Venetian section, however, is particularly valuable for its descriptions of art and architecture (at this point Coryate was much in the company of Sir Henry Wotton, English ambassador to Venice and connoisseur of the arts). This hand-coloured, velvet-bound copy of the book was presented by Coryate to Prince Henry in 1611.

The scenes on the title page (illustrated here), are explained in a key on the following pages of the manuscript. Lower right, a Venetian courtesan pelts Coryate with eggs. Top right, a depiction of Coryate's clothes on a gibbet is a parody of the emblems that, accompanied by explanatory verses, were fashionable at court (see cat. 19). Coryate's verses emphasise the hardships of travel: 'See our louse-bitten Trauellers ragged device,/ Of case, shoes and stockings, and Canniball lice'. C.M.

PROVENANCE
Prince Henry; his chaplain, Mr Pomfret; by descent to Mr N. Pomfret Williams; given in 1796 to the Rev. Hugh Cholmondeley; at his death given by his brother Thomas Cholmondeley to Sir Thomas Grenville, 1816; bequeathed to the British Library, London, and received 1847.

LITERATURE
J.T. Payne and H. Foss (Pts I and II) and W.B. Rye (Pt III), *Bibliotheca Grenvilliana* (Shakespeare Press, London, 1842–72, part I, vol.I, p.164); Wilks 1987, p.83; O'Callaghan 2007, pp.85–103.

25

John Harington, 2nd Baron Harington of Exton (1591–1614)

UNIDENTIFIED ARTIST, *c.*1613–14

Engraving on paper, 313 × 221mm

The British Museum, London (1849,0315.17)

Like Robert Devereux, 3rd Earl of Essex (see cat. 14), Harington was a chosen companion to Prince Henry. His father was Princess Elizabeth's governor, and it was probably the father who commissioned the double portrait of the Prince with his son in 1603 (see pp.35–6). Harington and Prince Henry evidently developed a close friendship, and when the time came for Harington to travel abroad in 1608 (an aspect of his education in which the Prince could not share), he travelled in part on the Prince's behalf, sending back detailed accounts of the sights he had seen, and the politics, state occasions and cultural developments in the places he visited. In June 1609 the Earl of Salisbury (see cat. 16) wrote, 'I find every week, in the Prince's hand, a letter from Sir John Harington, full of news of the place where he is, and the countries as he passeth' (BL Landsdowne MS 108, fol. 94, cited in Hearn 2003, p.222.) In 1609–10 he was in Venice, where he was presented to the Doge, to whom he showed a miniature portrait of the Prince. The Venetian ambassador, Sir Henry Wotton, described Harington as the 'right eye of the prince', and speculated that as such, he would one day 'govern the kingdom' (*CSP Venetian, 1610–13*, XI, pp.215–16).

Like Prince Henry, however, he was to die young, his promise unfulfilled. Grief at the loss of Harington echoed that expressed at the Prince's death two years earlier; poetry (including that of John Donne), sermons and posthumous biographies described him as an ideal nobleman, with every virtuous quality, and a staunch Protestant.

This print, apparently made during Harington's lifetime, depicts him holding a baton signifying military command, but dressed, along with his horse, more appropriately for a tournament than for battle. Like so many of Prince Henry's portraits, Harington's shows him as a virtuous Protestant knight. C.M.

PROVENANCE
Richard Grenville, 2nd Duke of Buckingham and Chandos; the Stowe sale, Christie's, 15 August–7 October 1848, lot 363; bought by 'Evans' (presumably the dealers A.E. Evans & Sons); purchased by the British Museum, London, 1849.

26

Henry, Prince of Wales, Practising with the Pike

WILLIAM HOLE after ISAAC OLIVER, 1612

Engraving on paper, 198 × 125mm
The British Museum, London (1868,0822.1148)

The French ambassador Antoine le Fèvre de la Boderie, visiting England in 1606, described Prince Henry's daily timetable: 'He studies two hours a day, and employs the rest of his time in tossing the pike, or leaping, or shooting with the bow, or throwing the bar, or vaulting; or some other exercise of that kind; and he is never idle' (cited in Birch 1760, p.76). The Prince's love of military exercises was commented on by others, and his prowess at the 'push of pike' in particular was displayed to great effect at *Prince Henry's Barriers* of 1610 (see cat. 37). Such exercises were an important part of his education, not just to prepare him for possible warfare, but also to set an example to his court and to complete his image as a prince with all the necessary virtues and accomplishments of a potential military hero.

This print was based on a drawing by Isaac Oliver, now lost, which was subsequently acquired by Inigo Jones, Surveyor of the Prince's Works, and then passed on to Charles I. The head of the Prince is very close to that in Oliver's miniature (see cat. 44) and it seems likely that the drawing of the Prince's head was based on the miniature. The pose, holding the pike, is, as Timothy Wilks has shown, based on a contemporary Dutch print from a book of military exercises. William Hole's print was used as the frontispiece to Michael Drayton's *Poly-olbion* (1612), which was dedicated to Henry. It was evidently seen as a particularly appropriate image of the young Prince, as variants made by other engravers continued to be produced after his death, some used as frontispieces to his biographies (see Wilks 2007 and cat. 81). C.M.

PROVENANCE
Felix Slade (1790–1868); bequeathed
to the British Museum, London, 1868.

LITERATURE
Hind 1955, II, pp.321–22; Wilks
2007, pp.180–211.

27

Letters Patent of James I, creating his son
Henry Prince of Wales and Earl of Chester

Attributed to ISAAC OLIVER and two other unidentified hands, 1610

Illuminated manuscript, 533 × 700mm

The British Library, London (Additional MS 36932)

Henry was formally created Prince of Wales on 4 June 1610, during a solemn Parliamentary ceremony. Along with his princely regalia, he was presented with the Letters Patent, symbolic of his new office. At first glance, the Patent's imagery appears to be a straightforward celebration of Henry's titles and militant persona. The coats of arms that decorate its border represent the dignities of the Prince in ascending order: the badges of the Earl of Chester, the Duke of Cornwall and the Prince of Wales. The uppermost central arms are those of King James, while to their right are Henry's royal arms. Below the initial portraits are the ancient arms of the Principality of Wales. Interlaced with these heraldic devices are illustrations of armour and weaponry. Yet the plumed helmets and suits of armour with their coloured sashes, the pasteboard shields, banners and pavilions were all associated with the tilt yard, rather than the battlefield.

The initial portraits depict the moment of investiture, when the King handed the Patent to the kneeling Prince. The letter 'J' in which this scene is illustrated serves to highlight James's achievements. Depicted among the golden knots and scrolls is a lion's head and the lizard body of a wyvern, the supporters of the Scoto-Danish arms of James and his wife, Anne of Denmark.

These two creatures symbolise the union of the King and Queen, a match that had borne fruit and produced Henry. The cornucopia and foliage, which decorate its first line, continue this theme of fertility and denote the benefits of peace and plenty under James. Thus the Patent constitutes a carefully managed statement, representing the Prince's martial interests under the veil of the chivalric tournament and containing his figure within the iconography of his father's government. The faces of the King and his son have been attributed to the miniaturist Nicholas Hilliard, with the rest of the decoration ascribed to a second inferior hand (Strong 1983, p.147). However, comparison with other illuminated manuscripts attributed to Hilliard reveals marked stylistic differences. Indeed, it would also appear that the manuscript displays evidence of at least three separate artistic hands. The first artist, most probably a heraldic painter, was responsible for the coats of arms and tournament paraphernalia. The second was responsible for rendering the robes, figures, putto and setting of the initial portraits. The third – who executed the delicately modelled faces of James and Henry – remains elusive, although similarities in modelling and finish suggest Isaac Oliver. C.A.M.

PROVENANCE
Presumably commissioned by James I and part of Prince Henry's collections until his death in 1612; [...]; bought by the British Library in 1904 from Francis P. Wheeler.

LITERATURE
Daniel 1610, Sig. A3v–Sig. D3v; Strong 1983, p.147; Croft 1992, pp.177–93.

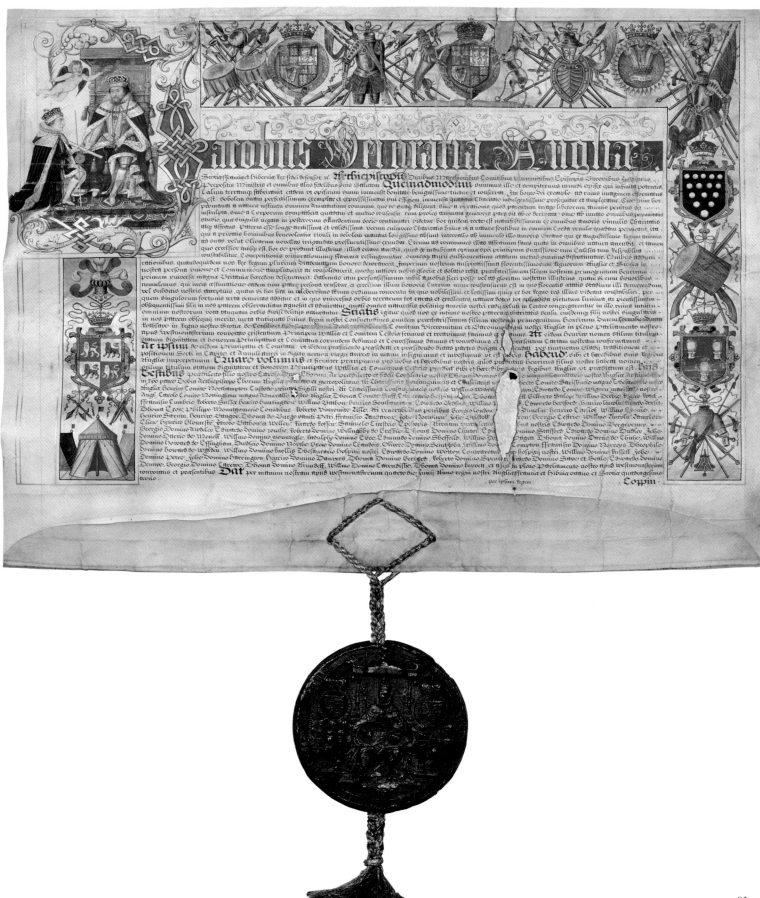

Festivals, Masques and Tournaments

Festivals and other kinds of entertainments were an essential part of life at the court of James I. They were not merely a means of passing the time, or of displaying the wealth of the monarch. They were a way of signalling the importance of the King and the royal family to courtiers and the wider public in Britain, and to foreign rulers and their courts abroad. Their lavish display was always presented within a framework of symbolism, which alluded to the virtue, power, honour and glory of the monarch and his family. They ranged from the ceremonial entry into London designed for James I in 1604, for which huge temporary triumphal arches were built, to martial jousts and tournaments in which military prowess was displayed in a context of chivalric symbolism, to the magnificent theatrical performances of court masques. Whatever the notional theme, the glorification of the monarch was always, ultimately, the aim.

Prince Henry was the focus of these celebratory occasions from early in his life. His baptism at Stirling Castle, in the summer of 1594, included an elaborate feast and a tournament in which the King himself participated, wearing 'a Lyons heade with open eyes'.[1] Henry made his first appearance in the tilt yard, armed and mounted, in 1606, on the occasion of the visit of his uncle, Christian IV of Denmark. Even at this stage it was evident to commentators that the Prince's own inclinations coincided with a general wish to present him at every opportunity as an idealised warrior prince. It was not, however, until *Prince Henry's Barriers* of 1610 (an indoor tournament with allegorical text by Ben Jonson) that he was really able to show his prowess at military exercises.

Gifts of horses and elaborate armour, intended for such displays, were known to be particularly acceptable to the young Prince, and Henry was given armour by both

Prince Henry on Horseback, Robert Peake the Elder, *c*.1606–8? (detail of cat. 28)

English courtiers and foreign princes. Henri IV of France also sent Henry a riding instructor, the Seigneur de St Antoine, to teach him French riding skills. In practising for and performing in tournaments and tilts, Henry was following the advice of his father James: 'Use therefore to ryde and daunton greate and coragious horses, that I may saie of you (as PHILLIP said of great ALEXANDER his son) [*Macedonia has not room for thee*] & use specially such games on horse-back as may teach you to handle your armes thereon, such as the Tilte, the Ring, and lowe ryding for handling of your sword'.[2]

Other entertainments staged for the Prince did not involve military exercises, but usually presented him in some kind of chivalric context. Jonson wrote an entertainment in honour of Prince Henry and his mother, Anne of Denmark, which was performed at Althorp during their journey south from Edinburgh to London in 1603, and reflected hopes that Henry's reign would be crowned with military success. The celebrations for his creation as Prince of Wales in May and June 1610 included a river fete, a tilt, a mock sea battle and firework display on the River Thames, and a masque, commissioned from Samuel Daniel by the Queen, entitled *Tethys Festival*.

Masques were elaborate, theatrical, courtly entertainments in which music, dance, poetry and sometimes prose, all set within an allegorical narrative, were performed by magnificently costumed participants, often including members of the royal family. A development of earlier Tudor entertainments, they also took elements from festivals held at the great courts of Europe. Some took place at courtiers' homes, but most were staged at court. The sets, almost always designed by Inigo Jones, were an integral part of the performance and frequently involved complex and spectacular effects, including moving scenery,

coloured lights and illusionistic transformations. While the characters and narratives differed, all the masques had certain elements in common: they drew on an eclectic mix of classical and chivalric, Arthurian sources both for their designs and their texts; they were extremely expensive, often costing over £1,000 to stage; they were almost always performed only once.

Henry's interest in entertainments of this kind is testified to by books in his library, his correspondence on the subject of foreign court festivals, and his own patronage. He commissioned *Oberon, the Faery Prince*, in which he took the lead role, for the Christmas celebrations in 1610–11; it had a text by Ben Jonson and designs by Inigo Jones. Henry was much involved in the planning stages of the festivities that later accompanied the marriage of Princess Elizabeth to the Elector Palatine, Frederick V, and, had he lived, he would have played a central role in the proposed masques and tilts. As it was, the chivalric figures he had played in life became the themes of poetry mourning his death. C.M.

1 Henry W. Meikle (ed.), *The Works of William Fowler*, 3 vols, Scottish Text Society, Edinburgh, 1914–40, vol. II (1936), p.174, cited by Deborah Howard, *Scottish Architecture: From the Reformation to the Restoration 1550–1650*, Edinburgh University Press, 1995, p.34.
2 James VI of Scotland, *Basilikon Doron*, Edinburgh, 1599, p.144.

28

Prince Henry on Horseback

ROBERT PEAKE THE ELDER, *c.*1606–8?

Oil on canvas, 2286 × 2184mm

From the collection at Parham House, Pulborough, West Sussex

This magnificent portrait is the earliest known full-size equestrian portrait of an English sitter. While equestrian portraits had been used on royal seals and in prints, and small images of Henry VIII on horseback can be seen in *The Field of the Cloth of Gold* and *The Meeting of Henry VIII and the Emperor Maximilian I* (both Royal Collection), this type of full-size equestrian portrait was without precedent in English painting at this date, although more familiar in France. It is the third of Robert Peake's innovative portraits of the Prince (see fig. 12 and cat. 60). As well as looking at French equestrian royal portraiture, of which there was at least one example in the Royal Collection (Wilks 2007, pp.173–9), it has been pointed out that Peake probably had Albrecht Dürer's print *Knight, Death and the Devil* of 1513 in mind (see fig. 13 and Weigl 2007, pp.163–4). Instead of the monstrous figures accompanying Dürer's knight, however, Prince Henry drags along a figure of Father Time, whose forelock is tied to the favour on the Prince's arm. Father Time carries a lavishly plumed helmet, part of an otherwise unrecorded suit of parade armour, decorated with mysterious *imprese* depicting hands rising from a grassy plain, holding anchors (Weigl 2007, pp.153–6). Perhaps in response to this portrait, equestrian portraits of the Prince were made by Henry Peacham for his *Minerva Britanna* and for James Cleland's manuscript *Le Pourtraict de Monseigneur le Prince*.

The extraordinary iconography of this portrait has been used in the past as evidence of Prince Henry's visual sophistication in commissioning his own portraiture, but there is no evidence that this picture was commissioned by him, or was ever in the Royal Collection. Instead, it probably reflects the response of the artist and the patron – quite possibly Henry Howard, 1st Earl of Northampton (1540–1614) – to the great promise for the future that the young Prince seemed to embody.

It has previously been assumed that this painting must date from 1610 at the earliest, presumably because this was the year that Henry was created Prince of Wales, and the so-called Prince of Wales feathers and coronet are shown on the wall behind him. However, it is clear that the heir apparent's feathers, as they are more properly known, were used in association with the Prince long before this date; see, for example, cats 58 and 59, and John Norden's *A Description of the Honor of Windesor ...* of 1607 (Royal Collection). It seems more likely, given the apparent age of the Prince, that this portrait dates from before 1610.

The unusual iconography of this painting was evidently found uncomfortable by its owners at some point in the later seventeenth or early eighteenth century. The wall, landscape and Father Time were painted over with a new, wooded landscape, and the heavy tilting horse transformed into the kind of elegant mount shown in Van Dyck's equestrian portraits. This overpaint was removed in 1985–6 and the original appearance of the painting revealed for the first time in 300 years. C.M.

PROVENANCE
Probably commissioned by Henry Howard, 1st Earl of Northampton; recorded in his collection in 1614; Sir Robert Cotton; [...]; Hengrave Hall, Suffolk, in the early 19th century; Godfrey Williams, St Donat's Castle; Christie's, 4 October 1946 (lot 131); Mrs P.A. Tritton; by descent at Parham Park.

LITERATURE
Woudhuysen-Keller et al 1988, pp.15–22; Strong 1986, p.115; Weigl 2007, pp.146–72; Wilks 2007, pp.173–9.

29

Prince Henry's Armour for the Field, Tilt, Tourney and Barriers

ROYAL ARMOURY, GREENWICH,
under JACOB HALDER (d.1608), c.1608

Blued steel, gilt, brass, copper-zinc alloys; height 1590mm

The Royal Collection (RCIN 72831)

This armour was presented to Prince Henry in July 1608 by Sir Henry Lee (1533–1611). Lee had been a favourite of Elizabeth I and, as the Queen's Champion, was responsible for the elaborate and visually spectacular Accession Day tilts. These festivals were precursors of the Jacobean festivals that combined classical and chivalric symbolism to draw parallels between the Stuart royal family and heroes of mythology and history. Henry was a particular focus of these entertainments and his appearances in the tilt yard were central to the militaristic reputation he acquired.

Lee's gift of armour served to encourage the Prince's martial interests and demonstrate his loyalty to his future sovereign. However, the court gossip John Chamberlain questioned the wisdom of buying such a splendid armour for the fourteen-year-old Prince: 'Sir Henry Lea [sic] ... went to present the prince with an armour that stood him in £200: and within a yeare or two will serve his turne neither for jest nor earnest' (quoted in Wilks 1987, p.208).

The suit consists of a relatively light and flexible field armour for use in battle, to which additional pieces could be attached for greater protection in the tilt (jousting), tourney (tournaments) and barriers (combat with sword and pike across a barrier). The armour is shown in its tourney configuration with tasset extensions over the hips and reinforced gauntlets, visor and gorget (neck piece). The extravagant colouring and decoration is characteristic of Greenwich armour. The blued steel is embellished with gilt and etched bands of strapwork bearing the Prince's cipher, 'HP' (*Henricus Princeps*), interspersed with Tudor roses, thistles and fleurs-de-lys. The design scheme conspicuously promotes the Scottish thistle above the emblems of the preceding royal dynasty and the French crown (to which the English monarchy made a notional claim). The enduring significance of the armour is indicated by its appearance in portraits of Prince Charles and in Van Dyck's posthumous portrait of Henry (fig. 9). R.M.

PROVENANCE
Presented to Henry, Prince of Wales, by Sir Henry Lee, 1608; believed to have been rescued from Greenwich by Edward Annesley, 1644; displayed at the Tower of London following the Restoration (1660); recorded at Windsor Castle from 1742.

LITERATURE
Laking 1904, cat. no. 678; Strong 1986, p.67; Wilks 1987, p.208; Evans 1998, p.37.

30

Prince Henry's Armour

DUTCH, *c.*1608

Iron, embossed, etched, chased gilt; height 1510mm
Royal Armouries (11.88)

This outstanding example of decorated Dutch armour was presented to Prince Henry in 1608 by Sir Francis Vere (1560–1609). The dimensions of the armour indicate that Henry's height, aged fourteen, was approximately 1445mm (4ft 9in). Though not intended for use in the field, the armour could have been worn during the training exercises at which the Prince excelled. Beyond its practical application, such an armour was appreciated for its craftsmanship, material worth and, above all, as a symbol of the chivalric honour and high social standing of its owner.

Armouries in Renaissance courts were treasure houses as much as weapon stores and were generally prized above art collections and *kunstkammern*. A martial disposition was considered essential in a prince and, in this spirit, a self-consciously militaristic culture developed around Henry from a young age. The earliest instance of his court soliciting a gift of armour was in 1607, when Claude de Guise, Prince de Joinville, presented a suit, which may be that worn by Henry in Nicholas Hilliard's miniature (see cat. 31). Further gifts of armour were sent by Henri IV and Maurice of Nassau, although the latter arrived after Henry's death. Vere's gift of Dutch armour was made at the end of thirty years of distinguished service in the Dutch War of Independence. Initially fighting under the Earl of Leicester and Maurice of Nassau, he served from 1589 as the chief commander of the English force. His participation in famous victories, such as the Battle of Nieuwpoort in 1600, made him a celebrity at home. Re-enactments of his most heroic actions were performed on the London stage and *Commentaries*, his posthumously published autobiography, was a bestseller.

The armour is richly decorated with bands of chased and gilt strapwork in which exquisitely rendered scenes illustrate the life of Alexander the Great (356–323 BC). The scheme was no doubt designed to compliment the Prince by associating him with the most celebrated warrior of antiquity. This flattering comparison was frequently employed in verse in praise of Henry; a fine example is Henry Peacham's *Minerva Britanna* (1612) (quoted in Strong 1987, p.67):

> ...thus young HENRY, like Macedo[n]'s son,
> Ought'st thou in armes before thy people shine.
> A prodigie for foes to gave vpon,
> But still a glorious Load-starre vnto thine ...

R.M.

PROVENANCE
Presented by Sir Francis Vere to Prince Henry in 1608; appears in the Greenwich inventory of 1629: 'one feilde armou[r] complete guilte and chaced given by Sr Francis Veare [sic] unto Prince Henry in a chest lyned within and without with red cloth'; probably transferred to the Tower of London by Edward Annesley in 1644 or 1649.

LITERATURE
Strong 1986, pp.66–70; Thom Richardson, *Stuart Royal Armours from the Royal Armouries* (forthcoming publication).

FIG. 18
Vambrace from Prince Henry's Dutch Armour, showing the Battle of the Hydaspes River

31

Prince Henry in French Armour

NICHOLAS HILLIARD, 1607

Watercolour, bodycolour, powdered gold and silver
on vellum laid on card, 60 × 50mm
Inscribed: *Año Dñi 1607 . Ætatis suae 14.*

The Royal Collection (RCIN 420642)

This miniature and a smaller example of
approximately the same date (both Royal
Collection; see fig. 23) are the only known
miniatures of Prince Henry by Nicholas Hilliard,
the favoured miniaturist of Queen Elizabeth I
and also of King James (see cat. 5). All Henry's
surviving subsequent miniature portraits seem to
have been painted by Isaac Oliver (see cat. 6); it
may be that the change in patronage came about
after Henry's creation as Prince of Wales in 1610.
In this work he wears a suit of French armour
that survives in the Royal Collection today.
It is probably the armour that was given to him
by the Prince de Joinville in 1607, the date of
the miniature. Hilliard's graphic, linear style
is enhanced by the use of tiny applications of
gold and silver, imitating the sparkling effect
that must have been created by the highly
decorated armour.

Henry was given a number of armours by
English courtiers and by foreign monarchs and
aristocrats (see cats 29 and 30). In 1607, apart
from that given to him by the Prince de Joinville,
he was given another by King Henri IV. These
armours were particularly appropriate gifts for
the young Prince; expensive and magnificently
decorated, they were intended for display in the
tilt yard or other settings for military sports,
rather than on the battlefield, and perfectly
suited Henry's developing image as a potential

military hero. The Prince de Joinville, among
numerous others, also gave Prince Henry gifts
of horses (Strong 1986, p.235, note 178).

Hilliard's authorship of this miniature has
been disputed (see Strong 1983, p.140) but the
style is comparable with other late works by the
artist, and the attribution to 'ould Hilliard' is
recorded in the catalogue of works belonging
to King Charles I by Abraham van der Doort
(d.1640), who was in consultation with Hilliard's
son (Millar 1960, p.108, no. 20 and p.216, B3).
C.M.

PROVENANCE
In the collection of Charles I; lost
from the Royal Collection during
the Commonwealth but recovered by
Colonel Hawley at the Restoration;
by descent in the Royal Collection.

LITERATURE
Strong 1983, p.140; Strong 1986,
pp.66, 118, 236, note 199; Wilks 1987,
pp.101, 207–8; Reynolds 1999,
no. 35, p.76.

32

Henry, Prince of Wales

ISAAC OLIVER, *c.*1610–12

Watercolour and bodycolour on vellum laid onto card, 128 × 98mm
The Royal Collection (RCIN 420058)

This magnificent miniature of Prince Henry (overleaf) is one of Isaac Oliver's most compelling images, and one of those most repeated by the artist himself and members of his studio. A number of oval versions survive (including four in the Royal Collection) with a red curtain but without the scene in the background. The rectangular form of this miniature, however, lent itself to larger copies in oils. The most significant such copy is probably that by Daniel Mytens (*c.*1590–1647), painted for Henry's younger brother Charles, later Charles I (see cat. 82); the fact that it was this image by which Charles wished to remember his brother suggests that it was regarded as a particularly faithful likeness, and perhaps also particularly appropriate in its iconography.

Inevitably there has been debate about the mysterious military scene in the background. The figures are too small to be able to interpret with confidence; it is not clear whether they wear Roman or contemporary armour. Some kind of military leader sits in a tent, while outside other soldiers stand around, holding pikes. There is a cannon in the foreground. Henry himself wears contemporary armour, which may perhaps be identified with a black field armour owned by

Henry (Wilks 1987, pp.210–13). It is not possible to link the miniature to any specific masque or tournament, but as Graham Reynolds points out, it depicts Henry 'as the promoter of modern military prowess on the foundations of the past'.

Isaac Oliver was Queen Anne's miniaturist at the time this work was painted (see cat. 6). However, he seems to have been particularly favoured by Henry from at least the time of his creation as Prince of Wales in 1610. Records of payments to Oliver in the Prince's accounts from 1609 to 1612 have been interpreted as indicating that Henry commissioned numerous miniatures from the artist, but these are a mixture of payments for miniatures and payments for works by others; like many artists of the period, Oliver was also a picture dealer (Wilks 1987, pp.99–100). However, the survival of so many miniatures of the same type, and the fact that two were owned by Charles I, suggests that Oliver was producing these at least with the approval of Henry, if not always at his behest. Although there is no record of Oliver having an official appointment in Henry's household, he walked in the Prince's funeral procession as his 'paynter'. Henry's 'limner' or miniaturist was the otherwise little-known Mark Belford (Wilks 1987, pp.102–3). C.M.

PROVENANCE
First recorded in the collection of Charles I (Millar 1960, p.107, no. 17 and note 2; p.215); recorded in the collection of Charles II and possibly in the collections of James II and William III (see Reynolds 1999, pp.91–2); lost from the Royal Collection at an unknown date; in an unidentified sale in April 1751, from which purchased by James West (1703–72) for 27 guineas (Vertue, *Notebooks*, v, p.84); [...]; purchased for the Royal Collection by George IV from the jewellers Rundell, Bridge and Rundell on 7 August 1807; removed from the Royal Collection at an unspecified time and identified in the collection of an unidentified 'old man of excellent character', 1863; recovered before 1870 by Sir John Cowell (for details and full references see Reynolds 1999, p.92).

LITERATURE
Strong 1983, pp.153–4, no. 257; Wilks 1987, p.100, 210–12; Reynolds 1999, pp.91–3, no. 56.

CAT. 32

33

Henry, Prince of Wales

ISAAC OLIVER, *c.*1610–12

Watercolour on vellum laid onto a playing card,
77 × 56mm (oval)

The Royal Collection (RCIN 420057)

This is one of the finest surviving versions of the large rectangular miniature of Prince Henry (see cat. 32), all of which are in the more conventional oval format. This would have made them suitable for wearing in a locket, although miniatures were also kept in small boxes at this time, and sometimes displayed, framed, in cabinet rooms. The setting of a miniature within a locket, often richly jewelled or enamelled and usually made of gold, was a means of adding to its magnificence and value, as well as signifying the importance of the sitter to the wearer. Miniatures made ideal gifts for adherents and followers at the English court, or diplomatic presents for courts overseas, owing to their value and portability. This example, like most in the Royal Collection, has lost its original setting and is now housed in a nineteenth-century frame supplied by John Hatfield (1839–82).

Other versions of this miniature of Henry by Isaac Oliver include those in the Royal Collection (Reynolds 1999, cats 55 and 57);

the Victoria and Albert Museum, London; the National Museum and Gallery of Wales, Cardiff; and a private collection (formerly the Solly Collection, sold Bonhams, 23 November 2011, lot 9). The precision with which the armour is depicted, and the variations in the decoration as well as in the lace of the collar or ruff in the different versions, suggests that Oliver had access to Henry's armours and depicted them relatively faithfully. The Prince presumably only sat for the first of these miniatures, however, after which a pattern, kept by the artist in his studio, would have been used for the modelling of the face. As with most of Henry's portraits, there is little known about the circumstances of the commissions or acquisitions. It may be that the Prince commissioned the miniatures as gifts, or it may be that, like some of the large-scale portraits (see cats 32 and 82), these were ordered and paid for by courtiers as a sign of loyalty to the Prince, or as mementoes after his death. C.M.

PROVENANCE
[...]; Dr Richard Mead (1673–1754); purchased by Frederick, Prince of Wales; by descent in the Royal Collection.

LITERATURE
Vertue, *Notebooks,* IV, p.81; Reynolds 1999, pp.93–4, no. 56.

34

The Masque of Queens

BEN JONSON (1572–1637), 1609

Ink on paper, 20 folios, spine height 215mm

The British Library, London (Royal MS 18.A.XLV)

Ben Jonson was one of the great literary figures of the Elizabethan and Jacobean age, regarded in his own time and for much of the later seventeenth century as a writer of equal, if not greater, skill than William Shakespeare. He wrote poetry, plays, court masques and other courtly entertainments, and is perhaps most admired for his satirical comedies, including *Volpone* (1606) and *The Alchemist* (1610). In 1616, the year in which King James published his own collected writings, Jonson published his *Workes*, a new departure for an English writer at this period. Including nine of his plays, it created a new sense of authorial ownership over such material, which technically belonged to the theatre companies that staged them and were generally regarded as ephemeral.

Jonson's career as a playwright for the public theatre was well established by the time James came to the throne, but he worked hard to gain the patronage of the new court. He wrote an entertainment for Queen Anne and Prince Henry's visit to Althorp on their way from Edinburgh to London in 1603, various entertainments for the King at the behest of the Earl of Salisbury, and speeches for three of the eight pageants for the royal entry into the City of

London in 1604 (Donaldson, 'Jonson, Benjamin', ODNB 2004). His first royal masque was *The Masque of Blackness*, commissioned by Queen Anne and performed in January 1605. The success of this performance led to numerous other commissions: for the Queen, for Prince Henry and various courtiers. *The Masque of Queens celebrated from the House of Fame*, to give it its full title, was commissioned by the Queen and performed by her and her ladies at Whitehall on 2 February 1609. It was the first masque in which Jonson included an 'anti-masque', a representation of chaos and disorder, performed by actors dressed as witches, who vanished at the appearance of virtue and order in the form of the noble masquers.

This copy of *The Masque of Queens* was written out by Jonson himself at the behest of the Prince. As Jonson explains in his introductory letter, the Prince had asked him for a bibliography of the classical sources for his text, and his response was to provide this copy, annotated extensively in the margins with explanations of the sources. It provides an exceptional glimpse into the range of reference in this most erudite of literary forms. C.M.

PROVENANCE
Presented by the author to Henry, Prince of Wales; by descent in the Royal Collection; presented to the British Museum, London, by George II in 1757 as part of the Old Royal Library.

LITERATURE
Herford, Simpson and Simpson 1925–52, vol. VII, pp.277–317.

The Sunne, & the Wind had shrunke his vaynes:
I bit of a sinew, I clip'd his hayre,
& brought of his ragges, & daunc'd i' the ayre.

The Scrich-owles egges, and the fethers black.
The blod of the Frog, & the bone in his back.
I haue bene getting; & made of his skin
A purset, to keepe Sr Cranion in.

9.

And I ha' bene glucking, & plants among.
Hemlock, Henbane, Adders-tongue,
Night-shade, Moone-wort, Libbards-bane;
And, twise, by the Doggs was like to be tane.

church.

Church, or some such vast building (kept by Doggs) among ruines, and wild heaps.

10.

I, from the iawes of a Gard'ners Bitch
Did snatch these bones, & then leap'd y ditch:
Yet, went I back to the house agayne,
Kill'd the black cat; & here's y brayne.

11.

I went to the Toad, breedes under the wall,
I charmd him out, & he came at my call;
I scratchd out y eyes o' the Owle, before;
I tore the Batts wing: what would you haue more?

12.

DAME.

Yes, I haue brought (to helpe our vowes)
Horned poppie, Cypresse boughts,
The Figg-tree wild, that growes on tombes, not only to this,

And
more.

35

Set Design for Prince Henry's Barriers:
The Fallen House of Chivalry

INIGO JONES (1573–1652), 1610

Pen and brown ink and brown wash, 245 × 270mm
The Duke of Devonshire and
the Chatsworth Settlement Trustees

Inigo Jones was appointed Surveyor of Works to
Henry, Prince of Wales, in 1610, with a salary of
£50 per annum. Later, after the Prince's death,
his tour of Italy with the Earl of Arundel and his
appointment as Surveyor of the King's Works
in 1615, Jones was to become one of the most
famous and influential architects ever to work in
England. But at this early stage in his career his
most prominent achievements were his designs
for scenery, elaborate mechanical stage devices
and costumes for court masques. Jones's early
travels to France and Italy, his extensive knowledge
of continental prints and his familiarity with
foreign court entertainments, notably Italian
intermezzi, were all significant influences on the
style and content of his designs.

Prince Henry's Barriers of 1610 was not in
fact a typical masque, but a staged tournament,
intended to display the prowess of the young
Prince at military exercises shortly before his
creation as Prince of Wales, and to suggest the
great things that could be expected of him in the
future. The carefully controlled fighting was set
into an allegorical narrative based on Arthurian
mythology, blended with elements drawn from
classical antiquity. The first scene showed the
decayed 'House of Chivalry', which was to be
transformed, in effect restored, by a revival
of chivalry under the leadership of Meliadus,
Lord of the Isles, the character played by Prince
Henry. The 'House of Chivalry' is represented
in this drawing by an arrangement of ruins,
particularly classical ruins, some of which
resemble those Jones had seen during his early
travels, and some of which he based on prints
(see Peacock 1995, loc. cit.). C.M.

36

Set Design for Prince Henry's Barriers:
St George's Portico

INIGO JONES, 1610

Pen and brown ink and brown wash, 265 × 324mm
The Duke of Devonshire and
the Chatsworth Settlement Trustees

This drawing is a design for the second scene
in *Prince Henry's Barriers*: *St George's Portico*.
This scene symbolised the restoration of chivalric
values as brought about by Meliadus, played
by Prince Henry, and it was revealed when the
first scene was drawn aside. The reference to
St George underlines the saint's importance
to the concept of chivalry at this time, and the
significance of the Order of the Garter (the order
of chivalry to which the King, Prince Henry and
twenty-four other nobles belonged), of which
St George was the patron.

One of the most striking aspects of these
designs by Inigo Jones is the convincing use of
linear perspective to create a sense of depth and
recession. This was an unusual skill in an English
artist at this date, and it was taught as a branch
of geometry and engineering to Prince Henry by
the French architect-engineer Salomon de Caus
(see cat. 21). Jones used perspective, however,
to do more than create a convincing illusion of
space. The converging lines ensured that the
eye of the spectator was drawn to whatever
was in the centre of the design, thus giving that
object – or person, in the case of some of his
masques – a symbolic significance as the focal
point of the scene. C.M.

CAT. 35

CAT. 36

37

Costume Design for Prince Henry's Barriers: Helmet

INIGO JONES, 1610

Pen and brown ink and brown wash, 225 × 172mm

The Duke of Devonshire and the Chatsworth Settlement Trustees

This appears to be a design for the helmet worn by Prince Henry in his role as Meliadus in *Prince Henry's Barriers*. It is composed almost entirely of elaborate, fantastical elements, and derives closely from Antonio Tempesta's print of *Caligula* from his series The Twelve Caesars (see fig. 19, p.112). A winged sphinx forms the apex of the helmet; below, a coronet comprising obelisks sits on top of the upper part of an elephant's head. Such extravagantly plumed helmets were clearly thought to be Roman in origin, but plumes of this kind also seem to have been worn on contemporary helmets as part of tilting or tournament armour (see cats 29 and 30). The profile depiction employed by Inigo Jones, seen here, echoes Roman coins, medals and gems (as well as Isaac Oliver's profile miniature of the Prince in Roman costume, cat. 44) but it is also the logical way of showing the helmet design to best advantage. The profile also echoes earlier portraits of King Henry V, a famously martial king with whom Prince Henry is particularly compared in Jonson's narrative.

In the guise of Meliadus, Henry, with six companions, took on fifty-six opponents with pikes and with swords. Henry's Treasurer and later biographer, Sir Charles Cornwallis, recorded that he 'did admirably fight for his part, giving and receiving that night 32 pushes of pikes, and about 360 streakes of swords, which

is scarce credible in so young yeares, enough to assure the world, that Great Britaine's brave Henry aspired to immortality' (quoted in Wilks 2007, p.197).

Although the main action of the *Barriers* was this display of martial prowess, Jonson clearly felt that he had to balance the message about military might with the advocacy of civic virtues suitable for a ruler. The text spoken by Merlin includes the words:

> These were bold stories of our Arthur's age;
> But here are other acts; another stage
> And scene appears; it is not since as then;
> No giants, dwarfs or monsters here, but men.
> His arts must be to govern and give laws
> To peace no less than arms …

Norman Council argues that for Jonson, 'chivalry had lost its capacity to imitate British political ideals' (see Council 1980, no. 2, pp.259–75, especially pp.272–3); it has also been suggested that the apparent tension between civic and martial virtues in the *Barriers* is a reflection of the tensions between the Prince's and the King's agendas (Peacock 1987 and Strong 1986). It may be that Jonson included this element of balance in response to James's concerns about his son's martial image, but Henry's image continued to be predominantly that of a chivalric warrior prince. C.M.

PROVENANCE
As cat. 35.

LITERATURE
Orgel and Strong 1973, I, p.185, no. 52; Strong 1983, pp.141–2, no.229; Peacock 1987, p.187.

38

Set Design for Oberon, the Faery Prince: Oberon's Palace

INIGO JONES, 1611

Pen and brown and black inks and grey wash on paper, 333 × 393mm
Inscribed [by John Webb]: *2 sceane K; oberons Pallace*
The Duke of Devonshire and the Chatsworth Settlement Trustees

In 1610 Prince Henry commissioned his first masque, *Oberon, the Faery Prince*, which was to be performed in January 1611. The text was by Ben Jonson and the design by Inigo Jones. Like *Prince Henry's Barriers*, *Oberon* combined textual and visual references to ancient Rome and ancient Britain; it was, as John Peacock says, 'a synthesis of antique heroism and Christian chivalry' (Peacock 1995, p.74). Unlike the *Barriers*, it was a masque in the conventional sense, with music, singing and dancing as well as spoken poetry, spectacular sets and costumes.

Henry took the role of Oberon, a similar character to that of Meliadus in the *Barriers*. The theme of the masque was also close to that of the *Barriers*, although not expressed through military exercises: the establishment of a new order under a great new ruler, Oberon, with an emphasis on the unification of Britain. The movement from the old to the new was expressed through the designs and transformations of the sets, as well as the actions and speeches of the characters.

Oberon's palace has been described as 'a mixture of French Renaissance chateau, Italian palazzo and Elizabethan prodigy house' (Peacock 1995, p.77); this design also includes elements from medieval castles and a dome based on the Tempietto at San Pietro in Montorio by the Italian Renaissance architect Bramante, presumably alluding to God at the centre of, and above, all. Jones used incised lines in this drawing to ensure that the proportions were accurate. Jonson described the way in which the palace was to open up: 'There the whole palace opened, and the nation of fays [fairies] were discovered, some with instruments, some bearing lights, others singing; and within, afar off in perspective, the knights masquers sitting in their several sieges. At the further end of all, Oberon, in a chariot, which to a loud triumphant music began to move forward, drawn by two white bears, and on either side guarded by three sylvans, with one going in front' (Orgel and Strong 1973, I, p.288). William Trumbull, a diplomat who saw the masque, recorded seeing inside the palace 'a great throne with countless lights and colours, all shifting, a lovely thing to see' (Orgel and Strong 1973, I, p.206). C.M.

PROVENANCE
As cat. 35.

LITERATURE
Orgel and Strong 1973, I, p.216, no. 63; Strong 1983, p.142, no.232; Strong 1986, pp.169–70; Harris and Higgott 1989, p.46, no.8; Hearn 1995, p.162, no. 108; Peacock 1995, pp.74–81.

2 Horno K. oBrun Pallar

III

39

Costume Design for Oberon, the Faery Prince: Oberon

INIGO JONES, 1611

Pen and brown and black inks and grey wash on paper, 295 × 149mm. Inscribed below drawing: *A*.
The Duke of Devonshire and
the Chatsworth Settlement Trustees

This costume design for Prince Henry's role as Oberon, by Inigo Jones, is obviously Roman in inspiration, and takes elements from two prints of Domitian and Caligula by Antonio Tempesta from the series The Twelve Caesars (see Peacock 1995, pls 166, 168 on pp.284, 286 and fig. 19 below). However, the lower part of the costume is reminiscent of Jacobean trunk hose (see Orgel and Strong 1973, I, pp.220–1), and the designs for Oberon's attendants were even more obviously amalgamations of vaguely Roman armour, contemporary clothing, and Tudor or continental Renaissance elements (see Orgel and Strong 1973, nos 72 and 73 and cat. 41). This use of a mixture of sources was consistent with Jones's architectural designs for the masque, and also with Ben Jonson's text, in which Oberon represents a combination of chivalrous virtues and heroic qualities associated with ancient Rome. C.M.

FIG. 19
Caligula from The Twelve Caesars series,
Antonio Tempesta, 1596

PROVENANCE
As cat. 35.

LITERATURE
Orgel and Strong 1973, I, p.220,
no. 70; Strong 1983, p.142, no. 231;
Hearn 1995, p.163, no. 109;
Peacock 1995, p.282.

40

Costume Design for Oberon: Headresses for Oberon

INIGO JONES, 1611

Pen and grey ink, grey wash and black ink on paper
259 × 171mm
The Duke of Devonshire and
the Chatsworth Settlement Trustees

This drawing appears to present alternative designs for Oberon's headdress and neckwear. Although the cuirass and laurel wreath allude to Roman costume, the ruff and curious frill are fantastical adaptations of sixteenth-century dress. Jones's designs for Henry's costumes do not include portraits, strictly speaking, but idealised evocations of the young Prince.

The fluency and confidence of Jones's drawing, even in the most rapid of his designs, was unmatched by almost any native British artist at this time, and undoubtedly owes much to his study of continental prints, like that of the other great draughtsman of the period, Isaac Oliver. The high regard in which his draughtsmanship was held from the seventeenth century up to the present day accounts for the survival of such a large number of designs, of which those included here are just a small selection; over 450 drawings of costumes and scenery by Jones survive today, in addition to nearly 100 architectural drawings. C.M.

PROVENANCE
As cat. 35.

LITERATURE
Orgel and Strong 1973, I,
p.228, no. 71.

41

Costume Design for Oberon,
the Faery Prince: An Attendant of Oberon

INIGO JONES, 1611

Pen and black and grey inks and grey wash on paper,
293 × 154mm

The Duke of Devonshire and the Chatsworth
Settlement Trustees

Although the diplomat William Trumbull, who
was amongst the spectators who saw *Oberon*,
stated that the Prince and his attendants were
dressed like Roman emperors, this costume
design suggests that the Roman elements were
less prevalent in some of the designs than in
others. This figure, one of Oberon's attendants,
appears to be dressed in some sort of approxi‑
mation to a sixteenth‑century or medieval
costume, and, in spite of the cuirass and dagger,
appears much less martial than Oberon himself
(cat. 39). The mixture of styles was entirely
characteristic of these masques, and underlined
the presentation of Henry as the heir to all
that was great in both relatively recent British
history and ancient times. C.M.

PROVENANCE
As cat. 35.

LITERATURE
Orgel and Strong 1973, I, p.228, no. 73.

42

Costume Designs for Oberon, the Faery Prince:
Three Fays

INIGO JONES, 1611

Pen and light brown and black inks and light brown wash on paper,
188 × 290mm

The Duke of Devonshire and the Chatsworth Settlement Trustees

Many of Ben Jonson's masques included an 'anti-masque', a scene of disorder, wild dancing and music, which preceded the masque itself. The anti-masque represented the state of affairs before order and virtue were imposed by the noble masquers. The anti-masquers tended to be professional actors rather than courtiers, the latter, along with members of the royal family, taking more dignified roles. These three costume designs are thought to be for three of the 'fays', or fairies, which featured in *Oberon*. The fays were not in fact part of the anti-masque, but they fulfilled the same function in the masque itself, presenting a striking contrast in their extraordinary, fantastical costumes, to the Prince and his attendants, who were dressed nobly and magnificently as 'Roman emperors' (see cat. 39). Ben Jonson described the scene in which the fays made their first appearance: 'the nation of fays were discovered, some with instruments, some bearing lights, others singing'. C.M.

PROVENANCE
As cat. 35.

LITERATURE
Orgel and Strong 1973, I, p.220, no. 66; Peacock 1995, p.141.

43

Anne of Denmark in Masque Costume

ISAAC OLIVER, *c.*1610

Watercolour and bodycolour on vellum laid onto card, 52 × 42mm
(discoloured retouching on face)
Inscribed: *IO* in monogram, on left; *Servo per regnare*, on right
The Royal Collection (RCIN 420025)

This striking miniature shows Queen Anne in masque costume, her face depicted dramatically in profile. The choice of a profile depiction was unusual and links this image with a group of other miniatures by Isaac Oliver, mainly of men, produced at about the same time (see cat. 44). It has not been possible to connect the costume with any surviving design for a specific masque, but in spirit the headdress closely echoes those designed by Inigo Jones for Anne and her ladies. Anne was the most significant patron of masques at the Jacobean court. She commissioned and performed in six: *The Vision of the Twelve Goddesses* (1604); *The Masque of Blackness* (1605); *The Masque of Beauty* (1608); *The Masque of Queens* (1609); *Tethys Festival* (1610) and *Love Freed from Ignorance and Folly* (1611), the first and fifth of these written by Samuel Daniel (?1562–1619) and the other four by Ben Jonson. These lavish performances enabled Anne to indulge a number of her passions at the same time: music, dancing, fine clothes and jewellery. In spite of their often-complex allegorical literary and visual references, the masques all ultimately had the same theme: the restoration of peace, harmony, order and virtue by the Stuart royal family.

The Italian motto 'Servo per regnare' can be translated as 'I serve by reigning' and reflects the significance that the Stuarts placed on their belief in their divine right to rule. An oil painting of Anne made in 1614 by an artist in the studio of Marcus Gheeraerts the Younger, and a second oil by Paul van Somer, have a different Italian motto but one that conveys a similar message: 'La mia grandezza dal eccelso', which can be translated as 'My greatness comes from heaven' (Millar 1963, nos 98, 105). C.M.

PROVENANCE
Dr Richard Mead, when incorrectly identified as a miniature of Elizabeth I; bought by Frederick, Prince of Wales; by descent in the Royal Collection (seen by Horace Walpole at Buckingham House, *c.*1783); recorded in Royal Collection lists and inventories, *c.*1837, 1844, 1851, 1870, 1881 and 1910; first identified correctly as Anne of Denmark in 1870 list.

LITERATURE
Strong 1983, no. 225, pp.139–40; Reynolds 1999, no. 52, pp.89–90.

44

Henry, Prince of Wales, in Profile

ISAAC OLIVER, *c*.1610

Watercolour and bodycolour on vellum laid onto card, 53 × 40mm

Fitzwilliam Museum, Cambridge (3903)

In this distinctive and unusual miniature Prince Henry is shown in profile, in front of a niche topped with a scallop shell. The classicism of the architecture echoes that of the Prince's costume, which consists of Roman armour and a richly embroidered toga. The costume is conceivably that worn by the Prince in the masque *Oberon* (1611), although there are differences when compared with the surviving Inigo Jones drawings (see cat. 39). Henry also probably appeared in some type of Roman costume in the *Barriers* of 1610, in the text of which he is described as 'like Mars ... in his armour clad', although his costume design for this role does not appear to have survived. A further link with the *Barriers* is provided by another part of Ben Jonson's text, in which he alludes to the military accomplishments of Henry V, 'to whom in face you are so like' (Orgel and Strong 1973, I, p.162). Henry V's 'face' would have been known from the portrait sets of earlier English kings and queens, which were very popular at this time. Unusually for such portraits, Henry V is invariably shown in profile.

At least three other versions of this miniature of Prince Henry survive: in the collections of the National Portrait Gallery, London; the Queen of the Netherlands (signed by Peter Oliver, Isaac's eldest son); and the Mauritshuis (attributed to Peter Oliver). Although there may well be a link with Henry's masques, it also seems likely that these profile miniatures, with their consistently Roman iconography, reflected Henry's acquisition of the enormous collection of classical gems, coins and medals that had belonged to Abraham Gorlaeus (see cat. 54). Indeed, it appears that the National Portrait Gallery version of the present miniature was mistakenly identified at one point as a depiction of a Roman military leader (an old piece of paper in the back of the miniature is inscribed '*CNEIVS/POMPEIVS/MAGNVS*' (Pompey the Great). In addition, there are two very similar miniatures, attributed to Isaac Oliver, of men in identical poses, with slightly simplified costumes and niches behind. One, in the Royal Collection (Reynolds 1999, no. 64, pp.99–100), has been identified as Lord Herbert of Cherbury; the other, in a private collection (photograph, Heinz Archive and Library, National Portrait Gallery), is of an unidentified man, presumably also in the circle of the Prince. C.M.

PROVENANCE
Possibly the miniature in the collection of Charles I; [...]; William Montagu Douglas Scott, 6th Duke of Buccleuch; by descent; bought 1942 by the Fitzwilliam Museum with money bequeathed by Mrs Prichard in memory of her father Thomas Waraker, LL.D., and with a grant from the Art Fund.

LITERATURE
Kennedy 1917, p.11, pl.XIV; Millar 1960, p.107, no. 18; Strong 1983, p.142; Powell 1985, pp.166–7, pl.III; Hearn 1995, no. 84, p.137.

Princely Collecting

A mark of a virtuous Renaissance prince was that he gathered examples of all that was most rare and excellent, reason enough for Prince Henry to begin collecting. In this regard, he was unlike his father, James VI of Scotland and I of England, who showed little interest in art and none at all in forming art collections. It was, therefore, to Henry that the advocates of courtly collecting in England turned their attentions. He began to receive items for his new collections in 1609, as the court of the Prince of Wales began to take shape; some given by friendly states (Tuscany and the United Provinces), others by court well-wishers, among them Thomas Howard, Earl of Arundel, already a mentor to the Prince in artistic matters.[1]

These donations fell into the principal categories of 'magnificent collecting', as described by classical authors such as Pliny the Elder, Cicero and Suetonius, who in his *Twelve Caesars* (newly translated by Philemon Holland and dedicated to the mother of Henry's so-called 'right eye', John Harington) wrote of Julius Caesar: 'For to get and buy up pretious stones, engraved and chased pieces, Images, and painted Tables [i.e. pictures] of antique work, he was ever most eager and sharp set.'[2] Henry would be no less active than Caesar in acquiring just such objects. His main collections would be of paintings, sculptures, cabinet antiquities and books, categories in which the collector-princes of early seventeenth-century Europe competed with one another. Henry also became the recipient of various instructional, artificial wonders, such as Phineas Pett's intricate ship model and Edward Wright's 'Coelestiall Automaton', though he did not intentionally set out to collect them.

Among more recent authorities, Castiglione's *The Courtier* – a text recommended to Henry's own courtiers[3] – recounted how the Renaissance duke, Federigo di Montefeltro, had brought into his city-palace of Urbino 'a wonderous number of auncient Images of Marble and Metall, verye excellent paintings and Instruments of Musicke of all sortes'.[4] Nevertheless, by declaring that Urbino's 'chiefest ornament' was its library, Castiglione continued to give precedence to the word over the image.

Henry, Prince of Wales, Robert Peake the Elder, c.1610 (detail of cat. 45)

After Lord Lumley's death in April 1609, Henry received most of his 2,800 bound volumes and many of his manuscripts.[5] As Henry's court was to be a store of knowledge within which scholars would study under the Prince's patronage, even Lumley's great library was seen, after cataloguing, to be deficient. Sir William Maurice of Clennenau responded by donating 'select books of every kind out of Italy and France', while Robert Dallington, one of Henry's tutors, presented a cabinet of books.[6] Archbishop Bancroft pressured his bishops, richer clergy and diocesan officials to give money for the purchase of other needed titles, while Henry himself placed large orders for recently published works with two of London's leading booksellers, John Norton and Edward Blount.[7] A purpose-built library was constructed in St James's Palace, though Henry kept music books separately, and may also have established special collections in Richmond Palace and at his military yard.[8] Many of Henry's volumes were rebound in calf leather and gold-blocked with his arms, feathers and initials.

Henry's coroneted 'HP' cipher (*Henricus Princeps*) was also cut into the backs of his pictures, a practice that has revealed his ownership of several extant paintings.[9] Two such works – landscapes by Joos de Momper, with figures by Jan Brueghel the Elder – have only recently come to notice.[10] These, and other similarly marked landscapes, allegories and genre pieces by painters such as Hendrick Goltzius, Vredeman de Vries and Jacob de Backer were probably bought from visiting Dutch dealers, who may have hoped for a new market in the hitherto portrait-dominated galleries of England.[11]

Yet more adventurously, a group of pictures was purchased for Henry in Venice, a coup that would not have been conceived had the resident ambassador not been Sir Henry Wotton, one of the few Englishmen of his generation who thoroughly understood Italian art.[12] Several of these large Venetian canvases depicted classical or biblical acts of extreme violence, among them *Cain and Abel*, *Judith and Holofernes* and *Sacrifice of Isaac*, all by Leonardo Corona. It was the Shock Art of the time. With them came more sensuous works: *Mary Magdalene*, attributed to Titian, and *Ceres, Bacchus and Venus*, probably from the studio of Tintoretto.[13]

Henry was introduced to the finest quality bronze sculptures by the Medici court, which sent a gift of ten statuettes and five smaller figurines cast by Giambologna's pupil, Pietro Tacca (see cat. 53).[14] This mixed group of mythological figures, genre pieces and animal studies, received at Richmond, delighted Henry, who arranged them himself. A group of four Florentine bronzes followed, and a second group, the *Labours of Hercules*, was in preparation at the time of Henry's death.[15]

Exceeding in value all his other collections were Henry's antique coins, medals and gems. One cabinet, purchased for the huge sum of £2,200, had belonged to Abraham van Goorle of Delft, known to scholars and antiquaries as Gorlaeus, while his cabinet of finger rings set with engraved stones – some authentic ancient specimens, others recent skilful imitations – was acquired separately.[16] Gorlaeus had published descriptions of his collections, which had made them famous and desirable throughout Europe. But even these prestigious purchases did not provide the range of examples that Henry required, and so a rare Elizabethan collection of 'gould and silver coynes and medalles of antiquity', formerly belonging to the Cambridge scholar William Fulke, was also obtained.[17]

In all these areas, Henry laid the foundations for the collections of the Stuart court and for subsequent royal collections. Granted a period ten times longer in which to form his own taste, Charles I did not allow sentiment to stand in the way of creating his own unrivalled collection, disposing of many works inherited from his brother. More essentially, however, Henry had imparted to Charles his general passion for art, evident when a distraught Charles brought the smaller bronze horse, which they both admired, to his dying brother's bedside.[18] T.W.

1 TNA, SP.14/57/87.
2 Holland 1606.
3 See Cleland 1607; new impressions: *The Scottish Academie* (London, 1611); *The Instruction of a Young Noble-man* (Oxford, 1612), p.153, all recommending Bartholomew Clerke's Latin translation, *Bathasaris Castilionis comitis, De curialis sive aulici libri quatuor* (London, 1603; 1612); cf. Hoby 1561; new impression: *The Courtier*, London, 1603); *pace* Benvenuto Italian, *The Passenger* (London, 1612), p.484.
4 Hoby 1603, C.2 r–v.
5 Jayne and Johnson 1956.
6 For Maurice, see Smith 1707, p.13; Ward 1740, p.250; for Dallington, see TNA, SP14/57/87.
7 Cardwell 1839, II, pp.128–9; TNA, E.351/2793; *CSP Domestic: James I, 1603–10 (1857)*, p.398; Devon 1836, p.164.
8 St James's: TNA, E.351/3244, SP14/57/34, SP.14/62/50, SP14/63/55,

The King's Works, III (i), 124; music books: TNA, E.351/2793, E.351/2794; Richmond: TNA, E.351/3244, SP14/57/34; military yard: 'An account of the several libraries … in or about London', *Gentleman's Magazine*, 86, 2 (1816), p.214.
9 See Millar 1960, xiv; Wilks 2005, pp.149–72.
10 Museo Nacional del Prado, nos 1588, 1590.
11 TNA, E.351/3294.
12 See Wilks 1989, pp.167–77.
13 Tierney 1834, II, p.488.
14 Watson and Avery 1973, pp.493–507.
15 Lee 1972, p.136.
16 Inner Temple MS 538/17, f. 425; TNA, E.351/2793; HMC Salisbury (Cecil), XXI, p.352; Sweerts 1628, p.87.
17 Acts of the Privy Council of England, 1616–17, pp.98–9.
18 Millar 1960, p.92; cf. Watson and Avery 1973, p.501.

45

Henry, Prince of Wales

ROBERT PEAKE THE ELDER, *c.*1610

Oil on canvas, 1727 × 1137mm

National Portrait Gallery, London (NPG 4515)

Among Peake's portraits of Prince Henry this is unusual in showing him neither in the robes of a Knight of the Order of the Garter, nor brandishing a sword, nor wearing armour. Rather than alluding to his militaristic nature and chivalric qualities, the sumptuousness of his costume, jewellery and surroundings are the subject of the painting. Henry's expenditure on such items, like his assembly of a magnificent collection of paintings and sculpture, and his commissioning of lavish architecture and garden design, was not merely a matter of self-indulgence. The magnificence of his court was intended to reflect his wealth and power, his judgement and discrimination, his learning and wisdom. All his possessions, commissions and garments contributed to his image as an ideal prince, potentially boosting his status among his European counterparts. The intention was to fill his courtiers with respect and awe, and to impress foreign diplomats with the value of allegiance with Britain. The fabric of Henry's doublet in this portrait has been identified as Italian brocaded silk; diplomatic correspondence of the time reveals how foreign ambassadors interpreted the wearing of fashions associated with their country as a sign of favour on the Prince's part (Ribeiro 2005, p.27).

Henry's jewels feature prominently in this painting, perhaps in part testifying to Robert Peake's early training as a goldsmith. In addition to the jewelled garter and the badge of St George around the Prince's neck, his hat is decorated with a richly jewelled band and brooch, as are his sword belt and hilt. Even his gloves are set with diamonds and his shoes with enormous pearls. It is not possible to link any surviving Jacobean jewellery with Prince Henry; on the whole each generation of the royal family re-set the jewels they inherited in more up-to-date settings, and of course the English Civil Wars (1642–51) and Interregnum (1649–60) interrupted this kind of inheritance. But we know that Henry spent enormous sums on jewellery. Between November 1610 and October 1612 the jeweller Sir George Heriot was paid nearly £3,500 for jewellery for Henry, and another £4,000 for a hat-band and chain set with diamonds was owing to Heriot at Henry's death (Wilks 1987, p.115).

The garden seen through the window is probably that of Richmond Palace, on which Henry's 'Architect' Salomon de Caus was employed from 1610, and subsequently so was the Italian artist and designer Costantino de' Servi. Large sums of money were spent on this project, although not the enormous figure of £10,000 that has been stated in the past (see Strong 1986, pp.91–2, 107–8; Wilks 1987, pp.138–40, 143–9).

The provenance in the Craven collection suggests that this painting belonged to Henry's younger sister, Princess Elizabeth; the ownership, and perhaps commission, of the portrait by a close member of the royal family may explain its composition and iconography. It is reminiscent of portraits of James I by John de Critz (see cat. 3), but the curtain and view through the window echo more strikingly a portrait of Edward VI when Prince of Wales in the Royal Collection (fig. 11). A further link with the portrait of Edward VI is the presence of a layer of metal leaf under the red glaze of the curtain; this echoes the technique of the earlier painting but is a most unusual inclusion in a portrait of this date. The two portraits of princes may perhaps originally have been intended to hang near one another in one of the royal palaces. C.M.

PROVENANCE
By tradition from the collection of Elizabeth of Bohemia; believed to have been given or bequeathed by her to William, 1st Earl of Craven (1606–97), or otherwise acquired by him from Prince Rupert, her son; by descent (along with other paintings with the same provenance) in the collection of the Earls of Craven; purchased with help from the Art Fund, 1966.

LITERATURE
Strong, *Tudor and Jacobean Portraits*, 1969, 1, p.162; Wilks 1987, p.139; Ribeiro 2005, pp.27–9.

46

Thomas Howard, 14th Earl of Arundel (1585–1646)

SIR PETER PAUL RUBENS (1577–1640), 1629

Oil on canvas, 686 × 533mm

National Portrait Gallery, London (2391)

Thomas Howard was the heir to the great but disgraced sixteenth-century Howard family; his great-grandfather, the poet Earl of Surrey, had been executed by Henry VIII; his grandfather, the 4th Duke of Norfolk, had been executed by Elizabeth I; and his father, Philip Howard, had been imprisoned for treason and died in the Tower. The accession of James VI to the English throne, and the political success of members of other branches of the Howard family, provided an opportunity for the rehabilitation of the family. In 1604, Thomas regained the Arundel title, lost when his father was convicted of treason, and was allowed to attend court.

Arundel soon became associated with the entourage of Prince Henry, and he named his second son, born in 1608, after the Prince. He may have been initially drawn to Henry's court by the potential he saw there for pursuing and forwarding his own interests, but he must have soon realised that the Prince shared with him – or was willing to learn to share with him – an interest in art collecting. An early indication that Arundel was seen as a suitable advisor to Prince Henry in this regard came in March 1610, when the Earl of Salisbury was planning to show a group of recently acquired pictures to Henry.

Sir David Murray, the Prince's Groom of the Stole (see cat. 15), wrote to Salisbury to say that if he could not come, 'you may send my Lord of Arundel as deputy to set forth the praise of your pictures' (Salisbury MSS, 24 vols, 1883–1976, xxi, p.39). Arundel was the first to bring a gift for Henry's new gallery at St James's Palace on 30 January 1610 (CSP 14/15/87, cited in Wilks 1987, p.38)

Arundel became perhaps the most remarkable collector and connoisseur of paintings in early Stuart England. This extraordinary portrait by the Flemish artist Peter Paul Rubens, one of the most admired artists of all time, was produced seventeen years after Prince Henry's death, when the artist came to London on a diplomatic mission. But it is an indication of the central role played by members of the Prince's circle in European art developments of the following decades. The contacts, money and enthusiasm available to Prince Henry had allowed a number of those around him to start their careers as collectors and patrons vicariously; their subsequent activities, and those of his brother Prince Charles, later Charles I, hint at what Henry's collecting and patronage might have become had he lived.
C.M.

PROVENANCE
John, 4th Duke of Argyll by 1765; by descent to his son Lord Frederick Campbell (1729–1816), who gave it or left it to 1st Earl Amherst; by descent; deposited on loan from 4th Earl Amherst in 1926; purchased by the National Portrait Gallery, London, 1929.

LITERATURE
Piper 1963, p.15; Humer 1977, p.110, no.56; Jaffé 1989, p.314, no.971.

47

Thomas, 2nd Baron Vaux of Harrowden (1509–56)

HANS HOLBEIN THE YOUNGER (1497/8–1543), *c*.1533

Black and coloured chalks, pen and ink, brush and ink,
white and yellow bodycolour, and metalpoint on
pale pink prepared paper, 279 × 295mm
Inscribed: *silbe* [twice], *rot, w. sam, Gl, carmin* [colour notes];
upper left corner, cut off: *UX*

The Royal Collection (RL 12245)

When Prince Henry acquired the library of
John, Lord Lumley, probably in 1609 before the
latter's death, it appears that one of the volumes
that came into his possession was a 'great booke'
containing drawings by Hans Holbein the
Younger, the great Augsburg-born court artist to
Henry VIII. The drawings all seem to have been
portraits of individuals in and around Henry
VIII's court, made as preparatory studies for
painted portraits. Some were made during the
artist's first stay in England from 1526 to 1528;
others – the majority – from his longer English
period from 1532 until his death in 1543. The
collecting of such works was very unusual in
England at this time, so sixteenth-century
English preparatory drawings tend not to have
survived. The existence of such a large group
by Holbein reflects the exceptional esteem
with which the artist was regarded during his
lifetime and beyond.

The 'great booke' of Holbein drawings
contained more than one drawing of a small
number of individuals, including Thomas, 2nd
Baron Vaux, the sitter in this work. The two
drawings of Lord Vaux are quite distinct from
each other; it is not clear whether they were
intended as two alternative studies for the
same painting, or whether they were entirely
independent portraits drawn at different times.
Either drawing may have been intended as a
companion to the portrait of Lady Vaux (cat. 48).
Vaux, a nobleman on the fringes of Henry VIII's
court, was most notable as the author of courtly
poetry, mainly on the subject of love. Working
notes on the drawing indicate the colours and
fabrics Vaux is wearing, for reference when
Holbein came to make the oil painting, but no
oil version of either of Holbein's drawings of
Vaux survives. C.M.

FIG. 20
An Allegory of Prudence, Hans Holbein the Younger,
1532–6

PROVENANCE
Possibly Henry VIII; probably
Edward VI, 1547; Henry FitzAlan,
12th Earl of Arundel; inherited
by John, 1st Baron Lumley, 1580;
assumed to have passed with his
library to Henry, Prince of Wales,
1609; inherited by Prince Charles
(later Charles I); given in an
exchange to Philip Herbert, 4th
Earl of Pembroke, 1627/8; given to
Thomas Howard, 2nd Earl of
Arundel; [...]; acquired by Charles II
by 1675; by descent in the Royal
Collection.

LITERATURE
Foister 1983, p.41; Parker 1983,
pp.42–3, no. 24; Hearn 1995, no. 94,
p.147; Foister 2004 pp.229, 231, 246.

48

Elizabeth Cheney, Lady Vaux (b.1505?)

HANS HOLBEIN THE YOUNGER, *c*.1536

Coloured chalks, black ink, white bodycolour and
metalpoint on pink prepared paper, 281 × 215mm
Inscribed, top left: *The Lady Vaux*

The Royal Collection (RL 12247)

The sitter in this portrait, Lady Vaux, was
the daughter of Sir Thomas Cheney of Fen
Ditton, Cambridgeshire and Thenford and
Irthlingborough, Northamptonshire (not the
Sir Thomas Cheney, *c*.1485–1558, who was an
Esquire of the Body to Henry VIII, as stated
in most of the Holbein literature). She was the
ward of Nicholas, 1st Baron Vaux (*c*.1460–1523)
and married his son, Thomas, 2nd Baron Vaux
(1509–56), in 1523 (Woudhuysen, 'Vaux, Thomas,
2nd Baron Vaux', ODNB 2004; Ford, 'Vaux,
Nicholas, 1st Baron Vaux', ODNB 2004). No
oil painting by Holbein based on this drawing
survives, although there are painted copies of
the lost Holbein original (Royal Collection,
Hampton Court and Narodni Gardens, Prague).

In addition to the 'great booke' of drawings,
Henry owned at least one other work by Holbein,
a small panel painting entitled *An Allegory of
Passion* (J. Paul Getty Museum, Los Angeles;
fig. 20). This is identifiable as having come from
the Prince's collection by his brand on the reverse
(see cat. 126). While contemporary northern
European paintings were strongly represented
in Prince Henry's collection, these works by
Holbein were some of the finest he owned by an
artist of an earlier generation. Henry's interest
in Holbein's work does not seem to have been
shared by his brother Charles, however, to whom
the drawings apparently passed on Henry's
death. Charles exchanged the book of drawings
with the 4th Earl of Pembroke for a painting of
St George and the Dragon by Raphael, and in
a separate transaction gave away a *Portrait of
Erasmus* by Holbein (which had been given to
him by Adam Newton, Henry's tutor), along
with a painting by Titian, in exchange for
St John the Baptist by Leonardo.

Today eighty-five of Holbein's drawings
survive in the Royal Collection, having been
re-acquired by Charles II by 1675. Queen
Caroline had them removed from the book in the
eighteenth century. Many have seventeenth- or
early eighteenth-century inscriptions identifying
the sitters, based on earlier inscriptions that were
probably found on now-lost mounts or on the
pages of the book. The original identifications
are believed to have been made by Sir John
Cheke, tutor to Edward VI. C.M.

PROVENANCE
As cat. 47.

LITERATURE
Foister 1983, p.41; Parker 1983, p.42,
no.24; Foister 2004, pp.240, 246.

49

Boy Looking Through a Casement Window

UNIDENTIFIED NETHERLANDISH ARTIST, *c*.1550–60

Oil on panel, 738 × 616mm

The Royal Collection (RCIN 404972)

It is not known how this striking painting came
to be in Prince Henry's picture collection, but as
it is not recorded in the Royal Collection before
his lifetime it seems likely that it was bought
for or by the Prince; it is an example of a non-
contemporary work from Henry's collection.
Depicting a boy looking through a window, it is
intended to create an illusion that will, at least
for a moment, trick the viewer into believing that
he or she sees a real window with a boy behind
it. This kind of optical trick, known as *trompe
l'oeil*, was relatively popular in the sixteenth and
seventeenth centuries. Although there are no
other *trompe l'oeil* paintings known to have been
in Henry's collection, other works suggest that
he had an interest generally in optical effects
(see cats 50 and 51).

The depiction of smiling or laughing figures in
painting was unusual at this time and breached
the etiquette of formal portraiture, in which
individuals were almost invariably shown with
sober expressions. This painting was identified
in the 1616 inventory of Anne of Denmark's
collection at Oatlands Palace as 'A picture of a
Buffone [buffoon]'; it was paired with 'An other
of a Buffone in a fooles coate & Coxecombe'.
It may be intended as a representation of a
professional jester, and, along with Henry's copy
of *Coryats Crudities* (cat. 24), it provides a rare
glimpse into the humorous side of court life.
C.M.

FIG. 21
Brand showing Prince Henry's cipher

PROVENANCE
Henry, Prince of Wales (branded
with his cipher 'HP' on the reverse);
Anne of Denmark; by descent to
Charles I; sold 16 January 1651 to
Houghton and others; recovered
for the Royal Collection at the
Restoration; by descent in the
Royal Collection.

LITERATURE
Campbell 1985, pp.131–2, no. 83;
Evans 1998, pp.28–9, no. 6.

50

A Bearded Old Man with a Shell

MICHIEL JANSZ. VAN MIEREVELT
(1567–1641), *c.*1606

Oil on panel, 876 × 673mm

The Royal Collection (RCIN 403956)

Two works by the Dutch painter Mierevelt are known to have been in Prince Henry's picture collection: a portrait of the Protestant hero Maurice of Nassau, which was sent by the sitter as a diplomatic gift in 1610 (see cat. 70), and this portrait of an unknown sitter, which is an uncharacteristically theatrical painting within Mierevelt's oeuvre. It is possible to surmise that the picture's chiaroscuro would have appealed to the Prince as his collection included a number of works with dramatic lighting (e.g. *A Sea Battle at Night* by Jan Porcellis and *Head of an Old Woman Blowing Charcoal*).

This work is an early example of a Dutch portrait entering the Royal Collection on account of the celebrity of the artist rather than the sitter. It has been suggested that the sitter is the artist's father, Jan van Mierevelt (1582–1612; White 1982, p.74), but this has been rejected by Anita Jansen of the Museum Het Prinsenhof, Delft, based on a comparison with the portrait of his father included in Mierevelt's *Militia Banquet* (1611) (Museum Het Prinsenhof; private correspondence). The prominence of the shell identifies the sitter as a collector. Shells were admired for their rarity and expense, and their display simultaneously celebrated the wealth and erudition of the owner. Shells were also frequently included in contemporary Netherlandish paintings as *vanitas* symbols, their fragility suggesting the transience of life.

Prompted by the gift of Maurice of Nassau's portrait, Henry's court made strenuous, though ultimately unsuccessful, attempts to persuade Mierevelt to work for the Prince in London. Negotiations were led by Sir Edward Conway, the Governor of Brill, with support from Sir Edward Cecil, who had sat for the artist in 1610 (see cat. 18). In early 1611, a date of arrival –

apparently agreed by Mierevelt – was set for April but the artist postponed and prevaricated until the initiative faded out the following year. Conway's surviving letters reveal his frustration with the artist, writing that 'the man is naturally phantastical' (quoted in Wilks 1987, p.95). Mierevelt was an exceptionally successful portraitist with a large studio in Delft. He may well have been reluctant to exchange the steady and profitable patronage of the House of Orange for the uncertainties of employment by the Stuart court. R.M.

PROVENANCE
Collection of Henry, Prince of Wales (branded with his cipher 'HP' on the reverse); Charles I (branded with his cipher 'CR' on the reverse); sold to Peter Lely, 2 April 1651; returned to Charles II at the Restoration and thus by descent in the Royal Collection.

LITERATURE
Millar 1960, p.194; White 1982, p.74; Wilks 1987, p.184; Evans 1998, p.30.

51

Christic in the House of Martha and Mary

HANS VREDEMAN DE VRIES (1527–1609) and
ANTHONIS BLOCKLANDT (c.1534–83), 1566

Oil on panel, 794 × 1092mm
Signed, on step beneath arch: *NS* [in monogram] *VRIESE 1566;*
on plaque beneath oval picture: ΦΡΕΔΕΜΑΝ ΦΡΗΕΣ

The Royal Collection (RCIN 405475)

This painting illustrates a passage from the Gospel of St Luke, in which Christ visited the house of the sisters Martha and Mary: 'but Martha was cumbered about much serving, and came to him, and said, Lord, dost thou not care that my sister hath left me to serve alone? bid her therefore that she help me. And Jesus answered and said unto her, Martha, Martha, thou art careful and troubled about many things: But one thing is needful: and Mary hath chosen that good part, which shall not be taken away from her' (Luke 10: 40–2). The subject was popular among Dutch painters of the sixteenth and seventeenth centuries as it could be interpreted as supporting the Protestant doctrine that placed faith (represented by Mary, who sat listening to Christ) above good works (represented by Martha) in achieving salvation.

The composition was significantly changed at an early date. Originally Martha, now seen as a small figure in the kitchen to the right, was a large figure standing in front of the arch. Lorne Campbell has suggested that the original figure was by Vredeman de Vries, and that Blocklandt (whose involvement in the painting was noted by Abraham van der Doort) altered the painting after it had been finished by de Vries, presumably at the request of an early owner. Such a change

may have been brought about for doctrinal reasons, to emphasise the importance of Mary, or it may have been made to reveal the linear perspective of the receding architecture more clearly.

Architectural perspectives of this type were a novelty in England in the late sixteenth and early seventeenth centuries, and a speciality of de Vries, who also wrote and illustrated treatises on the subject, including *Perspective* (1604–5). The importance of this aspect of the painting is underlined by its description in the inventory of Anne of Denmark's collection in 1619, where it is listed as 'a small Prospective of Christe Mary and Martha'. Prince Henry was taught the art of perspective by Salomon de Caus (see cat. 21) and architectural settings drawn in perspective were important elements of Inigo Jones's designs for masques at court (see cats 35 and 36). Henry owned other perspective paintings, including that of 'A Vaulted House, wherein several are wrestling with each other; perspectively painted rather than artistically painted' (see Wilks 2005, p.161) and another of 'Two palaces perspectively painted on two tables [panels]', according to the descriptions of the Duke of Saxe-Weimar, who saw the Prince's collections in 1613 (Rye 1865, pp.161–2). R.M. and C.M.

PROVENANCE
Henry, Prince of Wales (branded with his cipher 'HP' on the reverse); Anne of Denmark; by descent to Charles I; sold to de Critz and others, 18 November 1651; recovered at the Restoration; by descent in the Royal Collection.

LITERATURE
Millar 1960, xiv; pp.52, 205; Campbell 1985, pp.118–20, no. 73; Strong 1986, p.193; Wilks 1987, p.166; Evans 1998, pp.29–30, no. 7.

52

Cesarini Venus

Seventeenth-century cast after a model by
GIAMBOLOGNA (JEAN BOULOGNE; 1529–1609)

Bronze, height 338mm (without plinth)
The National Trust, Fairhaven Collection, Anglesey Abbey

The Cesarini Venus is named after Giovanni Giorgio Cesarini (?1549–85), the first owner of a nearly life-sized marble statue of the bathing Venus carved by Giambologna in about 1583. A reduced version, possibly derived from the same cast as this statuette, was one of fifteen bronzes given to Prince Henry by Cosimo II, Grand Duke of Tuscany, in 1612. This unprecedented gift was the culmination of the decade-long marriage negotiations on behalf of Prince Henry and the Grand Duke's sister, Caterina de' Medici (1595–1629), in order to secure an Anglo-Florentine alliance. It was hoped that the gift would encourage the Prince to overcome the obstacles of religion and allegiance.

The offer of choice pieces of Italian art had initially been made to the Prince by the Florentine Court in 1609. It is a credit to the connoisseurship within Henry's circle that the Prince requested statuettes of works by Giambologna, the greatest sculptor of the age. The resultant group of bronzes, cast after models by the artist, amounted to a concise survey of Giambologna's remarkable range: the mythological and allegorical in *Hercules* and *Fortuna*; genre figures in *Birdcatcher* and *Bagpiper*; and animal models including *Bull* and *Pacing Horse* (see cat. 53). These may have been the earliest Renaissance bronzes to arrive in England and comprised the single most important consignment of bronzes after Giambologna ever to reach these shores.

The shipment was received by the Prince on 28 June 1612 at Richmond Palace, where he was joined by the Grand Duke's agent, Andrea Cioli, the influential supporter of the Florentine match, Sir Edward Cecil (see cat. 18), his Chamberlain Sir Thomas Chaloner and his Gentleman of

the Bedchamber Sir David Murray. Henry was delighted by the bronzes and Cecil informed Cioli that a second order should be made on condition that they be paid for, this being the 'English way of doing things'.

The second consignment of statuettes, consisting of the *Labours of Hercules*, was destined never to arrive as Henry's death on 6 November brought the marriage negotiations to an abrupt end. The fifteen bronzes passed to Prince Charles, later Charles I, and were dispersed along with the rest of his collection during the Commonwealth. None of the bronzes from the Florentine gift can now be identified with absolute certainty, although many casts of the models are extant. Such statuettes became an essential feature of European courtly collections and they were produced in quantity at Giambologna's workshop after his death. This bronze was once owned by Louis XIV.
R.M.

PROVENANCE
Collection of Louis XIV and by descent; appears in French royal collection inventories from 1669 until 1796; marked on pedestal with inventory numbers 'No. 48' and 'No. 210'; collection of Huttleston Broughton, 1st Lord Fairhaven (1896–1966).

LITERATURE
Watson and Avery 1973, pp.493–507; Strong 1986, pp.194–7; Avery 1987, pp.133–45; Wenley 1999, pp.3–12; Strozzi and Zikos 2006, p.127.

53

Pacing Horse

PIETRO TACCA (1577–1640), after GIAMBOLOGNA
(JEAN BOULOGNE), *c.*1600

Bronze, 273 × 280 × 115mm
The Royal Collection (RCIN 35467)

This bronze statuette of a horse is derived from
the monumental equestrian statue of Cosimo I
de' Medici (d.1574), erected by Giambologna and
his assistant Antonio Susini in the Piazza della
Signoria, Florence, in 1594. This work was itself
based on the antique equestrian statue of Marcus
Aurelius in the Piazza del Campidoglio, Rome.
Numerous bronze reductions after Cosimo I's
mount were produced by the Giambologna
workshop. Their popularity among princely
collectors attests to the pre-eminent status of
the horse as an indicator of social rank and
military command.

A bronze version of this model was part of
the Florentine gift of fifteen statuettes presented
to Prince Henry by Cosimo II, Grand Duke
of Tuscany, to further the marital negotiations
between the Prince and Caterina de' Medici,
granddaughter of Cosimo I. The *Pacing Horse*
was evidently a particular favourite of the Prince,
whose reaction was vividly described by the
Florentine agent Andrea Cioli in a letter to
Belasario Vinta, the Secretary of State to the
Grand Duchy of Tuscany. He recounts that
Henry protested sharply at Sir Edward Cecil's
suggestion that the *Pacing Horse* might be given
to his brother Charles, saying: 'No, no, I want
everything for myself' (translated from the
Italian in Watson and Avery 1973, p.501).

Horses and horsemanship were a major
preoccupation of the Prince. A number of books
on the subject were dedicated to him, including
Nicholas Morgan's *The Perfection of Horse-manship*
(1609), and he is presented on horseback in
Robert Peake the Elder's ambitious portrait
(see cat. 28). Between 1607 and 1609, Henry
oversaw the construction of a 'riding house' at

St James's Palace, in which the Prince hoped to
establish an academy of horsemanship. Edward
Cecil referred to the school when informing
Cioli of the Prince's desire for a second batch
of bronzes. He recommended that the Grand
Duke should also send a pair of real horses.

Henry's affection for the *Pacing Horse* was
poignantly articulated on 1 November 1612,
when Prince Charles gave it to his brother to
hold during their final meeting before Henry's
death. The moment was significant enough to
be recalled almost three decades later in Abraham
van der Doort's inventory of Charles I's collection:
'a little horse being one of the no: of 18^{en} W^{ch} your
Ma^{ty} did send–for to Richmond in the last sicknes
time and there yor Ma^{ty} gave it wth your owne
hands to the Prince' (Millar 1960, p.92). R.M.

PROVENANCE
Probably given to Henry, Prince of
Wales, in 1612; presumably sold
under the Commonwealth and
recovered at the Restoration; first
recorded at Kensington Palace, 1818.

LITERATURE
Millar 1960, xiv, pp.98–9; Watson
and Avery 1973, pp.493–507; Avery
and Radcliffe 1978, no.152; Avery
1987; Strozzi and Zikos 2006, p.127.

Aetatis Suæ 52. An⁰ 1601.

J.Hein fe.

Gorlæus hîc in ære scalptus, æs cui,
Argentum, & aurum, Roma quod vel Græcia
Signauit vnquam, gemmaque & carus lapis
Olim vetustis destinatus annulis
Perennitatis gratiam debent suæ.
Nunc experitur an Metalla a sæculis
Qui vindicata sæculo nostro dedit,
Ipsum futuris dent Metalla sæculis.

H.Grot,

54

Abraham Gorlaeus (1549–1608)

JACOB DE GHEYN II (*c*.1565–1629), 1601

Engraving, 170 × 113mm
Inscribed: lettered below right, *DGheÿn. fe.*;
below coat of arms, *Aetatis Suæ 52, An. 1601*;
in the margin eight lines of text, *Gorlæus hic ... sæculis*
by *H.Grot* [Hugo Grotius]

The British Museum, London (o,6.130)

Abraham Gorlaeus, whose real name was Van Goorle, was a native of Antwerp who emigrated to the northern Netherlands, where he worked for the Stadtholder of Utrecht and Gelderland. After his retirement from political life, he focused on his antiquarian and collecting interests, assembling a large and very important collection of antique gems, medals and coins. In 1601 he published a book about his collection of gems and seals set into finger rings, entitled *Abrahami Gorlaei Antverpiani Dactyliotheca seu Annulorum sigillarium* ...; this print formed the frontispiece. It shows Gorlaeus as a gentleman collector, studying his collection in a richly furnished interior, his coat of arms depicted on the wall behind him. Gorlaeus's book was published in various editions and, along with his later work *Thesaurus numismatum Romanorum* (1607), made his collection famous in antiquarian circles throughout Europe (see Henig 2008).

After Gorlaeus's death, a substantial part of his collection was purchased for Prince Henry.

The evidence is confusing, but it would seem that there were two acquisitions, one of which was a group of coins and medals for £2,200, the most expensive single purchase known for Prince Henry's collection (TNA E351/2793). It would appear that Gorlaeus's finger rings were acquired separately. Henry also purchased a collection of coins and medals that had belonged to the Cambridge scholar William Fulke (1536/7–1589; information supplied by Timothy Wilks, from article forthcoming; see also introduction to this chapter, 'Princely Collecting', pp.118–19). Although more impressive, finer collections of such items were acquired in succeeding decades by others, Prince Henry's collection of antique coins, medals and gems was, as far as is known, the first substantial collection of its kind in England. It must have had a significant impact on those in Henry's circle, feeding and stimulating a thirst for knowledge of the art of classical antiquity. C.M.

PROVENANCE
Pierre Mariette II (1634–1716); acquired by the British Museum, London, by 1837.

LITERATURE
Hollstein 2000, the de Gheyn Family, pt.2, no.245, pp.103–4.

55

Ring depicting Augustus and Livia

UNIDENTIFIED ARTIST, 16th century

Silver relief with intaglio behind;
mounted in an iron swivel ring,
the shoulders decorated in gold; the bezel gold,
20 × 15mm (relief); 19 × 15mm (intaglio)

Belvoir Castle

Among the gems acquired by Prince Henry from the collection of Abraham Gorlaeus, some appear to have been genuine Roman gems and others were skilful imitations made at a later date. This ring, which is recorded in Gorlaeus's book *Dactyliotheca* as number 103 (see fig. 22), is a fine Renaissance imitation of a classical gem.

FIG. 22
Ring with busts of the Emperor Augustus
and Livia, illustration 103 in *Dactyliotheca*,
Abraham Gorlaeus, 1609

It shows the Roman Emperor Augustus and his wife Livia. The depiction of the heads in profile was characteristic of ancient gems of this type, but very unusual in early seventeenth-century English portraiture. Henry's acquisition of such gems probably influenced a group of miniature portraits made in about 1610–12 showing the Prince and members of his circle in profile (see cats 43 and 44).

It would appear that Prince Henry acquired Gorlaeus's cabinet of finger rings through an agent recorded as 'Hans von Dirbige', who may have been the Dutch jeweller Jan van de Beecke (information supplied by Timothy Wilks, from article forthcoming). At some point this ring became part of the large and magnificent collection of gems assembled subsequently by the 14th Earl of Arundel, who was an influential member of Henry's circle; it may have been given by the Prince or acquired by Arundel after Henry's death. This transfer of ownership out of the royal collection saved it from the Whitehall Palace fire of 1698, which probably destroyed most of the remaining collection of Prince Henry's gems. It is now one of only two known surviving gems owned by Prince Henry, the other being a ring in Devizes Museum, Wiltshire (Henig 2008, p.281). C.M.

PROVENANCE
Abraham Gorlaeus (Van Goorle); purchased for Henry, Prince of Wales; probably given to the 14th Earl of Arundel; by descent as part of the Arundel collection of gems to Henry Howard, 6th Duke of Norfolk (1628–84); collection sold by the widow of Norfolk's brother to Henry, Earl of Peterborough; by descent to the second husband of Peterborough's daughter, Sir John Germain; given by his wife Lady Betty Germain to her niece the Hon. Mary Beauclerk on her marriage to Lord Charles Spencer (1762); passed to his brother George Spencer, 4th Duke of Marlborough (1739–1817); by descent; Marlborough collection (including Arundel collection) sold in 1899; this gem purchased by Captain Lindsay, brother of the wife of the 8th Duke of Rutland; by descent in the collection of the Dukes of Rutland.

LITERATURE
Gorlaeus (Van Goorle) 1601, no. 103; Boardman 2009, pp.3, 6, 11 (note 18), 56, no. 56.

56

Gold Medal of Prince Henry

UNIDENTIFIED ARTIST, *c.*1607?

Gold, diameter 28mm
Inscribed on obverse: *HENRICVS . . PRINCEPS*
(separated by fleurs de lys, annulets and a rose);
inscribed on reverse: *FAX . MENTIS . HONESTÆ . GLORIA .*
(separated by annulets and a rose)

The British Museum, London (M. 7022)

Medals depicting members of the royal family represented a relatively small but increasingly important aspect of portrait production in early seventeenth-century Britain. Like engravings, they could be manufactured in some numbers, but particularly when made in gold, they had a measurable value and were likely to last for a long time. They thus made ideal royal gifts. The growing interest in classical antiquity was a factor in the growth of medal production, although at James I's court there was also a strong link between portrait miniature production and medals, which resulted in three-quarter-face depictions, rather than the more classical profile, being favoured. There are a number of surviving payments from James I's accounts for medals, particularly to Nicholas Hilliard, the miniaturist (see Barclay and Syson 1993, pp.3–11, especially pp.5–9; and Farquhar 1908, p.348). In addition, in 1604 the jeweller Sir George Heriot was paid from the Queen's accounts 'for making of the Prince's picture in gold, vi li [six pounds]' (Wilks 1987, p.107) and Charles Anthony, chief engraver to the Mint, was paid 'for the stamps for one medal which his Highnes hath seen' (Farquhar 1908, p.351).

There are now only two known surviving medallic portraits of Prince Henry. One is represented by this medal; the other, which may be slightly earlier, can be seen in two variants (Hawkins et al 1885, p.201, nos 30 and 31). The image of the Prince on the present medal is very close to a miniature of him by Hilliard (Royal Collection; fig. 23), probably painted in 1607, depicting him in armour that had been given to him that year. The medal is not, however, stylistically like those of James, Elizabeth I and Elizabeth of Bohemia, attributed to Hilliard, and it may be that the miniaturist provided an image that was used by another designer; collaborative efforts seem to have been the norm in medal manufacture (see Barclay and Syson 1993, p.5). Helen Farquhar suggests that Charles Anthony may have been involved (p.351). C.M.

PROVENANCE
Probably acquired before *c.*1830.

LITERATURE
Hawkins et al 1885, pp.200–1, no. 29;
Farquhar 1908, pp.324–56.

FIG. 23
Prince Henry, Nicholas Hilliard, 1607

57

De Conscribendis Epistolis

DESIDERIUS ERASMUS (*c.*1467–1536),
published by Hero Alopecius, Cologne, 1523

Printed book; 387 pages, spine height 165mm
(open at title page)
The British Library, London (1083.d.1)

The great libraries of the sixteenth century
in England had been assembled by individuals
outside the royal family, including Thomas
Cranmer, Archbishop of Canterbury (1489–1556),
and John, Lord Lumley (*c.*1533–1609). King
James and Henry both wished to create for the
Prince a royal library that superseded these.
In part, the collecting of books was an aspect of
display and patronage, presenting Henry as a
learned prince on the European stage. Henry's
library was also intended to be a working tool,
assembled for the benefit of his education and
that of the aristocratic boys who were educated
with him, as well as for the academy that was
planned under his patronage (see 'The Making
of the Prince', pp.68–9). A large part of the
great library of Thomas Cranmer, author of the
Book of Common Prayer, had been acquired by
Henry FitzAlan, 12th Earl of Arundel (1512–80),
in the middle of the sixteenth century; Arundel's
books were inherited (and greatly added to)
by his son-in-law, Lord Lumley; and Lumley's
books, housed at Nonsuch Palace where Henry
was living before he became Prince of Wales,
passed to Henry, probably shortly before
Lumley's death in 1609 (see Jayne and Johnson
1956, pp.13–17).

This volume, Erasmus's *De Conscribendis
Epistolis*, had belonged to both Cranmer and
Lumley; both signatures can be seen on the title
page. Henry's tutor, Adam Newton, followed
the teaching methods of Erasmus, which were
already well established in English grammar
schools where learning how to write effectively
and impressively in Latin was a key aspect of
education. One important means of practising
Latin vocabulary, grammar and compositional
techniques was through letter writing, the subject
of this book. Some of the letters, or epistles, that
Henry wrote were simply exercises, never sent.

But some were addressed and sent to members
of his family, and others to European heads of
state, thus serving the double purpose of engaging
Henry in European politics and drawing him
to the attention of continental rulers and their
advisors. Adam Newton's admiration for Erasmus
was such that he also owned a portrait of the
scholar by Hans Holbein (Louvre, Paris), which
he subsequently gave to one of the Princes,
probably Charles rather than Henry (Millar
1963, p.57). C.M.

PROVENANCE
John Toker [Tucker], Cranmer's
physician; Thomas Cranmer;
probably acquired by Henry
FitzAlan, 12th Earl of Arundel after
Cranmer's arrest in 1553; probably
inherited by John, Lord Lumley;
acquired with the majority of
Lumley's library by Henry, Prince
of Wales, 1609; by descent in the
Royal Collection; given to the
British Museum as part of the Old
Royal Library by George II in 1757.

LITERATURE
Selwyn 1996, p.120; Pollnitz 2007,
pp.22–64, especially pp.32–3 and
p.60, note 69.

58

Astronomiae Instauratae Mechanica

TYCHO BRAHE (1546–1601),

published by Levinus Hulsius, Nuremberg, 1602

Printed book, bound in brown calf, blocked in gold
with the arms of Henry, Prince of Wales in the centre;
107 pages, spine height 320mm

The British Library, London (Davis 95)

The great Lumley collection of books formed
the core of Prince Henry's library, but it was
supplemented by an enormous number of
purchases on a wide range of subject matter.
The mathematician Edward Wright (see cat. 67),
who had been a tutor to the Prince, was in
charge of acquiring the scientific books, and he
assembled an impressive and practical collection
on mathematics, cosmography, navigation and
related subjects. Altogether about 1,000 of the
books that belonged to Prince Henry, but not
to Lumley, survive in the British Library (see
Birrell 1986, pp.30–40). This book by Tycho
Brahe, the great astronomer, is one such volume.
Like most of Prince Henry's books, it has been
rebound in a standard binding with the Prince's
coat of arms in the centre and, in this case,
fleurs-de-lys in the corners. Variations with roses,
thistles or heir apparent's feathers in the corners
are also common, and other, more complex
and decorative bindings were also used.

Tycho Brahe worked between 1576 and 1597
under the patronage of Prince Henry's grandfather, Frederick II of Denmark. He had an
observatory, Uraniborg, built on the island of
Hven near Elsinore, where he ran what was
in effect a research institute. Brahe's book,
Astronomiae, describes the astronomical
instruments he designed and used there, which
enabled him to make remarkably accurate
measurements of the positions of the stars before
the invention of the telescope. After leaving
Denmark, following the death of Frederick II in
1588, he lived for a time with Heinrich Rantzau,
the Stadtholder of Schleswig-Holstein, where
he had the first edition of *Astronomiae* privately
printed. Subsequently Brahe moved to Prague
and worked under the patronage of Rudolf II.
This, the second edition of the book, was
printed commercially after his death. C.M.

PROVENANCE
Prince Henry; [...]; Sotheby's,
20 June 1960 (lot 213); acquired by
Henry Davis; given to the British
Library, London, 1968.

LITERATURE
Ræder, Strömgren & Strömgren
1946; Foot 1979, vol. II, pp.96–7,
no. 64.

59

Chemise Binding of Crimson Velvet

UNKNOWN BOOKBINDER, *c.*1605

Velvet, embroidered with seed pearls and silver thread,
trimmed with gold fringe, 285 × 415mm (including fringes)
The British Library, London (Royal MS 12.C.VIIIB)

This beautiful cover was made for a manuscript presented to Prince Henry on 29 August 1605 at Magdalen College, Oxford. The manuscript itself was a richly illuminated, early sixteenth-century copy of Pandolfo Collenuccio's *Apologues* and Lucian of Samosata's *Dialogues* (see McKendrick, Lowden and Doyle 2011, no.113). It had belonged to Henry VIII and subsequently to Nicholas Bond (1540–1608), President of Magdalen College. Prince Henry visited Oxford with his mother and father from 27 to 30 August 1605, and became the first royal prince to matriculate at university. His study consisted merely of a series of learned entertainments, including a short oration in Latin given by the eleven-year-old Prince, and a feast. At the end of the visit, the university expected him to proceed to the degree of Master of Arts but instead of attending the ceremony, Henry watched a play by Samuel Daniel with the Queen. It has been suggested that James I prevented Henry from graduating out of jealousy of his son's popularity (Strong 1986, p.14), but it seems more likely that, while wanting his son to have a reputation for learning, a degree represented to James 'the wrong kind of learning for a future ruler' (Pollnitz 2007, p.29).

Gifts of manuscripts and printed books were an important means of supplementing Prince Henry's library. The presentation of a book alluded to the learning of both the donor and the recipient. A manuscript such as this one paid great tribute to the Prince by virtue of its magnificence, which was augmented with a velvet chemise cover (a loose cover to be fitted over the leather binding), embroidered with the heir apparent's feathers in silver thread and seed pearls. This rare survival of a textile of this period gives us a glimpse of the richly decorated fabrics that would have surrounded Prince Henry – in his clothing and that of his courtiers, and in the furnishings of his palaces (see cat. 45). C.M.

PROVENANCE
Presented to Henry, Prince of Wales, 1605; by descent in the Royal Collection; presented to the British Museum as part of the Old Royal Library by George II in 1757.

LITERATURE
Anon., 'An Account of the Entertainment of King James, with the Queen and Prince at Oxford anno 1605', University Library, Cambridge, Add. MSS 34, fols 28r–45v; Warner and Gilson 1921, II, p.25.

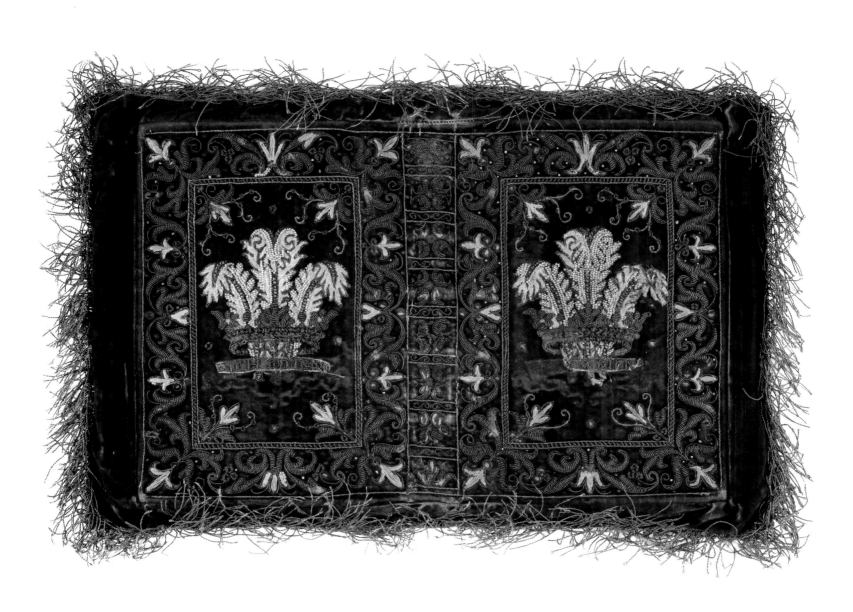

Prince Henry and the Wider World

The Venetian ambassador in London, Antonio Foscarini, gave a wide-ranging account of Prince Henry's relationship to the wider world:

> He was athirst for glory if ever any prince was. He lent fire to the King in the affairs of Germany, and aspired to be head of the confederate princes who include fourteen of the Hanseatic towns. Many predictions centred round his person, and he seemed marked out for great events. His whole talk was of arms and war. His authority was great, and he was obeyed and lauded by the military party. He protected the colony of Virginia, and under his auspices the ships sailed for the north-west passage to the Indies. He had begun to put the navy in order and raised the number of sailors. He was hostile to Spain and had claims in France. He would not suffer the Pope to be ill spoken of, and in his familiar conversation he declared that he admired him as a prince. His designs were vast; his temper was grave, severe, reserved, brief in speech. His household was but little inferior to the King's and kept in excellent order. He had few equals in the handling of arms, be it on horse or on foot; in fine all the hopes of these kingdoms were built on his high qualities. [1]

Foscarini's words reflected his own diplomatic agenda and the Venetian political context, but his description of the Prince, made shortly after Henry's death, indicates that by the time he was in his late teens, Henry had a role on

Prince Henry, Robert Peake the Elder,
c.1605–8 (detail of cat. 60)

the world stage, not just as a precocious collector and cultural patron, but also as a potential military leader with a particular interest in the navy and exploration. Henry's interest in ships had been secured early on by the presentation of a small ship, the *Disdain*, shortly after he arrived in England in 1603. The shipwright Phineas Pett went on to make a magnificent and enormous warship for Henry, the *Prince Royal*, the interior of which was decorated with elaborate history scenes by the painters Robert Peake the Elder and Paul Isaacson. Henry continued to take an active interest in the navy which, supported by his education in navigation and astronomy, led inevitably – at this time of the discovery and settlement of new lands – to the sponsorship of exploration.

Exploration was seen as a means of bringing honour and glory to the explorer and his country, as well as potential revenue from the exploitation of the natural resources – and sometimes native peoples – of the lands discovered. But the justification for exploration was often framed in terms of promoting the spread of Christianity, specifically, in the British context, Protestantism. Edward Wright, a mathematician and Henry's librarian, made this clear in his dedication addressed to the Prince in the second edition of his *Certaine Errors in Navigation*, in which he referred to 'the poore people there living in darkness and in the shadow of death, hauing hitherto been bred and brought up in most wofull and horrible idolatries and superstitions, deuoting themselues, and in diuers places sacrificing one another to Diuels, in stead of worshipping the euerliring God'.[2]

So, the navy, exploration, foreign politics and religion were closely connected in Henry's world. These were all areas of interest to the great Elizabethan polymath Sir Walter Ralegh, who was confined in the Tower of London for most of James I's reign, but saw Henry as a potential advocate for his release. Ralegh addressed treatises to Henry on the subjects of ships and the navy (he was a critic of Pett) and foreign marriage proposals for both the Prince and his sister Princess Elizabeth. Marriage proposals made between European courts were one of the most important kinds of diplomatic exchange, and a number of possibilities were considered for Henry, most of them with Catholic brides, which was a matter of some concern for him. Proposals were entertained from Spain, France, Florence and Savoy; the latter was the most likely to have succeeded, had Henry lived. Connections were secured with foreign courts by other means as well; Henry corresponded, and exchanged gifts, with foreign political and military leaders whom he admired, including Henri IV of France (his godfather), Maurice of Nassau and his uncle, Christian IV of Denmark. C.M.

1 CSP *Venetian, 1610–13*, XII, (1905), pp.441–54.
2 Edward Wright, *Certaine Errors in Navigation Detected and Corrected by Edw: Wright*, 2nd edition, 1610, p.7.

60

Prince Henry

ROBERT PEAKE THE ELDER, *c*.1605–8

Oil on canvas, 1330 × 900mm

Palazzo Reale, Turin (n. inv. 5209 rosso –1033DC)

This painting is the second of three innovative, large-scale portraits of the Prince produced by Robert Peake (see also cats 14 and 28). Its provenance suggests that it was acquired by Charles Emmanuel I, Duke of Savoy, during the marriage negotiations that were taking place on behalf of Henry and the Infanta Maria (1594–1656), the Duke's daughter, from January 1611 until Prince Henry's death in late 1612. Marriage negotiations between rulers were one of the most important types of diplomatic exchange to take place in this period. Marriages provided a means of amassing considerable revenue, as well as making strategic alliances with other powerful courts and countries. Other marriage possibilities were also considered for Henry, with a French princess, a Spanish princess, and a Medici princess from Florence. In the end the Savoy match seemed the most likely to go ahead, in spite of Henry's wish not to marry a Catholic (see Strong 1986, pp.81–3).

Peake was paid £50 in 1611–12 for 'Twoe great Pictures of the Prince in Armes at Length sent beyond the seas', no doubt in connection with marriage negotiations. However, the Prince appears much younger than seventeen in the present portrait and so it seems unlikely that this painting is one of those commissioned at that time. The feathers and motto of the heir apparent on the Prince's shield have been used in the past as a reason for dating this picture to 1610 or later, but as has been shown, this device was used in relation to the Prince much earlier (see cat. 28). Timothy Wilks has suggested that the painting may have been one of those owned by Sir Henry Wotton, and shown by him to the Duke of Savoy, who then may have acquired it as a stop-gap until a more up-to-date portrait could be produced (private communication).

Wotton, a keen advocate of the Savoy marriage, was a discerning judge of painting and it is possible that he commissioned this unusual image. The source for Peake's composition is clearly Hendrick Goltzius's print of the Roman hero Titus Manlius Torquatus, from his series Roman Heroes, published in 1586 (see fig. 24; also Leeflang, Luijten et al 2003, pp.89–92, specifically p.90, no. 29.6). The bridge in the background has been seen as a possible reference to Richmond Palace (Strong 1986, p.114), but there is also a bridge in the background of Goltzius's print. It is made clear in the account of Manlius's triumph over a giant Gaul from Quintus Claudius Quadrigarius's 'Annals', included in Aulus Gellius's *Noctes Atticae* (but not in Livy, which is usually assumed to have been Goltzius's source), that the action took place on a bridge. This David-and-Goliath-like episode seems a particularly appropriate allusion for a portrait of the young Prince. Peake combines this reference to a hero of classical antiquity with an allusion to the English, chivalric tradition by including a tilt-yard shield bearing the Prince's *impresa*. C.M.

PROVENANCE
Presumably commissioned by James I or by Sir Henry Wotton; presumably given to Charles Emmanuel I, Duke of Savoy; by descent; [...]; first recorded in 1879 Inventory of works of art given by the Crown (King Victor Emanuel II of Italy) in the Royal Palaces, Turin, no. 1099.

LITERATURE
Bertana 1983, pp.423–6; Strong 1986, p.114; Hearn 1995, pp.187–8, no. 127.

FIG. 24
Titus Manlius Torquatus from the Roman Heroes series, Hendrick Goltzius, 1586

61

Phineas Pett (1570–1647)

UNIDENTIFIED ARTIST, *c*.1612

Oil on panel, 1187 × 997mm
Inscribed: *ÆTAT SUE 43*

National Portrait Gallery, London (NPG 2035)

The shipbuilder and naval administrator Phineas Pett was one of the most celebrated members of a prominent family of shipwrights. He gained the young Prince's favour by presenting him with a small ship on the arrival of the new royal family in London in March 1604. Pett recorded in his autobiography how he accompanied the Prince, the Lord Admiral (Charles Howard, Earl of Nottingham) and 'divers other noblemen' for a sail on the Thames, during which Henry christened the ship *Disdain*. The following day Pett was sworn in as a Gentleman Servant to the Prince.

In November 1607 he presented Henry with a 'curious model' of a much more ambitious vessel. Pett was a pioneer of the shipwright's later customary practice of presenting a client with a scale model. The intricacy and skill of his workmanship was much appreciated and the model was kept in the Prince's cabinet room at Richmond Palace. The King was 'exceedingly delighted' with the model and ordered Pett to construct it at full scale. The resulting ship, named *Prince Royal* in honour of Henry, was the largest, most splendidly decorated and most powerful warship that had hitherto been built in England. Its construction is recorded in the background of Pett's portrait, where the Prince of Wales's feathers and cipher ('HP') are visible on the richly decorated stern.

It was only the third vessel to be entirely built by Pett and his rapid rise under the Prince's patronage provoked hostility from competing shipwrights. Accusations of malpractice in the ship's construction brought about an inconclusive naval inquiry, which in turn led the King and Prince to visit the Woolwich docks on 8 May 1609 in order to view the evidence and pass judgement. Pett recalled that, when he was cleared of all charges, such was Henry's devotion to his servant that he shouted of Pett's accusers, 'do they not worthily deserve hanging?' (Perrin 1918, p.62). R.M.

PROVENANCE
[...]; purchased at the sale of the 8th Earl of Hardwicke's collection, Christie's, 27 June 1924 (lot 133).

LITERATURE
Perrin 1918, pp.99–100; Piper 1963, pp.274–5; Strong 1986, pp.57–60.

This painting commemorates the departure
of Princess Elizabeth and Frederick V, Elector
Palatine, following their marriage in February
1613. The couple and their retinue arrived
at Flushing in the Netherlands on 29 April,
where they were greeted by Frederick V's
uncle, Maurice of Nassau. Following a period
of feasting and pageantry at The Hague, the
couple continued to the court of the Palatinate
at Heidelberg, where they lived until Frederick
accepted the crown of Bohemia in 1619 and the
couple were overtaken by the turmoil of the
Thirty Years War.

Adam Willaerts painted the *Embarkation* in
Utrecht in the year that Frederick and Elizabeth
returned to the Netherlands as exiles, having
been deposed by the imperial army in 1620. The
picture is one of a series of sea pieces celebrating
the voyage, which may have been painted for
the couple. The focus of the composition is
the magnificent ship the *Prince Royal*, built
by Phineas Pett in 1610 with the enthusiastic
support of Prince Henry (see cat. 61). It was
the largest and most heavily armed ship in
Britain and the flagship of the English navy.
The stern is decorated with the Prince of Wales's

62

*The Embarkation of the Elector Palatine in
the Prince Royal from Margate, 25 April 1613*

ADAM WILLAERTS (1577–1664), 1622

Oil on panel, 775 × 1372mm

National Maritime Museum, Greenwich,
Caird Collection
(BHC0266)

feathers and Henry's cipher 'HP' (*Henricus
Princeps*) with a figurehead of St George at the
prow. The ship is shown flying the Stuart Royal
Standard, Union flags and St George's Cross
pennants. The crowd on the deck watch as a
salute is fired on the starboard side.

The small ship to the left of the *Prince Royal*
appears to be the *Disdain*, presented to Henry
in 1604. The ship to the right is likely to be
the *Phoenix*, built by Phineas Pett in 1612 'as a
pinnace to the great ship, the Prince, in which
the Prince's Highness did purpose to solace
himself sometimes into the Narrow Seas'

(Perrin 1918, p.96), but was not completed
until after Henry's death. This shocking event
much diminished the celebratory voyage of
Elizabeth and Frederick. Henry had intended
to accompany them to The Hague on a visit
that would have marked his spectacular entry
onto the European stage and the occasion of
his first meeting with Maurice of Nassau
(see cat. 70). R.M.

PROVENANCE
[...]; collection of Sir James Caird
(1864–1954); acquired by the
National Maritime Museum, 1932.

LITERATURE
National Maritime Museum
catalogue 1937, p.20.

63

Astrolabe

HUMFREY COLE (d.1591), 1574

Gilt brass, diameter 88mm, thickness 6mm
Signed and dated: *Humfrey Cole, 1574*

The British Museum, London (MLA 1855, 12-1.223)

An astrolabe is a two-dimensional model of
the celestial sphere with the Earth at its centre.
In the Jacobean period, a skilled operator could
use it to carry out a multitude of essential
navigational tasks. These included charting the
movement of heavenly bodies, time-keeping,
surveying and determining latitude. As in this
case, they also frequently included information
about the zodiac, such as the temperaments
of planets, and could assist with the casting of
horoscopes. Such versatile instruments were
highly regarded by collectors for their utility,
complexity of design and beauty of fabrication.

This astrolabe was made by Humfrey Cole,
the most renowned maker of scientific instruments
in Elizabethan England. Cole began his career
as a die-sinker in the Mint before developing
his expertise to encompass map-making and
the construction of 'Geometricall instruments
in metall'. He is recorded as providing the
navigational instruments for Martin Frobisher's
voyage in search of the Northwest Passage in 1576.
The base of the astrolabe bears the markings of
a nautical square to assist mariners with navigational calculations. However, measuring just
8.9cm and carefully gilded, it is likely to have
been made for presentation rather than active
navigation. The identity of the original commis-
sioner or recipient has been lost but Henry's
ownership is indicated by the inscription on
the base: *Henr: Princ: Magn Brittan.*

It may have acquired its velvet-lined case
when the astrolabe came into the Prince's
possession. It is embellished with silver fastenings
and plates, the central of which is decorated
with the Prince's cipher 'HP', the heir apparent's
ostrich feather crest and his motto 'Ich Dien'
(I serve). Further inscriptions in Latin seem
to eulogise upon the Prince's qualities: on the
hinge-plate, *Inter omnes* (among all); and on the
subsidiary plates, *Scientia virtusque Autoritas
et ... virtus* (Knowledge, virtue, authority and

... virtue) and *faelicitas Illius crescat in eternum*
(His good fortune grows forever).

Under the instruction of his tutor, the
mathematician and navigator Edward Wright
(see cat. 67), the Prince was encouraged to take
an interest in the nascent scientific disciplines.
He was particularly appreciative of the glory
and material benefits that could be conferred
by overseas exploration. Wright supervised the
Prince's scientific library and *Wunderkammer*
(cabinet of wonders) at Richmond Palace.
Here, the astrolabe would have been part of his
large collection of navigational and cartographic
instruments, which included Wright's own
masterpiece, the 'Coelestiall Automaton' (quoted
in Wilks 1987, p.202). Through the handling and
study of these instruments, the young Prince's
boundaries were extended, both physically and
intellectually. R.M.

PROVENANCE
Prince Henry's ownership indicated
by inscription; [...]; collection of
Ralph Bernal (*c.*1785–1854);
purchased by the British Museum,
1855.

LITERATURE
Wilks 1987, p.203; Ackermann 1998,
pp.32–3; Turner 2000, pp.135–9;
Ackermann, 'Cole, Humfrey',
ODNB 2004.

64

Sir Walter Ralegh (1554–1618)

NICHOLAS HILLIARD, *c*.1585

Watercolour, bodycolour and silver on vellum
laid onto card, 48 × 41mm

National Portrait Gallery, London (NPG 4106)

Perhaps the most famous of Elizabethan
courtiers, Sir Walter Ralegh was a favourite of
Elizabeth I, a soldier, scholar, poet and explorer
who also dabbled in chemistry and wrote on
subjects as diverse as shipbuilding, politics and
the history of the world. He was frequently
rash in his dealings with others, and politically
naïve – Robert Cecil believed him to be against
James VI of Scotland's succession to the English
throne. When James did succeed in 1603 the
King already had a poor opinion of Ralegh.
Shortly after this, Ralegh was implicated in the
so-called Main Plot, an attempt to encourage
a Spanish invasion and remove James from the
throne. Tried and convicted in 1603, he was
sent to the Tower of London, where he was to
remain for the next thirteen years.

Ralegh's main concern while he was in the
Tower was to work for the restitution of honours
and property to his family, and his own release.
To this end, in the words of Mark Nicholls and
Penry Williams, he 'reinvented himself as a
kind of elder statesman, instructing Henry and
advising James' (Nicholls and Williams, 'Ralegh,
Sir Walter' ODNB 2008). Ralegh offered advice
in a number of prose works, some of which were
specifically addressed to Prince Henry. Among
these was 'Observations and Notes Concerning
the Royal Navy and Sea Service', dedicated to
Prince Henry in 1607, which was a revision of a
manuscript that he had presented to Elizabeth I.
Ralegh also wrote two treatises on the subject of
marriage negotiations, 'A Discourse Touching a
Marriage between Prince Henry of England and
a Daughter of Savoy' and 'Concerning a Match
propounded by the Savoyan, between the Lady
Elizabeth and the Prince of Piedmont'. The
latter treatise was stated by Ralegh to have been
written at Henry's request, and advised against a
marriage between Princess Elizabeth and Victor
Amadeus, son of Charles Emmanuel, Duke
of Savoy, advocating instead her betrothal to

Frederick V of the Palatine, a marriage that did
in fact take place the following year (see cat. 77).
The former treatise advised against the proposal
of a parallel marriage between Prince Henry
and the Duke's daughter, the Infanta Maria,
suggesting, instead, an Anglo-French alliance.

There has been much speculation about the
level of mutual admiration between Prince Henry
and Ralegh. Roger Coke, the political writer and
historian, reported that his father had told him,
'The Prince had an high Esteem for Sir Walter
Raleigh, and would say, No other King but his
Father, would keep such a Man as Sir Walter in
such a Cage, meaning the Tower' (Coke 1694, I,
p.61). However, there is no evidence that they
ever met, and on Ralegh's side the imperative
of getting himself released from the Tower gave
particular impetus to his cultivation of the Prince.
He apparently sent a 'quintessence' of his own
concoction to be administered to the Prince on
his deathbed, but believed that it had not been
given in time (McClure 1939, I, p.389). Ralegh
lamented Henry's death in the preface to his
History of the World (1614): 'For it was for the
service of that inestimable Prince Henry, the
successive hope, and one of the greatest of the
Christian World, that I undertooke this Worke.
It pleased him to peruse some part thereof, and
to pardon what was amisse. It is now left to the
world without a Maister: from which all that is
presented, hath received both blows & thanks'
(Raleigh 1614, 2nd edition, last page of Preface
[unnumbered]). C.M.

PROVENANCE
Earls of Carlisle at Castle Howard;
by descent at Castle Howard after
the division of the Howard Estates
following the death of the 9th Earl;
given to Charles Howard, Viscount
Morpeth in 1945; purchased by the
National Portrait Gallery with
help from the Art Fund and the
Pilgrim Trust, 1959.

LITERATURE
Strong 1983, p.74, no.81.

65

John Smith's Map of Virginia

WILLIAM HOLE, 1612

Engraving, 505 × 375mm
Inscribed: [left-hand illustration] *Powhatan held this state & fashion when Capt.*
Smith was deliuered to him prisoner 1607; right-hand image of a brave,
The Sasquesahanougs are a Gyant like people & thus atyred; [below the scale of leagues]
Virginia/Discovered and Discribed by Captayn John Smith/Grauen by William Hole

The British Library, London (Maps C.7.c.18)

PROVENANCE
Acquired in 1888.

LITERATURE
Hind 1955, pp.339–40; Farrell 2007,
pp.1–12; Crystal 2010, p.140.

Prince Henry was an enthusiastic sponsor of English expansion in the New World. Following the failure of Sir Walter Ralegh's Roanoke colony in the 1580s, the opportunity to re-engage with the region was revived by the peace with Spain in 1604. Letters patent for the foundation of colonies by the Virginia Company were granted by the King on 10 April 1606 and an expedition embarked later that year. On 26 April 1607 the fleet made landfall on the southern mouth of Chesapeake Bay, which was named Cape Henry in the Prince's honour (marked lower left on the map shown here).

The expedition continued up the Powhatan/James River, where colonists established Jamestown, the first permanent English settlement in America. The commander of the fleet, Christopher Newport, returned to England in June, carrying a letter for the thirteen-year-old Prince from Robert Tindall, his 'servante and gunner'. Addressing the Prince as 'heyre apparente' of Virginia, the letter included a journal of the voyage and a chart of the region's rivers: 'by us discovered where never christian before hathe beene ... whiche we have a taken a Reall and publicke possession in the name and to the use of your Royall father' (in the British Library, transcribed in Barbour 1969, pp.104–6).

This territorial claim is emphasised by the royal coat of arms on the map, drawn by the early governor of Virginia, John Smith (1580–1631), which was first published as *A Map of Virginia, With a Description of the Country, the Commodities, People, Government and Religion* (Oxford, 1612). This map features a mixture of indigenous and English toponyms and the illustrations recognise the existence of native peoples and their governance. However, the very act of mapping delineates the area as an English dominion. R.M.

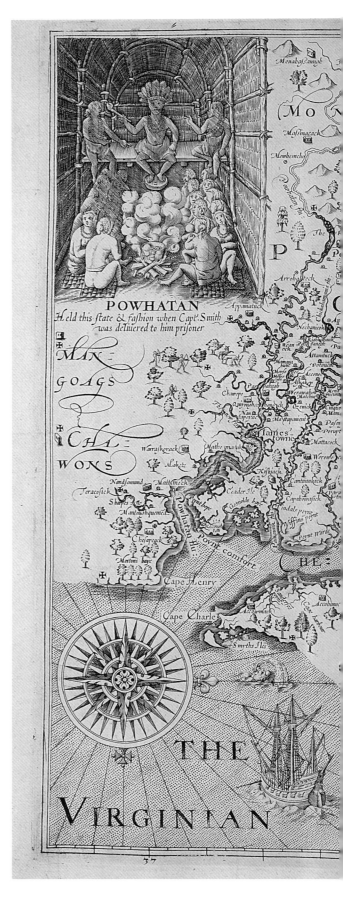

VIRGINIA

Maſſaw- Massawomeck Omecks

MANN AHOACKS

HONI SOIT QVI MAL Y PENSE

The Saſquesahanougs
are a Gyant like peo-ple &
thus a tyred

SASQVEHANOVGH

WHATAN

PEACK BAY

KVSKARAWA OKS

TOCK WOGHS

ATOV ANACC HVKES

and halfe

Scale of Leagues   Leagues

Diſcouered and diſcribed by Captayn Iohn Smith
Grauen by William Hole

SEA

38   39   40   41

151

66

Sir Thomas Button (*c*.1575–1634)

UNIDENTIFIED ARTIST, *c*.1615

Oil on canvas, 1005 × 865mm
Inscribed: NON MIHI SED PATRIA [Not for myself, but my country]
In the collection of Lieutenant Colonel Rhodri Traherne

Thomas Button was a naval officer who saw action in Ireland and the West Indies before being selected to lead Prince Henry's expedition to find the Northwest Passage in 1612. For over a century expeditions sponsored by the English crown had searched for a route to the prosperous trading nations of Asia that avoided the Spanish- and Portuguese-dominated trade routes to the south. The opening up of a new route would bring great riches to England and personal glory to the Prince.

Henry was anxious to avoid a repeat of the mutiny that had ended Henry Hudson's expedition the previous year. In a letter dated 5 April 1612, he issued strict orders to Button in his role as commander of the two ships, the *Resolution* and the *Discovery*. Alongside detailed navigational instructions, provided by the Prince's tutor, Edward Wright, the letter includes strongly worded guidance on religious devotion and the maintenance of the crew's behaviour:

> Let there be a religious care dailie throughout your shippes ... Especiallie provide that the blessed daies wch hee hath sanctified unto his service be Christianlike observed with godlie meditacions ... Let noe quarelling or prophane speeches, noe swearing or blaspheming of his Holie name, noe drunkenness or lewde behaviour passe unpunished, for fear of his most heavie indignacon.
> (Quoted in Rundall 1849, p.82)

The expedition reached uncharted areas of present-day Hudson Bay in Canada but failed to find the fabled passage. The *Resolution* was abandoned after being crushed by ice and many of the crew perished in the harsh conditions. Unable to endure a second winter, Button returned to Chatham in September 1613, almost a year after the death of the Prince.

This portrait was painted shortly after his return, possibly to commemorate his appointment as admiral in 1614 or his knighthood in 1616. He is presented as a man of refinement and action. His costume is expensive and elegant, consisting of a doublet decorated with an oak leaf pattern of gold embroidery, green breeches and a silk sash decorated with stars. His sword, gorget (neck piece) and baton identify him as a military commander and the globe under his left hand signifies his distinction as an explorer. Small inset images show a landscape with a passage of water to the left and a ship to the right, perhaps an allusion to his expedition in search of the Northwest Passage. R.M.

PROVENANCE
Presumably commissioned by the sitter; by descent in the Button family until acquired by the Traherne family in the eighteenth century; thus by descent.

LITERATURE
Steegman 1962, p.87; Thrush, 'Button, Thomas', ODNB 2004.

67

*Certaine Errors in Navigation Detected
and Corrected by Edw: Wright*

EDWARD WRIGHT (1561–1615),
printed by Felix Kingsto[n], London, 2nd edition, 1610

Printed book; 660 pages, spine height 190mm (open at dedication)
New College, Oxford (BT3.179.10.(1))

Edward Wright was an important mathematician and cartographer, who was employed first as a tutor, and then as librarian to Prince Henry. In this position he built up the Prince's remarkable scientific library, which was probably housed at Richmond Palace and consisted of modern and historical books on mathematics, cosmography, navigation, geography and other scientific subjects (see Birrell 1986, pp.32, 40). The library was intended as a practical tool, and reflected a considerable interest in these subjects on the part of the Prince and members of his household. Wright also made, or had made, a group of navigational and cartographical instruments for the Prince, including an extraordinary model of a 'Coelestial Automaton' (BL Cotton Titus B VIII; BL Sloane 651; Wilks 1987, pp.201–3). These instruments attested to both the ingenuity of their designer and maker, and to the dedication of the Prince to a branch of learning with particular contemporary significance.

The first edition of Wright's *Certaine Errors* was published in 1599, with a dedication to the Earl of Cumberland. Its most significant contribution was to set out the mathematical basis of Mercator's projection, which eventually became the standard map of the world used by navigators. The second edition of *Certaine Errors*, published in 1610, greatly expanded on the first, and was dedicated to Prince Henry. Wright explains that he was inspired to produce this edition by the building of the Prince's ship, the *Prince Royal*, in case 'it shall fall out to be either your Highnesse pleasure, or the desire of any other honourable and worthie Patriots … to set them foorth, for the discouerie of strange and forraine lands and nations yet unknown' (p.7). Wright's work certainly did make more accurate navigation possible, particularly his demonstration of the difference between magnetic north and true north. In spite of his significance both in the Prince's court and in the wider world of navigation, Wright did not achieve financial success and was described during Henry's lifetime as 'a very poor man' (CSP 14/71/47, cited in Wilks 1987, p.26). C.M.

LITERATURE
Waters 1978, pp.220–5; Wilks 1987, pp.80, 201–3, 259–60; Apt, 'Wright, Edward', ODNB 2004.

Certaine
ERRORS IN
NAVIGATION,
Detected and Corrected
By Edw: Wright.
with
Many additions that were
not in the former edi-
tion as appeareth
in the next
pages.
Printed by Felix Kingston at London 1610.

TO THE HIGH
AND MIGHTIE PRINCE
HENRY, Prince of *VVales*, Duke of
Cornwall, Earle of *Chester*, &c. and eldest
Son to our soueraigne Lord I A M E S,
King of great *Britaine, France*
and *Ireland.*

AS your Highnesse
honourable ac-
coūt of the Art of
Nauigation, hath
latelie appeared
to the world, in
building such a
goodly & prince-
ly Royall Ship, as
in the opinion of men of skill in that kinde,
may iustly be compared with the best that
floateth on the seas in these daies: So hauing
hitherto spent the best of my time in such
studies as containe the first and principall

✻ 3   grounds

68

Christian IV, King of Denmark (1577–1648)

Attributed to JACOB VAN DER DOORT

(*fl.*1606 – d.1629), *c.*1606

Watercolour and bodycolour on vellum laid on to card, 57 × 46mm,
set in a silver frame pierced and chased with berried foliage
(frame not illustrated)

Buccleuch Collection (21/7)

Christian IV succeeded to the Danish throne
at the age of eleven in 1588. His reign of almost
sixty years was a period of exceptional military
and cultural activity; he expanded the navy,
engaged in European conflicts and left a legacy
of artistic patronage, magnificent buildings
and new towns. Through his sister, Anne of
Denmark, Christian IV was Prince Henry's
uncle. His delight in regal display and his
ambitious foreign policy were of considerable
influence on the Prince.

Christian IV's visit to London in 1606 was
one of the great state occasions of the Jacobean
period and it was on this occasion that the
twelve-year-old Prince made his first appearance
in the tilt yard. Following a display of Christian
IV's skill jousting against Lord Effingham and
the Earl of Arundel, the Prince 'shewed himself
in his armour, gallantly mounted, and a hart as
powerful as any, though that his youth denied
strength' (Henry Roberts, 'England's farewell
to Christian the fourth', 1606, quoted in Nichols
1828, p.80). Henry's military interests were
further encouraged by Christian IV with the
presentation of a rapier and dagger enamelled

and set with diamonds. Henry appears to be
wearing the rapier in Robert Peake the Elder's
portrait of *c.*1610 (see cat. 45; Wilks 1987, p.204).

The present work may have been brought to
England by Christian IV during the state visit
of 1606. He wears the insignia of the Order of
the Garter, with which he was invested in 1603,
with a monstrance-like Star and an elaborate,
possibly customised, Lesser George (sash badge)
hanging from an unusual pearl sash. Jacob
van der Doort was a Dutch artist who had
a peripatetic career throughout the courts of
northern Europe. His service was recommended
to James I by Christian IV in 1624 and a full-
length painting by him of Charles I was recorded
in the Duke of Buckingham's collection in York
House (identified as the painting now in the
Royal Collection). Jacob's brother, Abraham
van der Doort, was the Keeper of Charles I's
collection from 1625 to 1640. He had earlier
been given a position at Prince Henry's court
as Keeper of the Cabinet Room but was deprived
of the post by Henry's early death. He was instead
commissioned to sculpt the wax hands and head
for the Prince's funeral effigy (see cat. 74). R.M.

PROVENANCE
In the collection of the Duke of
Buccleuch from before 1896;
thereafter by descent.

LITERATURE
Colding 1953, p.118; Millar 1962,
pp.325–6; Wilks 1987, p.259; Heiberg
1988, no. 61, p.33; Lloyd 2008,
pp.38–41.

69

Frederick, Elector Palatine, later Frederick V,
King of Bohemia (1596–1632)
ISAAC OLIVER, 1612–13

Watercolour and bodycolour on vellum
laid onto a playing card, 54 × 42mm
The Royal Collection (RCIN 420043)

The husband chosen for Princess Elizabeth was a matter of great political significance. Royal marriages were primarily about political allegiance, and James I was concerned to use the asset he had in his daughter to further his aim of European peace. This meant that he considered both Catholic and Protestant candidates, but Prince Henry was strongly in favour of a Protestant alliance. In the end a Protestant choice was made, that of Frederick V, Count Palatine of the Rhine and Elector of the Holy Roman Empire. Frederick was the leader of the Protestant Union, an association of German princes and free cities, and his betrothal to Elizabeth was part of a wider alliance that James made with the Protestant Union early in 1612. In spite of Frederick's significance politically – which was to increase dramatically but temporarily in 1619 when he was to accept the throne of Bohemia – Queen Anne regarded him as beneath her daughter in terms of rank and disapproved of the match. Elizabeth herself, supported by Henry, was happy with the proposal.

Frederick arrived in England on 16 October 1612, accompanied by a large party of followers and Count Henry of Nassau, the younger brother of Maurice (cat. 70). He and Princess Elizabeth seem to have liked each other from the start, and it was reported that Frederick 'seems to take delight in nothing but her companie and conversation' (John Chamberlain to Sir Ralph Winwood, 3 November 1612, cited in Strong 1986, p.176). Prince Henry was heavily involved in organising festivities and entertaining the guests: 'he was wonderfully busie in providing, and giving order for everything belonging to his care, for his Sisters Marriage, advancing the same by all meanes possible, keeping also his Highnes the *Palsgrave* [Frederick] company, so much as conveniently he could, together with Count *Henry*' (*The Life and Death* 1641, p.33; see cat. 81).

This miniature appears to have been based on one by Nicholas Hilliard (Victoria and Albert Museum, London). It would seem likely that King James commissioned Hilliard to depict his new son-in-law, and that Isaac Oliver, perhaps commissioned by Queen Anne or Princess Elizabeth, produced this version.
C.M.

PROVENANCE
Probably in the Royal Collection since at least the second half of the nineteenth century (see Reynolds 1999); by descent.

LITERATURE
Reynolds 1999, p.97, no. 61.

70

Maurice of Nassau (1567–1625)

MICHIEL JANSZ. VAN MIEREVELT
and STUDIO, *c.*1607

Oil on panel, 457 × 457mm
Private Collection

Maurice of Nassau became Stathouder of Holland and Zealand following the assassination of his father, William of Orange, in 1584. He would also become Prince of Orange following the death of his older brother, Prince William, in 1618. Maurice was perhaps the foremost general of the age. Under his command the Dutch rebellion against Spanish Habsburg rule developed into a coherent and ultimately successful war of independence. His military successes were due to a combination of his gift for strategy and his reorganisation of the Dutch force into a highly trained army.

This portrait of Prince Maurice is one of over a hundred versions that were produced by the studio of Mierevelt. The original was commissioned by the city of Delft in 1607 but Maurice's stature ensured a high demand for his likeness within the Netherlands and internationally. He wears an orange sash of command and the gilded armour with a chased laurel-leaf design that he received from the States General in recognition of his victory at the Battle of Nieuwpoort in 1600.

A full-length version of this portrait was sent to Prince Henry in 1610. Alongside Henri IV of France, Maurice was Henry's hero among the princes of Europe. His tutor, Adam Newton, wrote that those intimate with the Prince 'did obserue by the many questions his Hyghnes did make towcheing the cownte Moris his person, his great actions, his recreations, his paseing of his time, that the prince did take delight to heare Honnor of him and to approve hit' (letter to Sir Edward Conway, quoted in Strong 1986, p.73).

Maurice was keen to cultivate Henry as an important future ally. English forces had made a significant contribution to Maurice's campaigns and he was eager to maintain English support despite the cessation of hostilities between England and Spain in 1604. To this end Maurice actively encouraged Henry's martial interests by sending the Dutch engineer Abraham van Nyevelt to tutor the Prince in the construction of military fortifications. R.M.

PROVENANCE
Early provenance unknown; Sykes family at Sledmere House since before 1902 (1902 inventory); thence by descent.

LITERATURE
Strong 1986, p.73; Wilks 1987, p.164, p.211; Wilks 2007, pp.180–211; Jansen 2011, pp.109–26.

71

Henri IV of France (1553–1610)

HENDRICK GOLTZIUS (1558–1617),
published by Paul de la Houve, *c.*1600

Engraving on paper, 350 × 253mm
Lettered: *HGoltzius sculp,* in lower left corner, and *Avec privil; du Roy /es /Paul. de la Houve./excudebat/au Palais,* at right; below, in four lines of French, *Ce grand Roy que tuvoys est remply de la grace ...*

The British Museum, London (R,6.76)

Henri IV of France was one of the most powerful rulers in Europe and Prince Henry's godfather. As the King of Navarre, he was leader of the Protestant Huguenots in the French wars of religion. He succeeded to the throne of France on the death of Henri III in 1589, and converted to Catholicism in 1593 in order to unite his people. Famous for his military prowess, religious tolerance and the prosperity and cultural developments of his reign, he took a close interest in his godson.

Henri IV gave Prince Henry a number of presents that must have particularly appealed to the young Prince's interests. In 1603, the year of the Stuart royal family's move from Scotland to England, the French king sent Pierre Antoine Bourdon, Seigneur de St Antoine, to teach Henry the skilled art of horsemanship as practised at the French court, as well as six horses. M. de St Antoine was to bring further horses as gifts from France, and remained in England to serve eventually under Charles I

(with whom he is depicted in the famous equestrian portrait by Van Dyck in the Royal Collection). Henri also gave the Prince gifts of armour (1607) and sent a fencing master or tumbler (Strong 1986, p.64). Their correspondence suggests affection as well as respect, and when the French king was murdered in 1610, Henry was apparently genuinely distressed, declaring 'my second father is dead' (Birch 1760, pp.189–90, cited in Strong 1986, p.76).

Prince Henry owned a painted portrait of Henri IV, which hung in St James's Palace along with one of Maurice of Nassau (Strong 1986, p.191; Wilks 1987, p.164). Timothy Wilks has pointed out that there was also an equestrian portrait of Henri IV in Greenwich Palace during Prince Henry's lifetime, which, along with prints of similar portraits, may well have been an influence on the equestrian portrait by Robert Peake the Elder of the Prince (Wilks 2007, p.173; cat. 28). C.M.

PROVENANCE
Pierre Mariette II (signed and dated 1680 on the reverse); [...]; acquired by the British Museum, London, by 1837.

LITERATURE
Hollstein 193.II; Bartsch III.53.173; Strauss 1977, no. 357.

'Our Rising Sun is set': the Death of Prince Henry

The autumn of 1612 was a time of mounting anticipation and activity at the Stuart court, as the marriage of Princess Elizabeth to Frederick V, Elector Palatine, approached. Prince Henry was much involved in organising the welcome and entertainments for the young Elector and his entourage of European nobles, and in planning the festivities, including masques and tournaments, which would be part of the forthcoming wedding celebrations.[1]

In the midst of all the preparations, on 10 October, Henry fell ill with a fever. He was treated by his physician, Dr John Hammond, and, although he appeared visibly ill, continued against medical advice with his usual activities. On 25 October the Prince fainted and was finally forced to take to his bed. The King sent his own physician, Theodore Turquet de Mayerne, to attend him, and over the course of the next twelve days at least four more doctors joined Mayerne and Hammond. There was much debate about his treatment but nothing seemed to effect any real improvement. The King visited regularly and the royal family visited together on 1 November, when Prince Charles handed him a small bronze horse, presumably to try to comfort his brother (see cat. 53).

Finally, after much evidently excruciating suffering, on the evening of 6 November, Prince Henry 'quietly, gently, and patiently ... yielded up his Spirit unto his Immortall Maker'.[2] Henry's family were distraught. The Queen's grief was so great that it was thought to put her life in danger, and Princess Elizabeth went without food for two days and cried ceaselessly.[3] Of James I, it was reported months later that 'The King is doing all he can to forget his grief, but it is not sufficient; for many a time it will come over him suddenly and even in the midst of the most important discussions he will burst out with "Henry is dead, Henry is dead."'[4] The grief was widespread and deeply felt, both by those who knew Henry and those for whom he had simply represented hope for the future. Phineas Pett, Henry's shipwright, wrote:

Henry, Prince of Wales, Daniel Mytens
after Isaac Oliver, *c*.1628 (detail of cat. 82)

'Our royal and most loving master, departed his life, not only to the loss and utter undoing of his poor servants, but to the general loss of all Christendom of the protestant religion.'[5]

The overwhelming sense of loss and the rapidity of the Prince's decline led to rumours of malpractice on the part of the doctors, or, worse, of poisoning. In an attempt to rebut this, an autopsy was undertaken and Mayerne, the chief physician at his bedside, circulated the results and a detailed account of the progress of the Prince's illness. This quashed the rumours and vindicated the doctors, and nearly three centuries later, enabled typhoid fever to be diagnosed. The Prince's body lay in state and then, on 7 December, a funeral took place at Westminster Abbey that outdid even that of Elizabeth I in magnificence. In addition to the 2,000 official mourners, the streets were lined with the grieving populace, who, at the sight of the Prince's remarkably life-like effigy, lying on top of his coffin, let forth 'a fearefull outcrie ... as if they felt at the present their own ruine in that loss ... [their] streaming eyes made knowen howe much inwardly their harts did bleed'.[6] Parallel funerals were held on the same day in Bristol, Cambridge and Oxford.

Within twenty-four hours of the Prince's death an elegy on the subject was registered at Stationers' Hall, the first of approximately fifty publications of mourning poetry produced within the next couple of years, including anthologies of poetry by multiple authors.[7] Elegiac music was also composed, some of which took as its theme the biblical account of the death of Absalom, son of King David. The outpouring of poetry and music again completely eclipsed that for any previous English or Scottish monarch.

When the marriage of Princess Elizabeth and the Elector Palatine eventually did take place, on 14 February 1613, it was with much rejoicing but an awareness of a prince lost. Charles, Duke of York, then became the new focus of attention both in Britain and abroad, with foreign courts seeking to arrange allegiances with James I by means of a royal marriage. It was decided, however, that Charles would not step straight into Henry's shoes; instead of being given his own household, he was brought more closely into James I's court, and it was another four years before he was made Prince of Wales.

For many years, Henry remained in the collective memory as a paradigm of princely virtue. Several biographies were written and circulated in manuscript.[8] These were not published until Charles's reign, when the accounts of Henry's noble and martial qualities were used both to inspire the King and to criticise him. Charles himself clearly held his brother's memory dear; he commissioned a posthumous portrait of Henry from his court painter Daniel Mytens, which he hung in his bedroom, and subsequently another portrait by Sir Anthony van Dyck, showing Henry wearing his spectacular Greenwich armour (fig. 9). Both during Charles's reign and subsequently there has been much speculation about the course that British history would have taken under Henry IX, rather than Charles I; this is unknowable but it seems likely that it would not have been a peaceful one. C.M.

1 *The Life and Death* 1641, pp.28, 33.
2 *The Life and Death* 1641, p.75.
3 CSP *Venetian, 1610–13*, XII (1905), pp.441–54
4 CSP *Venetian, 1610–13*, XII (1905), pp.471–88.
5 *Autobiography*, p.100.
6 Kew, National Archives, SP 14/71, fol. 128r.
7 Goldring 2007, p.280.
8 *The Life and Death* (1641); Cornwallis 1641; W.H. 1634.

72

Sir Theodore de Mayerne (1573–1655)

UNIDENTIFIED ARTIST,

probably after 1625

Oil on canvas, 757 × 604mm
Inscribed around the inner edge of the oval, bottom:
AL BONÆ RECVN. MAG BRIT. IAC ET CAR ARCHIATR
National Portrait Gallery, London (NPG 6538)

Theodore de Mayerne was probably the most famous and admired doctor in Europe during his lifetime. In 1600 he was made Physician-in-Ordinary to Henri IV of France, but further progress to the position of Chief Physician was blocked by his religion (Mayerne was a Protestant) and his involvement in medical controversies. When his patron, Henri IV, was murdered in 1610, Mayerne decided to emigrate to England. He had visited England in 1606 and had impressed James I. In 1611, shortly after his return to this country, he was appointed Principal Physician to the King; the appointment marked the beginning of an exceptionally successful career. In addition to his work for the royal family, Mayerne had a thriving practice treating members of the court.

When Prince Henry fell ill with a fever in October 1612, he was initially treated by his own physician, Dr John Hammond. As the illness became more serious, however, the King's concern led him to send Mayerne to the Prince's bedside. A succession of additional doctors arrived after Mayerne, each making their own suggestions. Eventually the King offered to dismiss all the others and give Mayerne sole responsibility, but the physician declined, stating that 'it should never bee said in after Ages, that hee had killed the King's elder Sonne' (see cat. 81).

The treatment consisted mainly of the administering of 'juleps' (a sweet drink), cordials and 'clysters' (enemas); Mayerne described one of the juleps as containing, among other ingredients, 'behazar, unicorn, pearls, bone of stag's heart, &c.' (Moore 1882, p.9). The Prince was also bled, although not as frequently as Mayerne would have liked. As the illness progressed the remedies became more desperate. On the night of the tenth day, pigeons were applied to Henry's shaved head; on the night of the eleventh day, a cockerel was split and

applied to his feet. Finally, the Prince died two hours after midnight on 6 November.

This striking portrait dates from after Prince Henry's death, but Mayerne's depiction in a red robe like a Roman toga has echoes of portraits of the Prince and members of his circle (for example, cat. 44). By the time this work was painted, the interest in classical antiquity that had been growing during Henry's lifetime had become well established, and this portrait would have signalled both Mayerne's learning and his interest in, and knowledge of, the most sophisticated visual culture of the day. He died at the age of eighty-three, leaving a huge fortune and many manuscripts, which testify to his medical and other interests, including cookery, travel, alchemy and the materials and techniques of artists. C.M.

PROVENANCE
Christie's South Kensington,
9 March 2000 (lot 3); purchased
by The Weiss Gallery; purchased
by the National Portrait Gallery,
London, 2000.

LITERATURE
The Weiss Gallery, *A Life Delineat'd*,
2000, no.13.

73

Certain observations upon the opening of the body of Prince Henry, 7 Nov 1612

After THEODORE TURQUET DE MAYERNE, before 1631

313 × 208mm

The British Library, London (Cotton Vesp.F.ix., fol. 136)

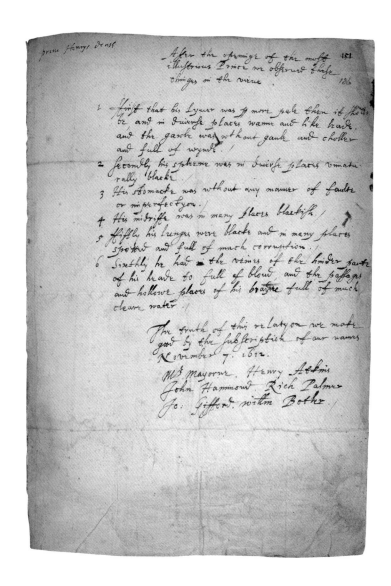

Prince Henry's death came as a terrible shock to the royal family, court and country. Inevitably there was a general urge to blame someone, and Theodore de Mayerne, as the chief physician at his deathbed, was accused of malpractice and even of poisoning. As Roger Coke wrote later in the century, 'it was observed, that poisoning was never more in Fashion than at this time' (Coke 1694, I, p.61). Mayerne wrote two extensive, detailed accounts of the progress of the Prince's illness and the treatment applied, one in French and one in Latin, in order to exonerate himself from these charges. Implicit in his accounts is the judgement that Henry himself was to a degree the cause of his own death, through his over-exertion in the heat of the preceding summer. Although he held some views on medicine that were unorthodox for the time, like most physicians of his day Mayerne believed that health was dependent on maintaining the balance of the four humours – blood, phlegm, choler (yellow bile) and melancholy (black bile) – each of which had various properties, combining heat or cold with wetness or dryness. He asserted that Henry had an excessively warm temperament, made worse by his behaviour: 'the Prince continually fatigued his body by exercises and violent occupations, hunting in the heat of the day, riding and playing tennis, and in consequence he often heated his blood extraordinarily' (Moore 1882, p.6). He also noted that the Prince ate excessive amounts of fruit, fish and oysters, and that he cooled himself down immediately after eating by plunging into the river and swimming for several hours. Mayerne went on to record, 'After all these irregularities he fell ill at Richmond on the 10th of October 1612'.

Mayerne also disseminated the results of the autopsy, which had been carried out by the six physicians who had attended Prince Henry on the day after his death. This is one of a number of surviving early copies. The autopsy in effect cleared Mayerne's name; as Francis Bacon wrote, 'Fame, which, as Tacitus says, is more tragical with respect to the deaths of princes, added a suspicion of poison; but as no signs of this appeared, especially in his stomach, which uses to be chiefly affected by poison, this report soon vanished' (Devey 1866, pp.493–5). In addition, Mayerne procured three written statements supporting his treatment of the Prince: from the King, the Privy Council, and the Gentlemen of the Prince's Household (Nance 2001, pp.181–2). Mayerne's detailed notes allowed another physician, 270 years later, to diagnose Prince Henry's illness as typhoid fever. C.M.

PROVENANCE
Sir Robert Cotton (1571–1631); by descent to Sir John Cotton (d.1702); transferred to the nation, 1701; transferred to the British Museum, London, 1753.

LITERATURE
Moore 1882; Nance 2001, pp.181–2; Trevor-Roper 2006, pp.171–7.

74

The Effigy of Henry, Prince of Wales

RICHARD NORRIS (*fl.* early 17th century), 1612

Pine or fir with iron nails, loops and screws, 1580 × 420 × 180mm

The Dean and Chapter of Westminster

Following Prince Henry's death, his bedchamber and the three rooms that led to it were hung with black cloth, and the coffin, draped in a pall of black velvet, was placed under a black velvet canopy (see McNamara in Wilks 2007, pp.266–7). The Prince's body lay in state for a month until his funeral on 7 December. For the purposes of the funeral procession and the funeral itself, an effigy of the Prince was made to lie on top of the coffin. The body, made out of wood with jointed arms and legs, was made by Richard Norris; the head and hands were made by Abraham van der Doort, a wax modeller and servant of Prince Henry's who was later to become Charles I's Surveyor of Pictures. Robert Peake the Elder's son, William, made a gilded staff. The effigy was dressed in the robes worn by Henry at his creation as Prince of Wales in 1610.

The effigy was much admired and was evidently felt to be a strong likeness: 'the goodly image of that lovely prince ... did so liuely represent his person, as that it did not onely draw teares from the severest beholder, but cawsed a fearefull outcrie among the people as if they felt at the present their owne ruine in that loss' (Isaac Wake, TNA SP 14/71, fol. 128r, cited in Strong 1986, p.1). This is the first occasion on which an effigy is known to have been made in England for the son of a reigning monarch, as opposed to a monarch or consort, and its manufacture was another sign of the exceptional circumstances surrounding the life and death of the Prince.

The after-life of the effigy was not so glorious. It was put on public display in Westminster Abbey, and the Prince's robes were soon stolen. By the eighteenth century, along with the other royal funeral effigies in the Abbey, it was so battered that collectively they were known as the 'Ragged Regiment' (Vertue, *Notebooks*, I, p.158). By the late nineteenth century the head had disappeared, and today the remains show the effects of woodworm infestation. In spite of elaborate plans, recorded by the Venetian ambassador Foscarini (*CSP Venetian, 1610–13*, XII, p.469), no monument was ever built in the Abbey for Prince Henry, but his effigy can be seen as symbolising both his significance in life and the obscurity into which his reputation has faded in the centuries since his death. C.M.

PROVENANCE
Westminster Abbey, since the funeral of Prince Henry in 1612.

LITERATURE
Harvey and Mortimer 1994, pp.59–62; Goldring 2007, pp.280–300.

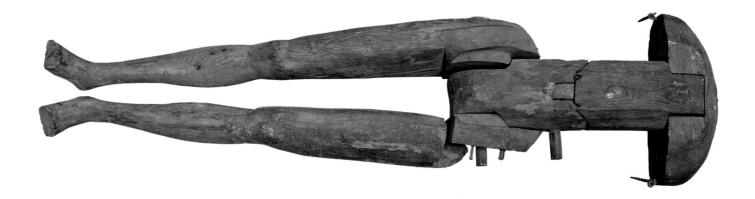

75

The Hearse of Henry, Prince of Wales

WILLIAM HOLE, 1612

Engraving on paper, 320 × 228mm
Inscribed with a Latin verse by Hugo Holland
and an English verse by George Chapman

The British Museum, London (1870,0514.2896)

This print records the appearance of the hearse
that carried Prince Henry's body and his effigy
to Westminster Abbey. It has been suggested
that the hearse may have been designed by Inigo
Jones, or possibly by Costantino de' Servi, an
Italian architect and painter in the service of
Henry (Peacock 1982, pp.1–5, cited in Goldring
2007, p.298, note 48). The canopy is shown
covered with royal coats of arms, and flags with
heraldic devices, representing the Prince's
various titles: Prince of Wales, Duke of Cornwall
and Earl of Chester. A scroll is inscribed with his
motto, '*Fax mentis honestae Gloria*', which can be
translated as 'Glory is the light of a noble mind'.
The second state of this print, with an additional
title, is usually found affixed in the front of
George Chapman's *Epicede or Funerall Song: On
the most disastrous Death, of the High-borne Prince
of Men, Henry Prince of Wales ...* (1613), and it
may have been made for this publication (see
Goldring 2007, pp.286–7).

There is only one earlier English print known
of a funeral hearse, that of Sir Philip Sidney (see
Goldring 2007, pp.286–7). It may be that in
making this engraving, William Hole had Sidney
in mind. He certainly held a similar place in the
popular imagination of the Elizabethan court to
that held by Henry at the Stuart court: as an
exemplar of the promising, militant Protestant
knight cut down in his prime.

Henry's funeral, on 7 December 1612, was an
extraordinary occasion. In addition to the main
event in London, parallel funerals were held in
Bristol, Oxford and Cambridge. Over 2,000
official mourners walked in the procession to
Westminster Abbey, 400 more than accompanied
Elizabeth I's body in 1603. Music was provided
by fife and drums, usually only heard at military
funerals. The people of London lined the streets:

There was to bee seene an innumerable
multitude of all sorts of ages and degrees of men,
women and children, whose wonderfull sorrow
who is able to expresse? Some holding in their
heads, not being able to endure so sorrowfull
a sight, all mourning, which they expressed by
severall sorts of lamentation and sorrow, some
weeping, crying, howling, wringing of their
hands, others halfe dead, sounding, sighing
inwardly, others holding up their hands,
passionately bewayling so great a losse,
with Rivers, nay with an Ocean of teares.
(*The Life and Death ...* 1641, p.86) C.M.

76

Anne of Denmark in Mourning

UNIDENTIFIED ARTIST, *c.*1628–44

Oil on panel, 572 × 438mm

National Portrait Gallery, London (NPG 4656)

Queen Anne was, inevitably, devastated by her son's death. The Venetian ambassador recorded that she wept alone in her room, and that her grief was such that there were concerns for her health. The following April he noted that 'she cannot bear to hear it mentioned; nor does she ever recall it without tears and sighs' (*CSP Venetian, 1610–13*, XII, p.521). When Prince Charles was created Prince of Wales four years later she did not attend the ceremony, fearing that it would bring back painful memories of a previous occasion (Strong 1986, p.166).

Anne had been interested in and collected art, particularly portraiture, before Prince Henry's death. After his death she seems to have inherited paintings from him, and her collection expanded and developed in different directions (see Wilks 1997, pp.31–48, especially pp.41–5). She continued to sit for portraits to a range of different artists, particularly patronising the more sophisticated immigrant artists from the Low Countries who came to work in England. During her last illness she had religious paintings from her palace at Oatlands transferred to Hampton Court, where she was confined until her death (Meikle and Payne, 'Anne of Denmark', ODNB 2008).

Recent dendrochronological analysis of the wood on which this portrait is painted indicates that the painting is posthumous, probably dating from the years between 1628 and 1644 (analysis undertaken as part of the Making Art in Tudor Britain project at the National Portrait Gallery). The quality of the work suggests that it was based on a portrait of the Queen, made in her lifetime but now lost, and it was certainly painted by an able artist. Unlike all the other known portraits of Anne, it shows her wearing deep mourning rather than her usual elaborate court dress (see, for example, cat. 4). This, combined with the provenance of the painting, suggests that it was commissioned by a close friend or member of her family, who wanted to commemorate not just the Queen herself, but also that particular moment in her life, likely to be the time of the death of Prince Henry.

C.M.

PROVENANCE
Possibly Elizabeth of Bohemia; possibly bequeathed to 1st Earl of Craven (or possibly to Prince Rupert, then bequeathed to Ruperta Howe, and purchased at her sale by 1st Earl of Craven); collection of the Earls of Craven, Coombe Abbey, by 1866 (cat. no. 14); by descent to Cornelia, Countess of Craven; sold Sotheby's, 15 January 1969 (lot 11); Leggatt Brothers; given by Dr Esmond S. de Beer to the National Portrait Gallery, London, 1969.

LITERATURE
Strong, *Tudor and Jacobean Portraits*, 1969, I, p.363.

168

77

Princess Elizabeth, Electress Palatine

UNIDENTIFIED ARTIST, 1613

Oil on panel, 784 × 622mm

National Portrait Gallery, London (NPG 5529)

After her early childhood in Scotland and subsequently at Coombe Abbey in Warwickshire (see cat. 8), Princess Elizabeth came to court late in 1608. She had lodgings at Hampton Court, Whitehall and Kew, and was able to see much more of her brother Henry, as well as the rest of her family. She and Henry developed a close and affectionate relationship, supported by frequent letters when they were apart. Henry's biographers testify to his fondness for his sister. The biographer 'W.H.' (possibly William Haydon) wrote that Henry 'loved her always so dearly, that hee desired to see her always by him' (W[illiam] H[Haydon], *The True Picture and Relation of Prince Henry* … Leiden, 1634, p.4). Francis Bacon recorded that he had 'an entire affection for his sister' (Bacon 1866, p.494). Henry was heavily involved in the preparations for Elizabeth's marriage to Frederick, Elector Palatine, when he was struck down by his final illness. The letter writer John Chamberlain recorded in a letter to Dudley Carleton, the English ambassador in Venice (12 November 1612) that 'the last wordes [Henry] spake in good sense (they say), were, Where is my deare sister?' (McClure 1939, I, p.390).

After Henry's death there was talk of delaying Elizabeth and Frederick's wedding until May (CSP *Venetian, 1610–13,* XII, no. 698) but in the event it took place on 14 February 1613, and inevitably Henry was still very much in everyone's minds. Nonetheless, an extraordinarily lavish spectacle was arranged, lasting many days, at a cost of £53,294 (Ribeiro 2005, p.351, note 22). Events included fireworks, a mock battle on the Thames (in which many of the participants were injured), processions, and a number of masques and plays. Among the latter was a performance of Shakespeare's *The Winter's Tale*, in which, co-incidentally, a prince dies, and (sixteen years later) a princess marries a prince of Bohemia, a country of which Frederick was later briefly to become king. It is difficult to believe, however, that any real parallels were being drawn with the actual events of the time; this would have been deeply insulting to James I, as it appears throughout most of the play that the suspicious and vengeful king is to blame for the death not just of his son but also of his wife and daughter.

Princess Elizabeth wore a wedding dress of cloth of silver, embroidered also with silver, so the dress shown in this portrait, with its coloured embroidery, is probably not the marriage gown. Yet the clear allusion to her British royal status in the royal coats of arms, lions, unicorns, and fleurs-de-lys of her lace standing collar and partlet (the lace around the neckline) suggest that the portrait was painted close to this event (Ribeiro 2005, pp.31–2). Around Elizabeth's left arm is tied a black armband, indicating that she is in mourning for Prince Henry. It seems likely that the black locket she wears pinned to her dress also contains a miniature of her dead brother. Elizabeth and Frederick's first son, born the following year, was named Frederick Henry after his father and Prince Henry. C.M.

PROVENANCE
Sotheby's, Gargrave House, 26–28 October 1982 (lot 51); purchased by the National Portrait Gallery, London, 1982.

LITERATURE
Ribeiro 2005, pp.30–2.

Elegies on the Death of Henry, Prince of Wales

78a

Lachrimae Lachrimarum or
The Distillation of Teares Shede
For the untymely Death of
The incomparable Prince Panaretvs

JOSUAH SYLVESTER (1562/3–1618),
2nd edition, printed by Humphrey Lownes,
London, 1613

Printed book; 34 pages, spine height 182mm
(open at page A2)
The British Library, London (G.18913)

78c

Three Elegies on the most lamented
Death of Prince Henrie

CYRIL TOURNEUR (d.1626),
JOHN WEBSTER (c.1578–1638?) and
THOMAS HEYWOOD (c.1573–1641),
printed for William Welbie, London, 1613
Printed book; 72 pages, spine height 190mm
(open at title page)
The British Library, London (1070.m.4.(3.))

78b

Two Elegies, consecrated to
the neuer dying memorie of
*Henry Prince of Wale*s

CHRISTOPHER BROOKE (c.1570–1628)
and WILLIAM BROWNE (1590/1–1645?),
printed by T.S. for Richard More, London, 1613

Printed book; 38 pages, spine height 176mm
(open at dedication)
The British Library, London (C.60.f.13)

78d

Teares on the Death of Moeliades

WILLIAM DRUMMOND OF
HAWTHORNDEN (1585–1649),
3rd edition, printed by Andro Hart,
Edinburgh, 1614

Printed book; 16 pages, spine height 272mm
(bound together with two other poems by the same
author, *Flowers of Sion* and *A Cypresse Grove*.
Edinburgh University Library, Special Collections
Department (De.4.54/2)

The death of Henry, Prince of Wales, led to an unprecedented outpouring of mourning literature. Elegiac poetry was published in single- and multiple-authored volumes; funeral sermons, ballads and madrigals were also printed. Altogether approximately fifty volumes were published within the first year or so after his death, far outnumbering the quantity of comparable literature produced, for example, following the death of Elizabeth I. As J. W. Williamson has written, 'A nation mourns its living symbols, those who stand more for *possibility* than for *actuality* ...' (Williamson 1978, p.173).

Among those who wrote poems were some of the most accomplished writers of the age, including John Donne, George Herbert, George Chapman and Thomas Campion. For some authors, such as Josuah Sylvester, the death of the Prince was a personal tragedy. Sylvester, a translator and poet, had dedicated translations to Prince Henry in 1605 and 1607, and had become the Prince's first court poet, for which he was granted a pension, in 1608. In addition to whatever personal sense of bereavement Sylvester might have felt, Prince Henry's death meant the loss of his income. For many others, including John Donne, who had probably not met the Prince, but whose *Elegy upon the untimely death of the incomparable Prince Henry* was included, along with others, in the third edition of Sylvester's *Lachrimae Lachrimarum*, Henry's death represented a shock to the nation and the symbolic loss of hope for the future. Poets could use elegies to explore wider ideas of loss and grief, both in the public and private spheres, and also to draw attention to themselves. By dedicating a poem to the King, another member

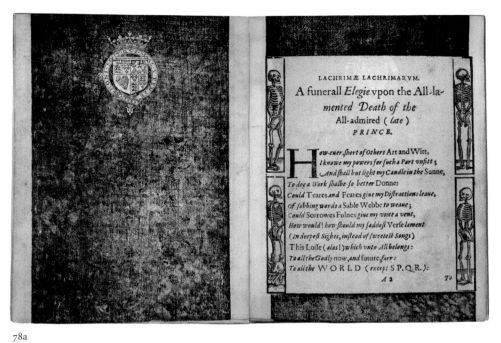

78a

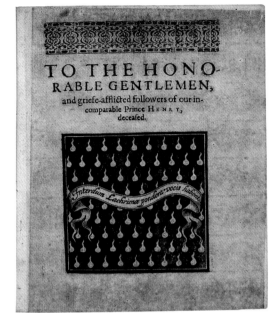

78b

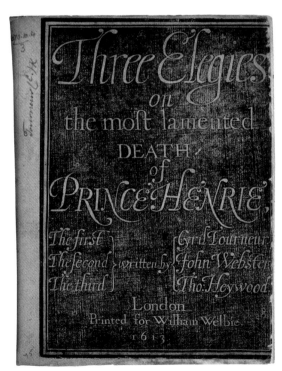

78c

78d

of the royal family or a prominent courtier, the author both paid respect to a grieving friend or relative of the Prince, and made a veiled plea for patronage.

The elegies took up many of the themes associated with Henry during his lifetime. William Drummond of Hawthornden cast Henry as Moeliades, the Arthurian figure he had represented in the *Barriers* of 1610 (in Ben Jonson's work spelled 'Meliadus'). Spelt Drummond's way, the name became, as the poet explained, an anagram of 'Miles a Deo' or 'Soldier for God', and Drummond's poem expressed the wish that Henry had died in the midst of a (crusading) battle rather than on his sickbed. Sylvester called Henry 'Prince Panaretus' meaning 'all virtue'. John Webster and Thomas Heywood, both, along with their co-author Cyril Tourneur, prominent playwrights for the Jacobean theatre, wrote of Henry as an actor on the world's stage, a metaphor that alluded not only to the Prince's importance, but also perhaps to an awareness that much of his life had been about playing a part.

A number of the books of mourning poetry published in response to Henry's death had strikingly decorated title pages and sometimes following pages as well. These were often made using woodcut prints, which were a cheap, quick form of printing (as opposed to engraving), but what makes these mourning volumes particularly special is their use of white-line woodcuts. In this process the lines are cut into the block rather than being left standing proud, so that when printed, the majority of the page is black, leaving outlines or lettering in white. This was an extremely unusual type of print at this date and its use seems to have been inspired by a feeling that simply creating poetry about Prince Henry's death was not enough; a new form of visual metaphor also had to be found that would suitably reflect the literary content of these volumes. At their simplest, these prints just recorded the title and names of the authors in white on black, as in the Tourneur, Webster and Heywood volume; Brooke and Browne's book has a more ambitious 'field of tears', representing the mourning of Henry's household; Sylvester's is the most ambitious of all, with each left-hand page printed entirely in black apart from the Prince's coat of arms, coronet and garter, while the right-hand pages carried the poem, bordered with skeletons and cadavers. William Drummond's volume does not use white-line woodcuts, but two shorter poems at the end are printed in the shapes of tomb monuments to the Prince. C.M.

78a
PROVENANCE
Rt Hon. Sir Thomas Grenville (1755–1846); bequeathed to the British Library, London, and received 1847.

LITERATURE
Payne, Foss and Rye, 1, vol. 4, p.704; Williamson 1978, p.179; Wilks 1987, pp.73–4; Snyder, 'Sylvester, Josuah', ODNB 2004; Pollnitz 2007, pp.27–8.

78b
PROVENANCE
Purchased by the British Library, London, 1859

LITERATURE
Williamson 1978, p.185; O'Callaghan, 'Brooke, Christopher', ODNB 2004; O'Callaghan, 'Browne, William', ODNB 2004

78c
PROVENANCE
Acquired by the British Library before 1837.

LITERATURE
Williamson 1978, p.182; Gunby, 'Tourneur, Cyril', ODNB 2004; Gunby, 'Webster, John', ODNB 2004; Kathman, 'Heywood, Thomas', ODNB 2004.

78d
PROVENANCE
Presented by the author to King James's College in Edinburgh, now the University of Edinburgh, 1630.

LITERATURE
MacDonald 1976, pp.3–7; Williamson 1978, pp.185–6.

79

Songs of Mourning: Bewailing the untimely death of Prince Henry

GIOVANNI COPRARIO (d.1626) and
THOMAS CAMPION (1567–1620),
printed by Thomas Snodham
for John Browne, 1613

Printed book; 20 pages, spine height 325mm
The British Library, London (k.2.g.8)

Music was an important element in Jacobean
court life, and a number of eminent musicians
were employed in various roles at Henry's court,
both before and after he became Prince of Wales.
Among these, the composer Alfonso Ferrabosco
(*c.*1575–1628) was employed to teach music to the
Prince from 1604, and the composer and organist
John Bull (*c.*1562–1628) was in charge of Henry's
musicians from the time of his creation as Prince
of Wales. Payments in the Prince's accounts
indicate various kinds of musical activity, and
music was an especially important component
in court masques (Strong 1986, pp.172–3). The
biographer 'W.H.' (possibly William Haydon)
recorded that Henry 'loued Musicke, and namely
good consorts of Instruments and voices ioyned
together' (*The True Picture and Relation of Prince
Henry*, 1634, p.31). It seems most likely, however,
that his real preference, as several commentators
noted, was for the martial music of fife and drums.

The Prince's death inspired not just elegiac
poetry, but also a significant amount of mourning
music. This volume, dedicated to the Elector
Palatine, contains a series of songs, to be
accompanied by a lute or viol, addressed to the
King, Queen, Prince Charles, Princess Elizabeth,
the Elector Palatine, 'the most disconsolate
Great Brittaine' and 'the world'. The words
were written by the poet and musician Thomas
Campion, and the music composed by Giovanni
Coprario, an English composer who had changed
his name from John Cooper after a visit to Italy.
Coprario worked for the Earl of Salisbury and
both he and Campion were involved after Henry's
death with the celebrations surrounding the
wedding of Princess Elizabeth and the Elector
Palatine in 1613; Campion wrote *The Lords'
Masque*, and Coprario was in the party that
accompanied the couple to Heidelberg.

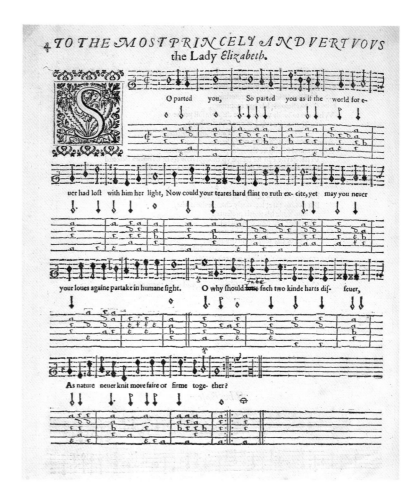

Other music mourning Henry's death
included an anthem for the Prince's funeral,
'Know ye not', by Thomas Tomkins (1572–1656)
and the elegy 'Fair Britain Isle' by William Byrd
(1539/40–1623). In addition to elegies that named
the Prince, a number of pieces were composed
shortly after his death – often in a fashionable
Italianate style – that took as their text the
biblical lament of King David for his son
Absalom. Although they do not mention Henry
by name it seems very likely, given the date and
the theme, that these were also intended as
elegies for him. Robert Ramsey (*c.*1595–1644),
Thomas Tomkins and Thomas Weelkes (d.1623)
were among those who wrote settings for words
that must have been particularly moving for
King James: '[When David heard that Absalom
was slain, he] went up to the chamber over the
gate, and wept: and [...] thus he said, O my son
Absalom, my son, my son Absalom! Would God
I had died for thee, O Absalom, my son, my son!'
(2 Samuel 18: 33). C.M.

PROVENANCE
Purchased by the British Library,
London, 1844.

LITERATURE
Pulver 1927 (57), pp.101–2; Parry
1981, pp.89–91; Irving, 'Coprario,
John', ODNB 2004.

80

Charles, Duke of York

ROBERT PEAKE THE ELDER, 1613

Oil on canvas, 1549 × 864mm
Inscribed: *CAROLE, TE MVSAE NAM TV DIGNATVS VTRVMQ/*
CEPIMVS HOSPITIO, PINXIMVS, OBSEQVIO/Academiam inuisens
Aᵒ Regni Paterni/Angliae 10ᵒ, die Martij 4ᵒ, cooptatus est/in ordinem Magistrorum,
admissusQ/hoc in Senatu, per Valentinum/Carey Procancellarium

University of Cambridge

Prince Henry's death left the twelve-year-old Charles as heir to the throne, and the attention of the court and the country as a whole soon refocused on the younger brother. Two weeks after his sister Elizabeth's marriage to Frederick, Elector Palatine, Charles travelled with the couple to Cambridge where he received the degree of Master of Arts. To commemorate this visit, the university commissioned this portrait of the Prince. The artist's receipt for payment of £13 6s. 8d from the Vice-Chancellor, Valentine Carey (or Carew, d.1626) survives, dated 10 July 1613. The commission and the occasion that it commemorates are also recorded on the painting, on the fictive slip of paper apparently pinned to the curtain to the Prince's right. In Latin, it has been translated as: 'Charles, we the Muses, since you deigned to agree to both, have both welcomed you as our guest and painted you in humble duty. Visiting the University in the 10th year of his father's reign over England, on 4 March, he was enrolled in the ranks of the Masters and admitted in this Senate House by Valentine Carey Vice-Chancellor' (Goodison 1955, p.117).

Robert Peake the Elder's portrait deploys all his most spectacular techniques in rendering jewels, embroidery, lace and rich textiles. But the composition – the Prince standing beside a draped table with curtains behind – is very traditional, even old-fashioned, compared with the portraits Peake had produced of Prince Henry. This presumably reflects the wishes of the patron; a composition of this type may perhaps have been thought to be most suitable for the relatively conservative university context. X-radiography has revealed that there is another portrait underneath; either the artist re-used an unwanted canvas, or he made significant changes to his original composition during painting.

Although Peake had painted Charles before (for example, cat. 9), the magnificence of this portrait and indeed the circumstances that prompted its commission reflect the Prince's newly enhanced status. He was not to be created Prince of Wales until 1616 (when Peake was paid for a further three portraits of him), but this portrait marks the beginning of the construction of his image as a worthy successor to the much-lamented Prince Henry. There is nothing in the portrait, however, to suggest the directions that Prince Charles, subsequently King Charles I, would take with his own art patronage. Charles, who inherited much of his brother's and mother's art collections, was to become the greatest ever royal art collector in England, and the patron of an entirely new kind of royal portraiture by Sir Anthony van Dyck (1599–1641). C.M.

PROVENANCE
Commissioned by the Vice-Chancellor of the University of Cambridge, 1613.

LITERATURE
Finberg 1920–1, pp.89–95; Toynbee 1949, pp.7–8; Goodison 1955, I, pp.16–17; *Hamilton Kerr Institute Bulletin*, i, 1988, p.117; Hearn 1995, pp.188–9, no. 128; Hearn, 'Peake, Robert', ODNB 2004.

81

The Life and Death of our Late most Incomparable and Heroique Prince,
Henry Prince of Wales

UNIDENTIFIED AUTHOR

printed by John Dawson for Nathanael Butter, London 1641

Leather-bound book, octavo; 106 pages, spine height 199mm

British Library, London (292.d.41)

Published in various forms throughout the seventeenth, eighteenth and nineteenth centuries, *The Life and Death* was the first extensive biography of Prince Henry, authored by an individual with close ties to his court. It provided anecdotes and character sketches to which later biographers would repeatedly return. From the outset, it presents Henry as a paragon of virtuous living – as a warrior prince, endowed from infancy with a martial spirit. The author informs us that, even from a tender age, no music was more pleasing to him than the sounding of the trumpet, beating of the drum and roar of the cannon. Similarly, Henry's sobriety and piety are emphasised. In an oft-quoted passage, the writer reports that Henry abhorred profanities, installing swearing boxes in his residences, the proceeds of which were given to the poor. Over a third of the text is concerned with the Prince's final sickness and his physicians' administrations. The account, which clearly derives from Theodore de Mayerne's description of Henry's illness and post-mortem, repeatedly attempts to exonerate the attending physicians from blame.

Written in 1613, *The Life and Death* was first circulated in manuscript form. The publisher of this printed version attributes the text to Sir Charles Cornwallis, Treasurer of Prince Henry's household. However, Cornwallis wrote his own biography of the Prince in 1626 (subsequently published by John Benson in 1641) and it is unlikely that he penned another. Based upon the dedication by John Hawkins of a manuscript copy in the British Library, Hawkins, a steward at the Tower of London, has been identified as the author (BL Add. MS 30075; Strong 1986, p.227). However, the existence of several similar and earlier manuscripts, at least one of which has a different dedicator, undermines this assertion (for example, NLS, Adv. MS 33.7.14). What can be gauged from the earliest surviving copy (dated 1613; BL Add. MS 11532) is that the author was intent upon maintaining his anonymity. Somewhat self-deprecatingly, he claims that many were more qualified to write Henry's biography but that this was his last duty to the Prince. The account's tone and detail suggest that it was written by a member of the Prince's household, with easy access to Henry and his circle.

This printed edition is dedicated to Henry's nephew Prince Charles, the future Charles II. The presentation of Henry as a suitable role model for Charles was timely. By the late 1630s and early 1640s the political fortunes of his father, Charles I, were in steady decline due, in part, to the King's own lack of judgement and inflexibility. Given the disillusionment that many of his subjects felt with regard to the King, it was, perhaps, not unnatural that hopes should be focused on Prince Charles as his uncle's spiritual heir. C.A.M.

PROVENANCE
Part of the bibliographic collections of King George III; included in the King's Library, gifted to the British Museum by George IV in 1832; transferred to the collections of the British Library, London, with its establishment in 1973.

LITERATURE
Strong 1986, pp.7–70 and 227.

ILLUST: HENRICUS PRINCEPS WALLIÆ.

W.M. Sculp:

THE
LIFE AND
DEATH OF OVR
Late most Incomparable
and Heroique Prince,

HENRY

Prince of WALES.

A Prince (for Valour and
Vertue) fit to be Imitated in
Succeeding Times.

Written by Sir CHARLES CORNVVALLIS
Knight, Treasurer of his Highnesse
Houshold.

LONDON,
Printed by Iohn Dawson for Nathanael
Butter. 1641.

82

Henry, Prince of Wales

DANIEL MYTENS (*c.*1590–1647),
after ISAAC OLIVER, *c.*1628

Oil on panel, 790 × 615mm
Private Collection

The Dutch artist Daniel Mytens was Charles I's principal 'picture-drawer' from 1625 until the arrival of Sir Anthony van Dyck in 1632. He was primarily employed as a portraitist but he also produced copies of the King's favourite paintings. This portrait after Isaac Oliver's exceptional miniature was such a commission (see cat. 32). It was described as 'Prince Henry with a Prospect' in a payment of £15, made to Mytens on 2 July 1628, and is branded on the back with the King's cipher 'CR' (*Carolus Rex*). The portrait hung in Charles I's bedchamber at Whitehall Palace, where it was placed alongside prized religious paintings and other portraits of his family.

A comparison between the panel and its source miniature reveals the pains taken by Mytens to replicate accurately details such as the gilt strapwork on the armour. There are, however, two significant deviations from Oliver's design: the masque-like scene in the background of the miniature is expanded into a more convincingly rendered military encampment, positioned on the coast with a fleet beyond; the flagship flies the White Ensign of the Royal Navy.

Mytens has also varied the Prince's features, lengthening the nose and darkening the hair and eyes. These changes suggest a subtle morphing of Henry's features into those of his younger brother, Charles. Such mutability between the two Princes' identities is not without precedent; see Robert Dallington's address of 1613 to Charles in the aftermath of Henry's death: 'men looke upon your worthy Brother in your princely self; holding you the true inheritor of his vertues as of his fortunes' (Dallington, quoted in Wilks 2007, p.202).

It is perhaps no coincidence that the painting was produced at the time of the then largest offensive in English naval history. In the summer of 1627 over 100 ships sailed from Portsmouth to break the French siege of the Huguenot stronghold La Rochelle. The expedition would ultimately end in failure but it is possible to hypothesise that Mytens's portrait flatters the King by suggesting that he has realised the promise of Prince Henry to become a militant-Protestant king.

Mytens's portrait marks a transition in Henry's iconography from that of a much-loved, or dearly missed, contemporary to a figure receding into history. In the context of Charles I's increasingly unstable reign, we can only speculate as to the extent to which this portrait became loaded with rich resonances, nostalgia and myth. R.M.

PROVENANCE
Commissioned by Charles I; sold at the Commonwealth Sale, 1651; bought by R. Houghton; recovered at the Restoration; given by King George III to Henry Addington, Viscount Sidmouth in 1804; thence by descent.

LITERATURE
Stopes 1910, pp.160–3; Belfield 1959, pp.175–6; Millar 1960, xiv, p.35; Oliver et al 1964 (cat. 47, p.38).

Prince Henry's Architecture and Garden Design

RAB MACGIBBON

The extent of Prince Henry's building and garden design ambitions cannot be judged from an assessment of surviving examples. His premature death brought all construction work being carried out in his name to an abrupt halt and any completed structures have since been destroyed or hidden beneath four centuries of modernisation and rebuilding at the royal palaces. Nevertheless, contemporary accounts and a small number of surviving visual records indicate that his ambition was considerable.

The provision of suitable accommodation for the heir to the throne and his court had not concerned the English monarchy for generations; the last formal investiture of a Prince of Wales had been the future Henry VIII in 1503. Following the arrival of the new royal family in the summer of 1603, Henry was installed in the Tudor palaces of Oatlands and then Nonsuch, where his household expanded to more than 300 people over the next six years (Wilks 2001, p.49). During this period work was undertaken at the larger palaces of St James's and Richmond to prepare them with the facilities necessary for a Renaissance prince.

The first new building to be erected for the Prince was a riding school at St James's Palace (fig. 25); it is also his only construction project for which a detailed visual record survives. Robert Smythson's survey of the recently completed building shows a substantial gabled-ended, seven-bay structure that provided 39 × 13 metres of uninterrupted interior space. This was the first riding school to be constructed in England and within it the Prince hoped to establish an academy of *haute école* horsemanship for young nobles.

The existing palace fabric at St James's also required a programme of refurbishment with the most significant alterations being the creation of rooms suitable for the storage and display of the Prince's rapidly expanding collections. Between 1609 and 1610 a library was constructed to house the large number of books received by Henry on the death of Lord Lumley, Keeper of Nonsuch Palace, in April 1609. At the same time a picture gallery was fitted out to hang contemporary continental art in addition to the dynastic portraits commonly found in Tudor long galleries; the combined cost of these projects exceeded £2,100 (Wilks 2005, p.150).

Work at the Prince's main country residence, Richmond Palace, began with relatively modest interventions such as the preparation of a tennis court, reinforcing the floor of a room for displaying artillery and converting a closet into a library to be presided over by Edward Wright (see cat. 67). Henry's investiture as Prince of Wales in 1610 enhanced both his financial independence and personal prestige. This change in status was reflected by the instigation of a bold programme to transform Richmond Palace and its grounds into a show-piece to rival the most sophisticated courts in Europe.

The first phase of the project was carried out by the Prince's Surveyor, Inigo Jones, and Salomon de Caus, the French polymath with a particular specialism in hydraulic engineering who had previously taught the Prince the art and science of perspective. Both Jones and de Caus had travelled in Italy and France and were alert to recent fashions

FIG. 25
*Plan and elevation of the Prince's
Riding School at St James's,*
Robert Smythson, 1609

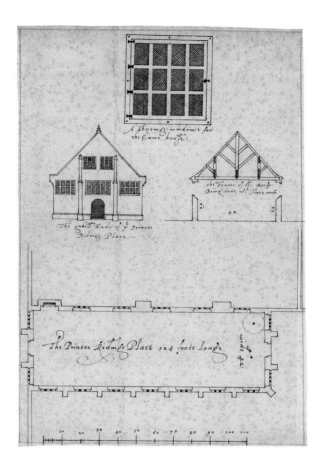

in courtly ornamentation. De Caus, and perhaps Jones,
had visited the Villa Medici at Pratolino, whose garden
by Bernardo Buontalenti was a masterpiece of Mannerist
design featuring an abundance of fountains, grottoes and
sculptures (Morgan 2007, p.43). These same features
were to play a central role at Richmond.

By the summer of 1611, Jones and de Caus had carried
out extensive structural work to the west of the palace.
Three islands were levelled and perhaps incorporated into
the 335-metre stretch of reclaimed and wharfed riverbank
(Wilks 2001, p.55), the Tudor moat seems to have been filled
in, a cistern house was built and underground pipes were
laid to supply the intended waterworks at a grotto called
the 'Rockhouse', then in the early stages of construction
(Morgan 2007, p.103). This is the low rectangular structure
at the left of Hollar's *View of Richmond*, 1638 (fig. 26).

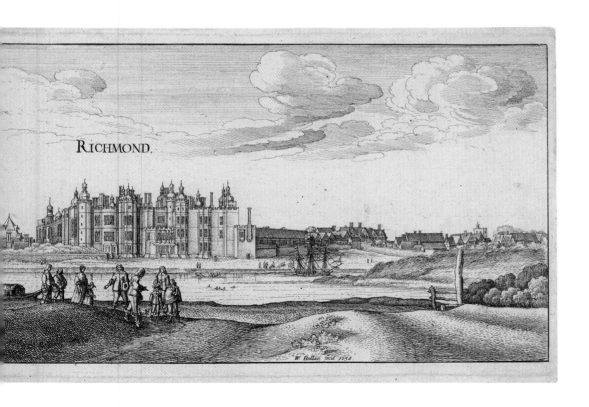

FIG. 26
View of Richmond,
Wenceslaus Hollar, 1638

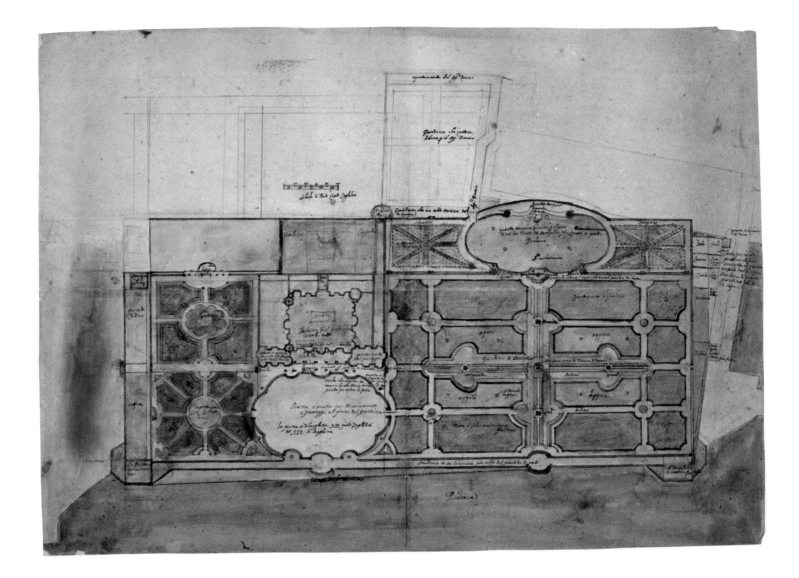

It seems that little progress was made following this initial spell of intense activity. The perennial Stuart problem of a lack of funds no doubt played a part in this disruption; so too did the arrival of the Florentine court artist Costantino de' Servi.

De' Servi was a late representative of the Renaissance ideal of the universal artist, who was equally accomplished in a number of disciplines. He was sent to the Prince by Cosimo II, Grand Duke of Tuscany, as part of a campaign of flattery and gifts intended to win Henry's support for a marriage alliance with the Medici. De' Servi's remarkable plan for the Richmond redevelopment was presented to the Prince in September 1611 (fig. 27). It incorporates the works already underway and expands it into a grandiose scheme that ignores property boundaries and requires the levelling of nearby buildings.

The proposal combines fashionable French parterres with Italian-influenced water and architectural features. New wings have been added to the palace, overlooking a large oval arena for tilts and pageants. To the west, gardens planted with heraldic devices surround a fountain and a 'Mount Parnassus'. To the east, avenues and pools are articulated with statues and pyramids with a column based on Trajan's Column in Rome at its centre. The climax of the garden is a large pool or 'Peschiera', decorated with sea monsters and overlooked by a giant statue of the Roman sea god Neptune, which was to be three times the size of the Appenino at Pratolino (letter from de' Servi to Andrea Cioli, 8 August 1611, cited in Eiche 1998, p.14). An indication of the colossal size of the statue may be given by the illustration to Salomon de Caus's *Les raisons des forces mouvantes* (1615), which incorporated designs prepared for Henry (fig. 28).

PRINCE HENRY'S ARCHITECTURE AND GARDEN DESIGN

FIG. 27
Plan of Richmond Palace Gardens,
Costantino de' Servi, 1611

FIG. 28
Design for a Giant, problem 14,
book 11, *Les raisons des forces
mouvantes*, unknown artist
after Salomon de Caus, 1615

During the course of 1612, de' Servi's proposal grew to include the complete rebuilding of the palace in a classical style (Strong 1986, p.94). The Prince was undoubtedly impressed and awarded him an annuity of £200, twice that of de Caus and four times Jones's salary. By the time of Henry's death nearly £4,000 had been spent on the gardens at Richmond (Wilks 1987, p.140). Had he lived it is not inconceivable that something approaching the richness and complexity of de' Servi's plan would have been produced.

As it was, de Caus created his masterpiece of garden design for Princess Elizabeth and Frederick V at their palace at Heidelberg; in England, de' Servi was 'chased from court with sticks' following his disastrous masque for the Duke of Somerset's wedding (Wilks 2001, p.64); and Jones returned from his second tour of Italy to an appointment as King's Surveyor, from which position he would fulfil the aspirations of Henry's court to build a new era of architecture in Britain.

Select bibliography

EDITORIAL NOTE

Published works are cited in the text using the short form of author + date; full details are given in the bibliography below.

Archival works frequently cited in the text have been identified by the following abbreviations:

CSP Calendar of State Papers; CSP *Venetian* refers to Papers Relating to English Affairs in the Archives of Venice; CSP *Domestic* refers to Papers Relating to Britain
HMC Historical Manuscripts Commission
ODNB Oxford Dictionary of National Biography
TNA The National Archives, Kew

'An account of the several libraries … in or about London', *The Gentleman's Magazine*, 86 (2), 1816

A true Reportarie of the most triumphant and royal acomplishment of the Baptisme of the most excellent, right high, and mightie Prince, Frederik Henry (Robert Waldegrave, Edinburgh, 1594 and Peter Short, London, 1594)

Silke Ackermann (ed.), *Humphrey Cole: Mint, Measurement and Maps in Elizabethan England* (British Museum Press, London, 1998)

Christy Anderson, *Inigo Jones and the Classical Tradition* (Cambridge University Press, Cambridge, 2006)

Charles Avery, *Giambologna: The Complete Sculpture* (Phaidon, Oxford, 1987)

Charles Avery and Anthony Radcliffe, *Giambologna 1529–1608: Sculptor to the Medici* (exh. cat., Arts Council of Great Britain, London and Kunsthistorisches Museum, Vienna, 1978)

Erna Auerbach and C. Kingsley Adams, *Paintings and Sculpture at Hatfield House* (Constable, London, 1971)

[Francis Bacon], *Henricum Principem Walliae Elogium*, in James Spedding et al. (eds), *The Works of Francis Bacon*, VI (Longman and Co., London, 1858)

[Francis Bacon], *The Praise of Henry, Prince of Wales*, in Joseph Devey (ed.), *The Moral and Historical Works of Lord Bacon* […] (Bell and Daldy, London, 1866)

Richard Badenhausen, 'Disarming the infant warrior: Prince Henry, King James, and the chivalric revival', *Papers on Language and Literature*, 31, 1995

Anna Banti (ed.), *Europa Milleseicentosei. Diario di Viaggio di Bernardo Bizoni* (Rizzoli, Milan, 1944)

Philip L. Barbour, *The Jamestown Voyages under the First Charter 1609–1609* (Cambridge University Press for the Hakluyt Society, Cambridge, 1969)

C. Barclay and L. Syson, 'A medal die rediscovered: a new work by Nicholas Hilliard', *The Medal*, Spring 1993

Illustrated Bartsch, The, Walter Strauss (ed.), III (Abaris, New York, 1978–)

E.M.G. Belfield, *The Annals of the Addington Family* (Warren & Son Ltd., Winchester, 1959)

Cesare Bertana, 'Il ritratto di uno Stuart alle corte dei Savoia', *Studi Piemontesi*, XIII, no. 2, 1983

Gilles Bertheau, 'Prince Henry as Chapman's "Absolute Man"' in T. Wilks (ed.), *Prince Henry Revived. Image and Exemplarity in Early Modern England* (Paul Holberton Publishing, London, 2007)

Thomas Birch, *An Historical View of the Negotiations between the Courts of England, France and Brussels from the year 1592 to 1617* (A. Millar, London, 1749)

Thomas Birch, *The Life of Henry Prince of Wales* (A. Millar, London, 1760)

Thomas Birch, *Court and Times of James I* (Henry Colburn, London, 1848)

T.A. Birrell, *Notes on English Monarchs and their Books: from Henry VII to Charles II*, Panizzi Lectures, British Library, London, 1986

John Boardman et al., *The Marlborough Gems. Formerly at Blenheim Palace* (Oxford University Press, Oxford, 2009)

Boderie to Piusieux, 21 June 1607, *Ambassades de Monsieur de la Boderie* […], 5 volumes, vol. II (edited by Paul Denis Burtin, Paris, 1750)

William Bouwsma, *Venice and the Defense of Republican Liberty* (University of California Press, Berkeley and Los Angeles, 1968)

Rick Bowers, 'James VI, Prince Henry, and *A True Reportarie* of Baptism at Stirling 1594', *Renaissance and Reformation*, XXIX, 4, 2005

Susan Bracken, 'Robert Cecil as Art Collector', in Pauline Croft (ed.), *Patronage, Culture and Power: the Early Cecils* (Yale University Press for the Paul Mellon Centre for the Study of British Art, New Haven and London, 2002)

Lorne Campbell, *The Early Flemish Pictures in the Collection of Her Majesty The Queen* (Cambridge University Press, Cambridge, 1985)

Edward Cardwell, *Documentary Annals of the Reformed Church of England*, 2 volumes, vol. II (Oxford University Press, Oxford, 1839)

Edward Chaney, 'The Italianate Evolution of English Collecting', in Chaney (ed.), *The Evolution of English Collecting: The Reception of Italian Art in the Tudor and Stuart Periods* (Yale University Press for the Paul Mellon Centre for Studies in British Art, New Haven and London, 2004)

George Chapman, *Chapman's Homer: The Iliad*, 1611 edn, series 41 (Allardyce Nicoll, Bollingen, 1998)

George Chapman, *Epicede or Funerall Song: On the most disastrous Death, of the High-borne Prince of Men, Henry Prince of Wales* […] (John Budge, London, 1613)

Ellen Chirelstein, 'Lady Elizabeth Pope: The Heraldic Body', in Lucy Gent and Nigel Llewellyn (eds), *Renaissance Bodies* (Reaktion Books, London 1990)

James Cleland, *Hero-paideia, or The stet of a Young Noble Man* (Joseph Barnes, Oxford, 1607; later editions 1611, 1612)

Bartholomew Clerke (trans.), *Bathasaris Castilionis comitis, De curialis sive aulici libri quatuor* (George Bishop, London, 1603; later edition 1612)

John Cloake, *Palaces and Parks of Richmond and Kew*, vol. 1 (Phillimore & Co., Chichester, 1995)

Roger Coke, *Detection of the Court and State of England*, 2 volumes, vol. I (London, 1694)

Torben Holck Colding, *Aspects of Miniature Painting* (Ejnar Munksgaard, Copenhagen, 1953)

H.M. Colvin (ed.) *The History of the King's Work*, vol . III (1975) and vol. IV (1982) (HMSO, London)

Sir Charles Cornwallis, *A discourse of the most illustrious prince, Henry late Prince of Wales. Written Anno 1626. by Sir Charles Cornwallis, Knight, sometimes Treasurer of His Highnesse house* (John Benson, London, 1641)

Norman Council, 'Ben Jonson, Inigo Jones, and the Transformation of Tudor Chivalry', *English Literary History*, 47, no. 2, Summer 1980

James Craigie, *The Basilicon Doron of King James VI*, 2 volumes (printed for the Scottish Text Society by W. Blackwood & Sons, London and Edinburgh, 1944–50)

Pauline Croft, 'The Parliamentary Installation of Henry, Prince of Wales' in *Historical Research*, vol. 65, issue 157, 1992

Pauline Croft (ed.), *Patronage, Culture and Power: the Early Cecils* (Yale University Press for the Paul Mellon Centre for the Study of British Art, New Haven and London, 2002)

David Crystal, *Evolving English: one language, many voices. An illustrated history of the English language* (British Library, London, 2010)

Charles Dalton, *Life and Times of General Sir Edward Cecil, Viscount Wimbledon* […] (Sampson, Low, Marston, Searle & Rivington, London, 1885)

Samuel Daniel, *The Order and Solemnitie of the Creation of the High and mightie Prince Henrie* (John Budge, London, 1610)

S. Daniel, dedication to *The Tragedie of Philotas*, published in *Certaine small poems lately printed with the Tragedie of Philotas* (printed by George Eld for Simon Waterson, London, 1605)

S. Daniel, *Tethys Festivall*, in Alexander B. Grosart (ed.), *The Complete Works of Samuel Daniel*, III (printed by Hazell, Watson & Viney Ltd., London, 1885)

Frederick Devon (ed.), *Issues of the Exchequer* (John Rodwell, London, 1836)

Michael Drayton, *Poly-olbion* (printed by Humphrey Lownes for Matthew Lownes, John Browne, John Helme and John Busbie, London, 1612)

Jean-François Dubost, *Marie de Médicis: La reine dévoilée* (Payot, Paris, 2009)

Albrecht Dürer, treatise, *Underweysung der Messung (Instruction in Measurement)* (Nuremberg, 1525)

M. Edmond, 'Limners and picturemakers', *Walpole Society*, vol. 47, 1978–80

Sabine Eiche, 'Prince Henry's Richmond. The project by Costantino de' Servi', *Apollo*, CXLVIII, no. 441, November 1998

Mark Evans (ed.), *Princes as Patrons: The Art Collections of the Princes of Wales from the Renaissance to the Present Day* (exh. cat., Merrell Holberton, in association with National Museums & Galleries of Wales and the Royal Collection, London, 1998)

Helen Farquhar, 'Nicholas Hilliard, "Embosser of Medals of Gold"', *Numismatic Chronicle*, 4th series, vol. viii, 1908

Cassandra Farrell, *Virginia, Discovered and Described: John Smith's Map of Virginia and its Derivatives*, Library of Virginia Research Notes, no. 28, 2007

A.J. Finberg, 'An Authentic Portrait by Robert Peake', *Walpole Society*, vol. 9, 1920–1

Susan Foister, *Drawings by Holbein from the Royal Library, Windsor Castle* (Johnson Reprint Corp., Harcourt Brace Jovanovich, London and New York, 1983)

S. Foister, *Holbein and England* (Paul Mellon Centre for Studies in British Art, Yale University Press, New Haven and London, 2004)

Mirjam M. Foot, *The Henry Davis Gift: A Collection of bookbindings*, 2 vols, II (British Museum Publications for the British Library, London, 1979)

Bruce Galloway, *The Union of England and Scotland, 1603–1608* (John Donald, Edinburgh, 1986)

Elizabeth E. Gardner, 'A British Hunting Portrait', *Metropolitan Museum of Art Bulletin*, New Series, vol. 3, no. 5, January 1945

George Gascoigne (general attribution), *The Noble Art of Venerie, or Hunting* [...] (1st edn imprinted by Henry Bynneman, for Christopher Barker, London 1575; 2nd edn printed by Thomas Purfoot, London, 1611)

Christine Gerrard, *The Patriot Opposition to Walpole: Politics, Poetry and National Myth, 1725–42* (Clarendon Press, Oxford, 1994)

Elizabeth Goldring, '"So iust a sorrowe so well expressed": Henry, Prince of Wales and the Art of Commemoration', in T. Wilks (ed.), *Prince Henry Revived. Image and*

Exemplarity in Early Modern England (Paul Holberton Publishing, London, 2007)

Julian Goodare, 'The Scottish Presbyterian Movement in 1596' in *Canadian Journal of History/Annales canadiennes d'histoire*, 45, 2010

J.W. Goodison, *Catalogue of Cambridge Portraits*, I (Cambridge University Press, Cambridge, 1955)

Abraham Gorlaeus (van Goorle), *Abrahami Gorlaei Antverpiani Dactyliotheca seu Annulorum sigillarium* [...] (Nuremberg, 1601)

Abraham Gorlaeus, *Thesaurus numismatum Romanorum* (Henrick van Haestens, Leiden , 1607)

Antony Griffiths, *The Print in Stuart Britain* (British Museum Press, London, 1998)

Hamilton Kerr Institute Bulletin, vol. I, 1988

Paul E.J. Hammer, *The Polarisation of Elizabethan Politics: The Political Career of Robert Devereux, 2nd Earl of Essex, 1585–1597* (Cambridge University Press, Cambridge, 1999)

Sir John Harington, *A Tract on the Succession to the Crown*, ed. Clements R. Markham (Roxburghe Club, London, 1880)

The Harriot, the newsletter of the Thomas Harriot Seminar, November 1999

John Harris and Gordon Higgott, *Inigo Jones: complete architectural drawings* (exh. cat., The Drawing Centre, New York & Royal Academy of Arts, London, 1989)

Anthony Harvey and Richard Mortimer (eds), *The Funeral Effigies of Westminster Abbey* (Boydell Press, Woodbridge, 1994)

Edward Hawkins, Augustus W. Franks (ed.) and Herbert A Grueber (ed.), *Medallic illustrations of the history of Great Britain and Ireland to the death of George II*, vol. I (British Museum Press, London, 1885)

W.H. [possibly William Haydon], *The True Picture and Relation of Prince Henry* [...] (William Christian, Leiden, 1634)

Karen Hearn, *Dynasties: Painting in Tudor and Jacobean England 1530–1630* (Tate Publishing, London, 1995)

K. Hearn, 'A Question of Judgement: Lucy Harington, Countess of Bedford, as Art Patron and Collector', in E. Chaney, *The Evolution of English Collecting* (Yale University Press, New Haven and London, 2003)

Steffen Heiberg (ed.), *Christian IV and Europe: the 19th Council of Europe Exhibition* (exh. cat., Frederiksborg et al., Foundation for Christian IV Year 1988, Denmark, 1988)

Julius Held, 'Le Roi a la Ciasse', *Art Bulletin*, XL, 2 June 1958

Martin Henig 'Gems from the Collection of Henry, Prince of Wales and Charles I', Appendix II, in Kirsten Aschengreen Piacenti and John Boardman, *Ancient and Modern Gems and Jewels in the Collection of Her Majesty The Queen* (Royal Collection Publications, London, 2008)

C.H. Herford and Percy Simpson (eds), *Works of Ben Jonson*, 12 vols (1925–52), vol. 7 (Clarendon Press, Oxford, 1941)

Thomas Heywood, *A Funerall Elegie on the Death of Prince Henry* (printed for William Welbie, London, 1613)

[Nicholas Hilliard], *A Treatise concerning the arte of limning*, ed. R.K.R. Thornton and T.G.S. Cain (Carcanet New Press, Manchester, 1981)

A.M. Hind, *Engraving in England in the sixteenth and seventeenth centuries*, II (Cambridge University Press, Cambridge, 1955)

Thomas Hoby, *The Courtyer done into Englyshe* (William Seres, London, 1561); new impression, *The Courtier* (printed by Thomas Creede, London, 1603)

Philemon Holland [trans.], *The Historie of the Twelve Caesars, Emperours of Rome, written in Latin by Suetonius Tranquillatus and newly translated in English* (printed by Humphrey Lownes and George Snowdon for Matthew Lownes, London, 1606)

F.W.H. Hollstein, *The New Hollstein: Dutch and Flemish etchings, engravings and woodcuts 1450–1700* (Koninklijke Van Poll, Amsterdam, 1949 [a revised 'New Hollstein' series underway since 1993]

Deborah Howard, *Scottish Architecture: From the Reformation to the Restoration 1550–1650* (Edinburgh University Press, Edinburgh, 1995)

John Ingamells, *Dulwich Picture Gallery: British* (Unicorn Press, London, 2008)

Benvenuto Italian, *The Passenger* (Thomas Snodham, London, 1612)

Mervyn James, 'English Politics and the Concept of Honour, 1485–1642', in James (ed.), *Society, Politics and Culture: Studies in Early Modern England* (Cambridge University Press, Cambridge, 1986)

M. James, 'At the Crossroads of the Political Culture: The Essex Revolt of 1601', in James (ed.), *Society, Politics and Culture: Studies in Early Modern England* (Cambridge University Press, Cambridge, 1986)

Anita Jansen (ed.), *De portretfabriek van Michiel van Mierevelt* (exh. cat., Delft, Museum Het Prinsenhof, 2011)

Sears Jayne and Francis R. Johnson, *The Lumley Library. The Catalogue of 1609* (Trustees of the British Museum, London, 1956)

[Ben Jonson], *The Entertainment at Althorp,* in C.H. Herford and Percy Simpson (eds), *Works of Ben Jonson*, VII (Clarendon Press, Oxford, 1941)

[Ben Jonson], *Oberon, The Faery Prince*, in C.H. Herford and P. & E. Simpson (eds), *Works of Ben Jonson*, VII (Clarendon Press, Oxford, 1941)

[Ben Jonson], *Prince Henries Barriers,* in C.H. Herford and P. & E. Simpson (eds), *Works of Ben Jonson*, VII (Clarendon Press, Oxford, 1941)

Brendan Kane, *The Politics and Culture of Honour in Britain and Ireland, 1541–1641* (Cambridge University Press, Cambridge, 2010)

H.A. Kennedy, 'Early English Portrait Miniatures in the Collection of the Duke of Buccleuch', *The Studio*, December 1917

David Laing, *Adversaria; Notices Illustrative of Some of the Earlier Works Printed for the Bannatyne Club* (Bannatyne Club, Edinburgh, 1867)

Peter Lake and Kevin Sharpe, *Culture and Politics in Early Stuart England* (Macmillan, Basingstoke, 1994)

G.F. Laking, *The Armoury of Windsor Castle* (Bradbury, Agnew & Co., London, 1904)

Maurice Lee (ed.), *Dudley Carleton to John Chamberlain, 1603–1624, Jacobean Letters* (Rutgers University Press, New Brunswick, 1972)

H. Leeflang, Ger Luijten et al., *Hendrik Goltzius (1558–1617), drawings, prints and paintings* (exh. cat., Rijksmuseum, Amsterdam, 2003)

The Life and Death of our late most incomparable and heroic Prince Henry, Prince of Wales [...], 1613 (Nathanael Butter, London, 1641)

Stephen Lloyd, 'Miniatures françaises et continentales dans des collections Ecossaises', in *La Miniature en Europe*: *Actes du colloque*, Chantilly, musée Condé (Institut de France, Paris, 2008)

Robert H. MacDonald (ed.), *William Drummond of Hawthornden: poems and prose* (Scottish Academic Press, Edinburgh, 1976)

Arthur MacGregor (ed.), *The Late King's Goods: Collections, Possessions and Patronage of Charles I in the Light of the Commonwealth Sale Inventories* (Alistair McAlpine in association with Oxford University Press, London and Oxford, 1989)

Eric S. Mallin, 'Emulous Factions and the Collapse of Chivalry: Troilus and Cressida', *Representations*, No. 29, Winter 1990

Alexander Marr, '"A Dutch graver sent for": Cornelis Boel, Salomon de Caus and the production of *La perspective avec la raison des ombres et miroirs*', in T. Wilks (ed.), *Prince Henry Revived. Image and Exemplarity in Early Modern England* (Paul Holberton Publishing, London, 2007)

Norman Egbert McClure (ed.), *The Letters of John Chamberlain*, 2 vols, I (American Philosophical Society, Philadelphia, 1939)

Peter McCullough, *Sermons at Court: Politics and Religion in Elizabethan and Jacobean Preaching* (Cambridge University Press, Cambridge, 1998)

Charles McIlwain (ed.), *The Political Works of James I* (Harvard University Press, Cambridge, Mass., 1918)

Gregory McNamara, '"Grief was as clothes to their backs": Prince Henry's funeral viewed from the Wardrobe', in T. Wilks (ed.), *Prince Henry Revived. Image and Exemplarity in Early Modern England* (Paul Holberton Publishing, London, 2007)

Henry W. Meikle (ed.), *The Works of William Fowler*, 3 vols (1914–40), II, Scottish Text Society, Edinburgh, 1936

Alan Melville, *Natalia Principis Scoti-Britannorum* (1594), trans. Paul J. McGinnis and Arthur Williamson, *George Buchanan: The Political Poetry* (Scottish History Society, Edinburgh, 1995)

Oliver Millar (ed.), *Abraham Van der Doort's Catalogue of the Collections of Charles I*, Walpole Society, vol. 37, 1960

O. Millar, 'Some Painters and Charles I', *Burlington Magazine*, vol. 104, 1962

O. Millar, *The Tudor, Stuart and Early Georgian Pictures in the Collection of Her Majesty The Queen*, 2 vols (Phaidon Press, London, 1963)

O. Millar et al., *The Orange and the Rose: Holland and Britain in the age of observation 1600–1750* (exh. cat., Victoria and Albert Museum, London, 1964)

Norman Moore, *The Illness and Death of Henry Prince of Wales in 1612. A Historical Case of Typhoid Fever* (printed by J.E. Adlard, London, 1882)

Luke Morgan, *Nature as Model: Salomon de Caus and Early Seventeenth-Century Landscape Design* (University of Pennsylvania Press, Philadelphia, 2007)

Nicholas Morgan, *The Perfection of Horse-manship* (E. White, London, 1609)

Sir David Murray, *The Tragicall Death of Sophonisba* (printed for John Smethwick & Co., London, 1611)

National Maritime Museum Catalogue (National Maritime Museum, London, 1937)

Brian Nance, *Turquet de Mayerne as Baroque Physician: the Art of Medical Portraiture* (Rodopi, Amsterdam, 2001)

John Napier, *A plaine discovery of the whole revelation of St John* (Robert Waldegrave, Edinburgh, 1593)

John Nichols, *The Progresses, Processions, and Magnificent Festivities of King James I, His Royal Consort, Family and Court*, II (J.B. Nichols, London, 1828)

John Norden, *A Description of the Honor of Windesor* [...] (BL Harley MS 3749,1607)

Michelle O'Callaghan, 'Coryats Crudities (1611) and Travel Writing as the "Eyes" of the Prince', in T. Wilks (ed.), *Prince Henry Revived. Image and Exemplarity in Early Modern England* (Paul Holberton Publishing, London, 2007)

Stephen Orgel (ed.), *Ben Jonson: The Complete Masques* (Yale University Press, New Haven, 1969)

Stephen Orgel and Roy Strong, *Inigo Jones The Theatre of the Stuart Court*, 2 vols (Sotheby Parke Bernet, London and University of California Press, Berkeley, 1973)

Oxford Dictionary of National Biography (Oxford University Press, Oxford, 2004)

Caterina Pagnini, *Costantino de' Servi architetto-scenografo fiorentino alla corte d'Inghilterra (1611–1615)* (Società Editrice Fiorentina, Florence, 2006)

K.T. Parker, *The Drawings of Hans Holbein in the Collection of Her Majesty The Queen at Windsor Castle*, 2nd edn (Johnson Reprint Corp., Harcourt Brace Jovanovich, New York, 1983)

'The parliamentary installation of Henry, Prince of Wales', *Historical Research*, vol. 65, 1992

Graham Parry, *The Golden Age Restor'd: The Culture of the Stuart Court, 1603–42* (Manchester University Press, Manchester, 1981)

John Thomas Payne, William Brenchley Rye, Henry Foss, *Bibliotheca Grenvilliana* (William Nichol [part 1], British Museum, Dept. of Printed Books (parts 2&3), London, 1848–72)

[H. Peacham], 'Manuscript Emblem Books', *The English Emblem Tradition*, 5, Alan R. Young with Beert Verstraete (eds) (University of Toronto, Toronto, 1998)

John Peacock, 'Inigo Jones's Catafalque for James I', *Architectural History*, 25, 1982

J. Peacock, 'Jonson and Jones collaborate on Prince Henry's Barriers', *Word and Image*, III, 2, April–June 1987

J. Peacock, 'The Politics of Portraiture', in Peter Lake and Kevin Sharpe, *Culture and Politics in Early Stuart England* (Macmillan, Basingstoke, 1994)

J. Peacock, *The Stage Designs of Inigo Jones: The European Context* (Cambridge University Press, Cambridge, 1995)

Linda Levy Peck (ed.), *The Mental World of the Jacobean Court* (Cambridge University Press, Cambridge, 1991)

L. Levy Peck, 'Monopolizing Favour: Structures of Power in Early Seventeenth-Century English Court', in J.H. Elliott and L.W.B. Brockliss (eds), *The World of the Favourite* (Yale University Press, New Haven and London, 1999)

W.G. Perrin (ed.), *The Autobiography of Phineas Pett* (Navy Records Society, London, 1918)

David Piper, *Catalogue of Seventeenth-century Portraits in the National Portrait Gallery* (Cambridge University Press, Cambridge, 1963)

Peter van der Ploeg and Carola Vermeeren, *Princely patrons: the collection of Frederick Henry of Orange and Amalia of Solms in The Hague* (Mauritshuis, The Hague, 1997)

Ayshna Pollnitz, 'Humanism and the Education of Henry, Prince of Wales' in T. Wilks (ed.), *Prince Henry Revived: Image and Exemplarity in Early Modern England* (Paul Holberton Publishing, London, 2007)

Robert Lane Powell, *Catalogue of Portrait Miniatures in the Fitzwilliam Museum, Cambridge* (Cambridge University Press, Cambridge, 1985)

Daniel Price, *The Defence of Truth against a booke falsely called, The Triumph of Truth …* (Joseph Barnes, Oxford, 1610)

J. Pulver, 'Giovanni Coprario alias John Cooper', *Monthly Musical Record*, 57, 1927

H. Ræder, E. Strömgren & B. Strömgren, *Tycho Brahe's Description of his Instruments and Scientific Work* (Munksgaard International Publishers Ltd., Copenhagen, 1946)

Sir Walter Ralegh, *The History of the World* [...], 1st edn, 2 vols (1614)

Dr Jim Reeds, 'Harriot's Number and Letter Squares', 14 September 1999, in *The Harriot* (the newsletter of the Thomas Harriot Seminar), November 1999

Graham Reynolds, 'Portraits by Nicholas Hilliard and his Assistants of King James I and his Family', *Walpole Society*, vol. 34 (1952–4), 1958

G. Reynolds, *English Portrait Miniatures*, revised ed. (Cambridge University Press, Cambridge, 1988)

G. Reynolds, *The Sixteenth- and Seventeenth-Century Miniatures in the Collection of Her Majesty The Queen* (Royal Collection Enterprises, London, 1999)

Aileen Ribeiro, *Fashion and Fiction. Dress in Art and Literature in Stuart England* (Paul Mellon Centre for Studies in British Art, Yale University Press, New Haven and London, 2005)

Thom Richardson, *Stuart Royal Armours from the Royal Armouries* (Royal Armouries, Leeds, forthcoming publication)

Scot McKendrick, John Lowden, Kathleen Doyle, *Royal Manuscripts: The Genius of Illumination* (exh. cat, British Library, London, 2011)

Thomas Rundall, *Narratives of Voyage towards the North West in search of a passage to Cathay and India, 1496 to 1631* (Hakluyt Society, London, 1849)

W.B. Rye, *England as Seen by Foreigners* (John Russell Smith, London, 1865)

Diana Scarisbrick, 'Anne of Denmark's Jewellery; Old and New', *Apollo*, vol. 123, no. 290, April 1986, pp. 228–36

D. Scarisbrick, *Tudor and Jacobean Jewellery* (Tate Publishing, London, 1995)

David G. Selwyn, *The Library of Thomas Cranmer*, Oxford Bibliographical Society, 1996

Sebastiano Serlio, *The First Booke of Architecture* [...] (printed by Simon Stafford and Thomas Snodham for Robert Peake, London, 1611)

Walter W. Seton, 'The Early Years of Henry Frederick, Prince of Wales and Charles Duke of Albany (Charles I) 1593–1605', *Scottish Historical Review*, XIII, 1915–1916

Kevin Sharpe, *Image Wars* (Yale University Press, New Haven and London, 2010)

John Shearman, *The Early Italian Pictures in the Collection of Her Majesty The Queen* (Cambridge University Press, Cambridge, 1983)

John W. Shirley, *Thomas Harriot: a Biography* (Oxford University Press, Oxford, 1983)

Logan Pearsall Smith, *Life and Letters of Sir Henry Wotton*, 2 vols, 1 (Clarendon Press, Oxford, 1907)

Thomas Smith, *Vitae quorundam eruditissimorum et illustrium virorum* (David Mortier, London, 1707)

Malcolm Smuts, 'The Making of *Rex Pacificus*: James VI and the Problem of Peace in an Age of Religious War', in Daniel Fischlin and Mark Fortier (eds), *Royal Subjects: Essays on the Writings of James VI and I* (Wayne State University Press, Detroit, 2002)

John Steegman, *A Survey of Portraits in Welsh Country Houses*, vol. II (National Museum of Wales, Cardiff, 1962)

Charlotte C. Stopes, 'Daniel Mytens in England', *Burlington Magazine*, vol. 17, 1910

Walter L. Strauss (ed.), *Hendrik Goltzius 1558–1617: The Complete Engravings and Woodcuts*, 2 vols (Abaris Books, New York, 1977)

Roy Strong, *Portraits of Queen Elizabeth I* (Clarendon Press, Oxford, 1963)

R. Strong, *The English Icon* (Paul Mellon Foundation, London, 1969)

R. Strong, *Tudor and Jacobean Portraits in the National Portrait Gallery*, 2 vols (HMSO, London, 1969)

R. Strong, *The Renaissance Garden in England* (Thames and Hudson, London, 1979)

R. Strong, *Artists of the Tudor Court: The Portrait Miniature Rediscovered 1520–1620* (exh. cat., Victoria and Albert Museum, London, 1983)

R. Strong, *Henry, Prince of Wales and England's Lost Renaissance* (Thames and Hudson, London, 1986)

Beatrice Paolozzi Strozzi and Dimitrios Zikos (eds), *Giambologna: gli dei gli eroi* (exh. cat., Museo Nazionale del Bargello, Florence, 2006)

Pierre François Sweerts, *Athenae Belgicae* (Guilliam van Tongheren, Antwerp, 1628)

Werner Thomas and Luc Duerloo (eds), *Albert & Isabella 1598–1621*, 2 vols (Brepols, Turnhout, 1998)

Duncan Thomson, *Painting in Scotland 1570–1650* (Scottish National Portrait Gallery, Edinburgh, 1975)

Andrew Thrush and John P. Ferris (eds), *The House of Commons, 1604–1629*, 6 vols (Cambridge University Press, Cambridge, 2010)

Simon Thurley, *The Royal Palaces of Tudor England: Architecture & Court Life 1460–1547* (Yale University Press for the Paul Mellon Centre for Studies in British Art, London, 1993)

M.A. Tierney, *The History and Antiquities of the Castle and Town of Arundel*, II (George and William Nicol, London, 1834)

Edward Town, '"Whilst he had his perfect sight" – new information on John de Critz the Elder', *The Burlington Magazine*, July 2012.

Margaret Toynbee, 'Some Early Portraits of Charles I', *The Burlington Magazine*, vol. 91, 1949

Hugh Trevor-Roper, *Europe's Physician: The Various Life of Theodore de Mayerne*, ed. Blair Worden (Yale University Press, New Haven and London, 2006)

David Trim, 'Calvinist Internationalism and the shaping of Jacobean Foreign Policy', in T. Wilks (ed.), *Prince Henry Revived. Image and Exemplarity in Early Modern England* (Paul Holberton Publishing, London, 2007)

Gerard L'E. Turner, *Elizabethan Instrument Makers* (Oxford University Press, Oxford, 2000)

Sir Francis Vere, *Commentaries* (William Dillingham, Cambridge, 1657)

G. Vertue, *Notebooks* (1930–55), 6 vols, *Walpole Society*, vol. xviii, 1930

Hans Vredeman de Vries, *Perspective* (Lvgdvni Batavorum, Leiden, 1604–5)

Patrick Walker (ed.), *Letters to King James the Sixth*, xxxvii (Maitland Club, Edinburgh, 1835)

John Ward, *Lives of the Professors of Gresham College* (John Moore, London, 1740)

George F. Warner and Julius P. Gilson, *Catalogue of Western Manuscripts in the Old Royal and King's Collections*, 4 vols, II (British Museum, London, 1921)

David W. Waters, *The Art of Navigation in England in Elizabethan and Early Stuart Times, 3 vols, 2nd edn* (National Maritime Museum, London, 1978)

Katherine Watson and Charles Avery, 'Medici and Stuart: A Grand Ducal gift of "Giovanni Bologna" bronzes for Henry Prince of Wales (1612)', *Burlington Magazine*, vol. 105, 1973

Gail Capitol Weigl, '"And when slow Time hath mad you fit for warre": The Equestrian Portrait of Prince Henry', in T. Wilks (ed.), *Prince Henry Revived. Image and Exemplarity in Early Modern England* (Paul Holberton Publishing, London, 2007)

Sir Anthony Weldon, *The Court and Character of King James* (printed by R. I. and sold by John Wright, London, 1650)

Robert Wenley, 'French Royal Bronzes in Great Britain', *Apollo*, vol. XX, September 1999

Christopher White, *The Dutch Pictures in the Collection of Her Majesty the Queen* (Cambridge University Press, Cambridge, 1982)

Timothy Wilks, *The Court Culture of Prince Henry and his Circle, 1603–1613* (unpublished D.Phil dissertation, University of Oxford, 1987)

T. Wilks, 'The Picture Collection of Robert Carr, Earl of Somerset (c.1587–1645), Reconsidered', *Journal of the History of Collections*, 1, 2 (1989)

T. Wilks, 'Art Collecting at the English Court from the Death of Henry, Prince of Wales to the Death of Anne of Denmark', *Journal of the History of Collections*, 9, no. 1, 1997

T. Wilks, '"Forbear the Heat and Haste of Building": Rivalries among the Designers at Prince Henry's Court, 1610–1612', *Court Historian*, VI, no. 1, April 2001

T. Wilks, '"Paying special attention to the adorning of a most beautiful gallery": the Picture Gallery at St. James's Palace, 1609–1649', *Court Historian*, X, no. 2, December 2005

T. Wilks, 'The Pike Charged: Henry as Militant Prince', in Wilks (ed.), *Prince Henry Revived. Image and Exemplarity in Early Modern England* (Paul Holberton Publishing, London, 2007)

T. Wilks, '*Henry Prince of Wales, on Horseback:* A note on patronage and provenance', in Wilks (ed.), *Prince Henry Revived. Image and Exemplarity in Early Modern England* (Paul Holberton Publishing, London, 2007)

T. Wilks (ed.), *Prince Henry Revived. Image and Exemplarity in Early Modern England* (Paul Holberton Publishing, London, 2007)

J.W. Williamson, *The Myth of the Conqueror. Prince Henry Stuart: a Study of 17th Century Personation* (AMS Press, New York, 1978)

Peter Wilson, *The Thirty Years War* (Harvard University Press, Cambridge, Mass., 2009)

Jenny Wormald, 'James VI and I, *Basilikon Doron* and *The Trew Law of Free Monarchies*: the Scottish context and the English translation', in Linda Levy Peck (ed.), *The Mental World of the Jacobean Court* (Cambridge University Press, Cambridge, 1991)

Giles Worsley, 'A Courtly Art: the history of the *haute école* in England', *Court Historian*, VI, 1, 2001

G. Worsley, *Inigo Jones and the English Classical Tradition* (Yale University Press, New Haven and London, 2007)

Renate Woudhuysen-Keller et al., 'The examination and restoration of *Henry, Prince of Wales on Horseback* by Robert Peake', *Hamilton Bulletin*, no. 1, Cambridge, 1988

Frances A. Yates, *Frances Yates: Selected Works*, vol. iv (1975), *Shakespeare's Last Plays* (Routledge, London and New York, 2007)

Picture credits

The National Portrait Gallery would like to thank the copyright holders for granting permission to reproduce works illustrated in this book. Every effort has been made to contact the holders of copyright material, and any omissions will be corrected in future editions if the publisher is notified in writing. Credits for figures are given below. Dimensions for figures are given height × width (mm).

FIG. 1: *Nonsuch Palace*, unidentified artist, *c*.1620. Oil on canvas, 1518 × 3025mm. Photo: © Fitzwilliam Museum, Cambridge.

FIG. 2: *Prince Henry*, Robert Peake the Elder, 1604. Oil on canvas, 1340 × 1010mm (unframed). Collection of the Earl of Mar and Kellie.

FIG. 3: *Thomas Howard, 14th Earl of Arundel*, unidentified artist, 1611. Oil on canvas. Private Collection. Photo: © Stéphane Rocher Photography.

FIG. 4: *Henry, Prince of Wales*, Robert Peake the Elder, *c*.1612. Oil on canvas, 2032 × 1219mm. Photo: courtesy The President and Fellows of Magdalen College Oxford.

FIG. 5: See cat. 11.

FIG. 6: *Ben Jonson*, Abraham van Blyenberch, *c*.1617. Oil on canvas, 470 × 419mm. Photo: © National Portrait Gallery, London (NPG 2752).

FIG. 7: *Les raisons des forces mouvantes by Salomon de Caus* (title page), unidentified artist, 1615. Engraving on paper, 336 x 209mm. Photo: © The British Library Board (5355.l.23).

FIG. 8: See cat. 27.

FIG. 9: *Henry, Prince of Wales in Greenwich Armour* (posthumous), Sir Anthony Van Dyck, *c*.1633. Oil on canvas, 2158 × 1204mm. Photo: supplied by Royal Collection Trust/© HM Queen Elizabeth II 2012.

FIG. 10: *The Whitehall Mural Cartoon* (detail showing Henry VIII), Hans Holbein the Younger, *c*.1536. Ink and watercolour, 2758 × 1372mm. Photo: © National Portrait Gallery, London (NPG 4027).

FIG. 11: *Edward VI when Prince of Wales*, attributed to William Scrots, *c*.1546. Oil on panel, 1072 × 820mm. Photo: supplied by Royal Collection Trust/© HM Queen Elizabeth II 2012.

FIG. 12: *Henry, Prince of Wales and Sir John Harington*, Robert Peake the Elder, 1603. Oil on canvas, 2019 × 1472mm. Photo: © The Metropolitan Museum of Art/Art Resource/Scala, Florence.

FIG. 13: *Knight, Death and the Devil*, Albrecht Dürer, 1513. Paper/engraving, 248 × 191mm. Photo: © The Trustees of the British Museum.

FIG. 14: *Robert Devereux, 2nd Earl of Essex*, unidentified artist, *c*.1587. Watercolour and bodycolour on vellum,

248 × 203mm. Photo: © National Portrait Gallery, London (NPG 6241).

FIG. 15: Robert Devereux, 2nd Earl of Essex, Marcus Gheeraerts the Younger, *c*.1597. Oil on canvas, 2180 × 1272mm. Photo: © National Portrait Gallery, London.

FIG. 16: Illustration from p.133 of *The Noble arte of Venerie, or Hunting...*, George Gascoigne, 1575. Paper, 188 × 149mm. Reproduced by permission of The Huntington Library, San Marino, California.

FIG. 17: *Prometheus Chained to the Caucasus*, Palma Giovane, *c*.1570–1608. Oil on canvas, 1840 × 1606mm. Photo: supplied by Royal Collection Trust/© HM Queen Elizabeth II 2012.

FIG. 18: Vambrace from Prince Henry's Dutch Armour, showing the Battle of the Hydaspes River, *c*.1608. Photo: © Royal Armouries, Leeds, UK/The Bridgeman Art Library.

FIG. 19: Caligula from The Twelve Caesars series, Antonio Tempesta, 1596. Etching, 304 × 227mm. Photo: © The Metropolitan Museum of Art/Art Resource/Scala, Florence.

FIG. 20: *An Allegory of Prudence*, Hans Holbein the Younger, 1532–6. Oil on panel, 454 × 454mm (unframed). Photo: © The J. Paul Getty Museum, Los Angeles.

FIG. 21: Brand showing Prince Henry's cipher. Photo: courtesy Museo Nacional del Prado.

FIG. 22: Ring with busts of the Emperor Augustus and Livia, illustration 103 in *Dactyliotheca*, Abraham Gorlaeus, 1609. Photo: © The British Library Board (7706.b.15).

FIG. 23: *Prince Henry*, Nicholas Hilliard, 1607. Watercolour on vellum laid on to card, 34 × 28mm. Photo: supplied by Royal Collection Trust/© HM Queen Elizabeth II 2012.

FIG. 24: Titus Manlius Torquatus from The Roman Heroes, Hendrick Goltzius, 1586. Paper/engraving, 365 × 237mm. Photo: © The Trustees of the British Museum.

FIG. 25: *Plan and elevation of the Prince's Riding School at St James's*, Robert Smythson, 1609. Sepia pen on paper, 248 × 163mm. Photo: © RIBA Library Drawings & Archives Collection.

FIG. 26: *View of Richmond*, Wenceslaus Hollar, 1638. Paper/etching, 114 × 336mm. Photo: © The Trustees of the British Museum.

FIG. 27: *Plan of Richmond Palace Gardens*, Costantino de' Servi, 1611. Photo: © Archivio di Stato di Firenze.

FIG. 27: *Design for a Giant*, problem 14, book II *Les raisons des forces mouvantes*, unknown artist after Salomon de Caus, 1615. Engraving on paper, 232 × 280mm. Photo: © The British Library Board (5355.l.23)

EXHIBITION WORKS

1. (also p.10) Private Collection. Photo: courtesy Antonia Reeve.

2. The Trustees of the British Museum. Photo: © The Trustees of the British Museum.

3. By permission of the Trustees of Dulwich Picture Gallery, London. Photo: by permission of the Trustees of Dulwich Picture Gallery, London.

4. National Portrait Gallery, London: Purchased 2010. Photo: © National Portrait Gallery, London.

5. The Royal Collection. Photo: Supplied by Royal Collection Trust/© HM Queen Elizabeth II, 2012.

6. National Portrait Gallery: Purchased with help from The Art Fund, 1957. Photo: © National Portrait Gallery, London.

7. (also p.44) National Portrait Gallery: Bequeathed by Harold Lee-Dillon, 17th Viscount Dillon, 1933. Photo: © National Portrait Gallery, London.

8. National Maritime Museum, Greenwich, London. Acquired with the assistance of The Art Fund and the National Heritage Memorial Fund. Photo: © National Maritime Museum, Greenwich, UK.

9. Scottish National Portrait Gallery, Edinburgh. Photo: courtesy Scottish National Portrait Gallery, Edinburgh.

10. (also p.18) The Trustees of the British Museum. Photo: © The Trustees of the British Museum.

11. The British Library. Photo: © The British Library Board, Royal 18.B.XV.

12. The British Library. Photo: © The British Library Board, Harl 6986 fol.67r.

13. The British Library. Photo: © The British Library Board, Harl MS 7007 fol.20r.

14. (also frontispiece and p.68) The Royal Collection. Photo: supplied by Royal Collection Trust/© HM Queen Elizabeth II 2012.

15. Scottish National Portrait Gallery, Edinburgh. Photo: courtesy Scottish National Portrait Gallery, Edinburgh.

16. National Portrait Gallery: Given by David Laing, 1860. Photo: © National Portrait Gallery, London.

17. National Portrait Gallery: Purchased 1972. Photo: © National Portrait Gallery, London.

18. Private Collection. Photo: courtesy Private Collection.

19. The British Library. Photo: © The British Library Board, Royal.12.A.LXVI.

20. (also endpapers) The Master and Fellows of Trinity College Cambridge. Photo: © Master and Fellows of Trinity College Cambridge.

Index

ccc c c cn cccc

eeeeeeee eeeeeeeee

tanta est

t t tamen

s satis

Henricus M M M N M

temporibus

sententiis

Henricus

temporibus

mea quidem sententia

Maxima cunctarum victoria victa Voluptas.